Wars CNN Didn't Cover

Jack Muhlenbeck

Copyright © 2008 by Jack Muhlenbeck

ISBN 0-7414-4933-1

Published by:

INFINITY
PUBLISHING.COM

1094 New DeHaven Street, Suite 100
West Conshohocken, PA 19428-2713
Info@buybooksontheweb.com
www.buybooksontheweb.com
Toll-free (877) BUY BOOK
Local Phone (610) 941-9999
Fax (610) 941-9959

Printed in the United States of America

Printed on Recycled Paper

Published September 2008

Contents

Introduction

"Tell me something I don't know" is a weekly feature of the television show hosted by Chris Matthews.

On each show Matthews monitors a roundtable of four news people who discuss the events of the week. At the end of the discussion he asks each to "tell me something I don't know." These little nuggets can be what to look for in the weeks ahead or bits of Washington gossip. They are always interesting and add zest to the show.

"Wars CNN Didn't Cover" hopes to "tell you something you didn't know," but in print format. It is designed to inform the readers of some obscure bits of history little known outside the dusty stacks of major university libraries but which are germane to the world in which we live.

After reading the book, hopefully the reader will say words to the affect "I didn't know that." Should that happen, the book will have been a success.

A few words about style. This book will probably be an English teacher's greatest nightmare as spelling, grammar, and punctuation are, at time, fractured. This is by design.

A great deal of the material in this anthology is drawn from newspapers, magazines and books up to 150 years old and older. To give today's reader the flavor of what was being said and written at the time, few edits — only those required for clarity — have been made. The stacked headlines of the New York and New Orleans papers and the flowery rhetoric of the *Labor Argus* of Charleston, West Virginia, are presented unaltered. In the contemporary text, numbers ten or less are spelled out; those greater are in numerical format. Several versions are used in the original texts, which have not been changed.

Korean names can be written in three ways, i.e., Yi Sun-sin, Kim Il Sung, and Syngman Rhee. All are considered correct. Eliminating the hyphen is a more modern rendition. Some words are spelled more than one way in the quoted material, i.e. jingalls and gingals both being used to describe antique muskets. As neither word is found in modern dictionaries, both spellings appear as they did in the original text.

Likewise, the spelling of place names in Korea changes from time to time. Pusan is now sometimes spelled Busan. The author uses the more traditional versions.

A number of words used to describe the Russian Communists of the early twentieth-century are used interchangeably – Bolos, Bolshevik, Bolsheviks, Bolshiviki and even Bolshis. All spellings were found in original writings.

Stray commas and hyphens, renegade capitals and non-traditional spellings in the contemporary text are on the author.

Many people helped make this book possible. Sangsoo Ahn walked the terrain of Kanghwa Island and the southern coast of Korea with the author. Paul Kotakis, of U.S. Army Cadet Command, offered timely advice and helped debug the text. The librarians at the Main Street and Grissom Libraries in Newport News, Virginia were indispensable in obtaining books and articles through Inter-Library Loan.

JC Gooch of the Transylvania University Library offered valuable material pertaining to Hugh Wilson McKee and Shelia Blackburn of the Matewan Development Center provided critical material for the chapter *Revolt of the "Rednecks"*.

Many journalists and authors made this anthology possible. Specials thanks goes to the Marine Corps Gazette, the University of Pittsburgh Press, the Harvard University Asia Center and the Marine Corps Museum at Triangle, Virginia.

Citations

The battle at Kanghwa Island, Korea, pages 26–37, Chapter I, *Shinmiyangyo, America's "Weekend War,"* is credited to: Runyon, Maj. C.F., "Capt. McLane Tilton and the Korean Incident of 1871," *Marine Corps Gazette*, March 1958.

The "Red Seal" excerpts, pages 145–147, Chapter IV, *The Turtle and Samurai*, are from the book *Hideyoshi*, by Mary E. Berry, published by the Harvard University Asia Center, permission to reprint granted by the Center.

The *Massacre at Matewan* portion of Chapter V, *Revolt of the "Rednecks,"* pages 187–191 originally appeared as "*The Battle of Matewan"* in *Thunder in the Mountains: The West Virginia Mine War, 1920-21*, by Lon Savage, copyrighted 1985. Reprint by permission of the University of Pittsburgh Press.

The cover art is a rendition of the oil painting *Storming Fort Chojin, Korea*, by John Clymer. The original is on display at the Art Collection, National Museum of the Marine Corps, Triangle, VA. The Museum graciously provided the publisher with an electronic file from which the cover art was designed.

Fort McKee

Shinmiyangyo – America's "Weekend War"

June 25, 1950 sent Americans scurrying to their atlases to find out just where Korea was located. For on that day, America's "Forgotten War" began with a thunderous, early morning, artillery barrage as the Communist North cut across the 38th Parallel in an attempt to unify the peninsula by force.

Ask the typical citizen when the first American servicemen died in Korea and the answer most often given would be July of 1950 when the soldiers of the 24th Infantry Division's "Task Force Smith", commanded by LTC Charles Smith, were overrun by the North Korean Communists, spearheaded by their Soviet tanks, near Osan. The men of "Smith" did their best to stop the rapid move southward of the Communists and suffered 120 killed in action and 36 captured.

Those who answer Task Force Smith get partial credit.

While it is true that the first American *soldiers* to die in combat in Korea were members of Task Force Smith, the first American servicemen to lose their lives on the Korean Peninsula died almost 80 years *earlier* in what is known as the long-forgotten

"Weekend War." If the Korean War of 1950-53 is the Forgotten War, then the action that took place in 1871 could well be called the "Unknown War."

To the U.S. Navy it is the "Korean Incident of 1871," to the Koreans it is called *Shinmiyangyo* (Western Disturbance in the year Shinmi), and to students of Korean history it is sometimes called the *6/11 Incident*, as the Korean War of 1950-1953 is known as the *6/25 Incident*. The story unfolded like this:

The Participants

The United States had become a world power less than 100 years after gaining its independence. American forces had defeated the British twice. The American Navy and Marines had fought and defeated the Barbary States of North Africa. U.S. forces had routed Mexico and added the American Southwest to the growing nation.

The American Civil War had drained the armies of both the North and South of much of their manpower. The Navy and Marines played only relatively minor roles in the Civil War and were ready to carry out America's "Manifest Destiny" throughout the world.

In short, the United States was young, robust, and looking for new worlds to conquer. Admiral Matthew Perry had pried open Japan in 1854 with the signing of the Treaty of Kanagawa, leaving Korea being one of the few countries with which America had no contact. And the Koreans liked it that way.

Korea, on the other hand, was an almost 5,000 year-old civilization. It had been unified into one kingdom, the Silla Dynasty, in 688. The Chosun Dynasty that followed ruled continuously from 1392 until Korea was annexed by Japan in 1910 as part of the settlement of the Russo-Japanese War.

Korea was so obscure that as late as 1768, *The Encyclopedia Britannica* listed "Corea" as possibly being an island somewhere in the Pacific Ocean. (Spelling Korea exclusively with a *K* didn't begin until early in the twentieth-century). This obscurity didn't change much even with the outbreak of the Korean War in 1950.

In 1970, the hit movie *M*A*S*H* featured an American Army surgical hospital just behind the front lines in the Korean War. The rice farmers in the movie were depicted wearing conical hats. Close, but not right. Conical hats are common in Vietnam, not Korea.

Korea has long lived in the shadow of China, playing little brother to its huge neighbor. Geographically Korea is in a tough neighborhood. To the north it borders on both China and Russia. And just across the narrow strait is Japan. Koreans live by the maxim "when the whales fight, the shrimp are crushed."

Korea generally had correct relations with, and paid an annual tribute to, its larger neighbor China. But that did not keep Chinese as well as Japanese pirates from preying on its long coastline – just another reason why the "Hermit Kingdom" wanted to remain as isolated as possible.

The Koreans have a rich culture, having built an astronomical observatory in the seventh-century, began using movable type in the thirteenth-century and adopted their own phonetic alphabet in the fifteenth-century. They had used thermal heating for centuries to warm their homes.

Korea had a two-tiered society with a thin veneer of aristocrats (yangbans) ruling the country, while the songnams were the farmers, laborers, watermen and peasants.

To maintain its isolation, shipwrecked sailors who happened to wash up on Korean shores were repatriated as quickly as possible, usually through China, to prevent Western "contamination."

This, then, was the Korea of the nineteenth-century.

Prelude to War – The General Sherman

American merchants could not believe that any country could be as resolute as Korea against trade and making money. In 1866, the American sailing ship the *General Sherman* decided to put this reclusive policy to the test.

The *General Sherman* was built in England and began its sailing days as the Confederate blockade-runner *Princess Royal* in the American Civil War. She was almost 200 feet long by 30 feet wide. The ship carried two 30-pound cannons and four 24-pound howitzers.

The *Princess Royal* was captured by Union forces in the waters off Charleston, South Carolina in January 1863 and was reflagged as a United States Navy ship assigned to the West Gulf Blockading Squadron with Commander M.B. Woolsey at the helm.

Her crew captured, or played a part in the capture of seven Confederate blockade-runners. With the Confederate surrender, the *Princess Royal*, now outfitted as a cruiser, was sent to Philadelphia and sold at auction as "war surplus."

A year later, renamed the *General Sherman*, it was sailing around the rim of Asia, home-ported in China. In August 1866 the vessel made its ill-fated trip to Korea.

The incursion of the *General Sherman* into Korean waters was the subject of a fictionalized dramatization of an episode of the 1940s Mutual Broadcasting System radio drama *The Voyage of the Scarlet Queen* starring Elliot Lewis as skipper Philip Carney.

The crew of the *Scarlet Queen*, like that of the *General Sherman*, tramped around Asia looking for fun, adventure and profit.

In Korea, the crew of the *Scarlet Queen* went hunting for ginseng, a gnarly root looking much like an icicle radish with rumatoid arthritis and a suntan. The best roots grow in the deep shade of the forest. Vintage roots are highly prized in China and Korea as an aphrodisiac and can literally be worth their weight in gold, and more. A root, alleged to be more than 150 years old, and thought to have almost magical medicinal powers, recently sold in Seoul for more than $10,000!

The men of the *Scarlet Queen* may have spent some time with the kisangs (Korea's version of the geisha), filled some sacks with ginseng, scuffed up some of the "natives" – who fought to keep their roots – and made a run back for their ship.

They arrived just in time to clamor aboard their ketch and head back to the studio to rehearse for the following week's episode.

The crew of the *General Sherman* should have been so lucky!

As anyone who has been in Korea knows, the tides along the West Coast can be fierce and the summer monsoon rains can change the course and depth of rivers. As the crew of the *General Sherman* was presumably making its first voyage to Korea, it probably knew none of this. This lack of knowledge would prove fatal.

With a mixed crew of Americans, Englishmen, Chinese and Malayans, the *General Sherman* prepared to move up the Taedong River – swelled by the recent monsoons – toward the present North Korean capital of Pyongyang, some 50 miles away.

Korea had trade relations with China going back centuries. A limited number of Japanese merchants were allowed to set up shop along the southern coast of Korea.

But China and Japan were fellow East Asian nations. Trading with the "West" was strictly forbidden.

There were three reasons for this: The Korean monarchy and court stated that their country had existed for more than 5,000 years without trading with the West and could exist for a similar amount of time without Western goods.

They felt Korea was a poor country with nothing to offer the West. Conversely, they felt the decadent West had nothing to offer the Koreans.

The ruling class lived well and really didn't need the cheap tin, glass and colored cotton fabric and other trinkets the *General Sherman* had to trade. The elite dressed in colorful silk; the peasants wore white and probably would have welcomed a little color into their lives. But they had no vote.

The primary reason the elite did not want to trade with the West was the fear that Western ideas would sneak into the country wrapped in the colorful calico.

The invasions by the Japanese in the late 1500s and the Manchus in the 1600s had devastated the country and the Koreans feared more aggression.

The Koreans had one other reason to fear the West – the feeling among Occidentals that they could do as they pleased with the Orientals.

Dr. William Speer gives an example of this writing in the *Galaxy* magazine in March 1872. In his piece, *Corea: What Shall We Do With Her?* he wrote:

While cruising through these waters it became known to the British fleet that fine cattle abounded upon some of the islands bordering the Corean coast.

A twenty-gun vessel of war, the *Nimrod*, and a transport, the *Hooghly*, were dispatched there to capture a supply of fresh meat. It was counted a rare sport for the seamen to land upon an island, drive a number of cattle into a narrow place on the seashore, and when they attempted to break forth, with bellowing and terror, to trip them with ropes stretched taut, leap upon and tie them and then drag them to the boats.

The resistance, the threats, the tears of the poor Corean keepers, the information which was given to the British officers that the herds were the property of the King, and that those in charge of them had no right to let them go, and would be punished, for the loss of them, perhaps with death, only made the mirth more boisterous.

If something like this had happened in the American West during this time period, the *rustlers* would probably have been hanged. In the Korea in the nineteenth-century, the Westerners laughed and the *cowboys* suffered.

The *General Sherman* set off for Korea in June 1866. The ship was owned by the British firm Meadows & Company of Tinstsin, China. It was leased by the American merchant, W. B. Preston. When operating as a blockader during the American Civil War the ship carried as many as 80 crewmen. On the trip to Korea Preston was joined by two other Americans, known only as Page and Wilson, George Hogarth, a British citizen, 16 Chinese and two Malay sailors and a British missionary, the Rev. Robert J. Thomas.

The *General Sherman*, all 600 tons of her, arrived at the mouth of the Taedong River in July. The crew told the Koreans who met them that the ship planned to sail up river to Pyongyang and trade with Korean merchants. The Koreans were irate.

Presumably the *General Sherman* was flying the "Stars and Stripes." Should not the Koreans have known that it was an American vessel on a peaceful mission and not the British rustlers looking for more porterhouse steak?

When the words "**War in Korea!**" flickered across ten-inch black and white television screens in America on June 25, 1950, the odds of finding ten people in Bettendorf, Iowa who could make a color sketch of the Korean flag would have been astronomical. Add to it the North Korean flag, and the odds would have been off the chart.

How then, could anyone, except the jingoistic American media, have expected the Koreans, living in one of the most isolated areas in the world, to know what red and white stripes and white stars on a field of blue meant?

No matter. The crew of the *General Sherman* was told that the ship could anchor in open water and could expect supplies from shore. But as far as going up stream to trade – that was forbidden by the crown. In simple language – "Turn around and go back to China!"

Since no one aboard the *General Sherman* survived, the only reports of the destruction of the ship come from Korean sources. Some relate that the Rev. Thomas, who spoke some Chinese and a little Korean, was really the leader of the expedition with the intent of introducing Protestantism into Korea. He is quoted to have said the Koreans could not stop the ship from sailing up the river because the *General Sherman* was heavily armored and carried a variety of guns.

Probably the best summary of the burning of the *General Sherman* is an eyewitness account recorded in 1892:

In the seventh moon of the year Pyeng-in (July 1866), a black schooner was sighted on the Taedong River. The ship dropped anchor at Keupsa Gate at the border of Pyung-an and Whang-hae provinces.

Governor Park Kyoo-soo of Pyung-an sent an emissary to investigate the ship's presence. The emissary was told that the foreigners came to exchange goods with the Koreans. They came from the land of Miguk (the United States). There were nineteen persons on the ship, including several Orientals of about the stature of Koreans with dark complexions. They understood Hanja characters (Chinese) and so served as interpreters for the Americans.

The emissary informed them that Korea did not trade with Westerners and that only the King could change the law; and that the governor had no authority to deal with the foreigners. He then offered to provide them with some provisions. They asked for flour and eggs.

When the emissary left the ship to report to the governor, the foreigners weighed anchor and sailed up the river as far inland as Mangyung-dea, a hill some twelve li (four miles) from Pyongyang. The Crow Rapids stopped them from going any further.

(Ordinarily this would have been as far as the *General Sherman* could have sailed. Unable to cross the rapids, it would have had to return to open water and the incident could have been avoided.)

During the night, rain poured down on the mountains and the Taedong River rose rapidly. The day was the fifteenth of the lunar month and there were also high tides. These two factors combined swelled the water to a level seldom seen before. Thus the black ship was able to pass over the Crow Rapids and sailed further inland.

The foreigners apparently thought the high water was natural and kept on sailing until the reached Yank-jak Island. Governor Park and Lee Hyon-ik, the deputy commander of Pyongyang, went to the ship with four eggs and a message: "You have reached the walls of our city when asked to stay put at Keupsa Gate. You insist on trading with us, which is forbidden. Your actions have created a grave situation so much so that I must report to my King and let him decide what to do with you people."

This was the second year of the King's reign (the minor Kojong) and the powerful Taewongun was the regent of Korea. He believed that the foreign ship was a vanguard of another invasion of the Roman Catholic Church and commanded: "'Tell them to leave at once. If they do not obey, kill them!"

The day before the Taewongun's edict arrived the river's water level dropped and the ship was hopelessly stranded. The governor ordered the troops to attack the foreigners. We had wha-jun (fire arrows) that could travel eight hundred feet and then explode. Our troops were dressed in dragon cloud armor and marched past a cheering crowd. We had several cannons rolled out to fight the invaders.

The Americans saw our troops coming and made a hostage of Deputy Commander Lee, who was onboard the ship for a visit. Governor Park told his troops to attack the ship, notwithstanding Lee's safety.

The fighting continued for four days amidst a huge crowd of spectators. The foreigners fired large cannon balls that traveled more than ten li (three miles). The cannon's thunder could be heard as far away as one day's walk. They aimed at the spectators and showers of deadly shell fragments rained down on them. Our troops retreated to a safe distance, from where their guns and bows could do little harm to the foreigners.

We tried a Turtle Boat, a boat covered with metal sheets and cowhides. The bow of the boat had a covered port for a cannon hidden inside. The Turtle Boat approached the ship and fired many shots, but the shots bounced off the thick skin of the ship. The fight was not going well for us.

Then Drill Sergeant Park Choog-win tied three boats together by the East Gate and loaded them up with firewood. He then poured sulfur and saltpeter on the wood. Two long ropes were attached to both sides of the boats and the firewood was lit.

But the fire went out before the boats reached the ship. A second set of fireboats was pushed away by the Americans. But the third set reached the enemy ship with success at last. The enemy ship caught fire and began to burn. The crew faced suffocation by stench and vapor of the burning saltpeter and sulfur. They tried in vain to put out the flames and as the smoke grew thicker they were forced, one by one, to jump into the water.

Our troops in boats surrounded the enemy ship and captured the enemy as they tried to escape. Drill Sergeant Park boarded the ship and rescued Lee. Some of the invaders waved white flags. Most of them were hacked to pieces before they reached the shore. Others were dragged ashore alive. They tried friendly smiles and soft words to win the goodwill of our people – in vain.

The remains of the foreigners were trampled on and dragged around. Body parts were cut off for medical use and what was left was burned.

The enemy ship was totally burned and there remained only her iron ribs which looked like posts driven into the ground. These irons were melted down and used in various ways. We also recovered three cannons, which are displayed in the armory in Pyongyang. We also recovered the anchor chains that hang from the East Gate Tower.

There was a big celebration over this victory of ours. Governor Park provided food and wine. There was much joy but sadness over our losses. Governor Park sent a special messenger to the King with the news.

When the Taewongun read this note he laughed his heart out and made Park Chong-win his aide-de-camp in Ahn-ju. We lost one solider and thirteen civilians.

The Korean government, fearing the United States would seek compensation for the loss of the ship and the crew, claimed that a civilian mob was responsible.

Professor Han Gyu-mu of Kwangju University in Korea and Professor Robert Swartout of Carroll College in Montana, an authority on Korean history and culture, both feel that the missionary, the Rev. Thomas, played a key role in the voyage of the *General Sherman* and that evangelism was at least as important as commerce.

The consensus of opinion, however, is that the *General Sherman* was in Korean waters on a commercial venture and that evangelism was a sideline. Would the Americans and the additional British passenger have been willing to risk visiting a strange and forbidding country solely to spread the gospel and not make money? Doubtful.

For years after the destruction of the *General Sherman*, rumors circulated that some members of the crew, possibly Westerners, had survived. This theory also was never confirmed.

Dr. Bruce Cumings, in his book *Korea's Place in the Sun, a Modern History*, writes that upon visiting North Korea he was taken to a stone monument that marks the spot where the *General Sherman* was destroyed. Nearby is anchored the American spy ship the *Pueblo* which was captured off the East Coast of North Korea in January 1968. Together, the monument and the *Pueblo* are considered to be two instances of the "people" routing the imperialists.

The stone marker is said to be near the birthplace of Kim Il Sung, the first Communist dictator of North Korea, and father of the present "Dear Leader" Kim Jong Il.

North Koreans believe that one of Kim Il Sung's ancestors, Kim Ung U, not only took part in the destruction of the *General*

Sherman, but that he lead the charge. No one in North Korea disputes this version, at least no one who is still alive!

As translated by Dr. Cumings, the headline states: "MONUMENT TO THE DESTRUCTION OF THE AMERICAN PIRATE SHIP 'SHERMAN' ". The text reads: "At this spot on the Taedong River on September 2, 1866, the Pyongyang citizenry, with the ardent patriot Mr. Kim Ung U in the lead, destroyed the American pirate ship 'Sherman' which had aggressed upon our country."

Ask Americans about General Sherman and those who would answer would probably say something like he was an eccentric Union general during the Civil War who marched his army through Georgia. Outside the halls of academia, few would identify the *General Sherman* as part of nineteenth-century gunboat diplomacy.

The same is true in South Korea where an American re-searcher, working through an interpreter, asked two dozen students at random in a sushi bar near Seoul National University (Korea's Harvard, MIT, and Stanford combined) if they could identify General Sherman or *Shinmiyangyo*. The question elicited a few giggles and many blank stares. Neither term means much in South Korea.

Not so in the North.

In addition to the marker discussed by Dr. Cumings, the Communist North issued a commemorative stamp marking the centennial of the destruction of the *General Sherman*, albeit two years early, in 1964.

The stamp depicts a burning ship in the background and a group of a dozen and more men dressed in the white garb of peasants carrying long poles celebrating the torching of the vessel. The clothing of the men on the stamp is significant in that when the ship was actually destroyed, the Korean government blamed the incident on an angry mob of farmers, and not the Korean military.

Prelude to War

Following the burning of the *General Sherman* and the killing of its crew, the U.S. Navy sent two expeditions to seek an explanation from the Korean crown as to the fate of the crew of the American merchant ship and to seek a treaty of commerce. Both came back empty handed.

The Koreans did not want to sign a treaty and could not understand why the American government was pressing the matter of the *General Sherman*. The Koreans reasoned that common law holds that if an intruder enters one's house by force, the individual, if necessary, has the right to defend house and home with deadly force. The American ship had muscled its way, uninvited, into Korea and killed and wounded many Korean citizens. The crew of the *General Sherman* got what it deserved. Reluctantly the American government seemed to agree and the matter was dropped – for the time being.

The United States was not the only country with which Korea was having a problem. France was also an irritant.

French Catholic missionaries had been active in Korea off and on since the 1770s. Some Koreans had accepted Christianity but most government officials and intellectuals were against the "foreign" religion. The Catholic Church and its members were often persecuted and converts massacred. Included in the dead were French bishops and priests.

A major crackdown on Catholics took place in 1866, the same year as the *General Sherman* incident. French priests begged the French government to send the French Asiatic Squadron to "punish" the unbelievers.

French diplomat Henri de Bellonet, stationed in China, fumed that a French force would sail to Korea, depose the Korean king and that the French sovereign – Napoleon III – would decide who would fill the empty throne.

In October of 1866 the French landed a force of some 600 men commanded by Admiral Pierre-Gustave Rose. How could the French hope to defeat a nation of more than ten million with such a small force?

The French were probably using as their model the conquests of the Spanish conquistadors in the first quarter of the sixteenth-century.

In his book *War Made New*, Max Boot points out that Hernan Cortes, with a force of less than a thousand, was able to conquer the Aztec civilization of more than eight million souls. Francisco Pizarro took control of the even larger Inca nation with less than 200 conquistadors. What the Spanish could do, the French felt they could do better.

Diplomat de Bellonet's calculus was faulty on two counts.

For centuries China had considered itself to be the "Middle Kingdom", literally the center of the world, with all other civilization orbiting around it. The country cousins in Korea followed the Chinese lead and sealed the peninsula into the "Hermit Kingdom," shutting out Westerners whom they considered to be inferior.

And the Koreans were not unfamiliar with gunpowder.

When the conquistadors were overrunning Central and South America in the 1500s, they, and their "talking sticks" were considered a deity to be obeyed. When the French ventured into Korea, they were looked upon as devils to be obliterated. Unlike the peons in Nicaragua, the Koreas were not awaiting a "Grey-Eyed Man of Destiny" to make all well with them (see chapter three).

For more than 500 years the Koreans had been using gunpowder. Their naval ordnance shredded the Japanese fleet in the Seven Years War of 1592-1598 (see chapter four).

The French were successful in taking Kanghwa Island but the Koreans massed an army, said to be upwards of 10,000, on the mainland facing the island. Their guns were not as modern as those of the French but, considering the advantage they had in manpower, would be adequate.

Also in October the Taewongun issued a four-point declaration:

- Talking peace with the French is a betrayal of your motherland;

- Establishing "intimate" relationships with the French is inviting the gradual destruction of your motherland;

- Retreating in the face of the enemy is a cowardly act, and will encourage the French to endanger the survival of your motherland;

- Attempting to drive the French away by means of superstitious exorcisms is playing into the hands of the enemy.

The final blow to the French came when a Korean detachment of about 500 men ambushed and defeated a French force of 160 on Chongjuk Mountain. The French suffered some 50 casualties, while the Koreans toll was one man killed and three wounded.

Admiral Rose realized there was no way he could subdue or negotiate with the Koreans. He feared that they would soon launch an attack from the mainland against his small, isolated force on Kanghwa. On November 21, the French expedition sailed from Korean waters, but not before it transferred all its "war booty" to its ships and set fire to government buildings in Kanghwa City.

The French sailed away to concentrate on the colonization of another country that would bring grief to both France and the United States a century later – Vietnam.

There the situation stood for three years. The United States still wanted a treaty with Korea spelling out protection for shipwrecked sailors and trade relations. Korea was not interested. The *6/11 Incident* would come in 1871.

Prince Hungson and Navy Lieutenant McKee

Prince Hungson was born into the royal family that had ruled Korea since 1392; Lieutenant Hugh Wilson McKee, a Kentuckian, was a middle of the pack graduate of the U.S. Naval Academy. The prince, who resembled the 1940s inscrutable movie detective Charlie Chan, was a direct descendent of Prince Sado. Lieutenant McKee's father, Colonel William McKee, was killed at the battle of Buena Vista on February 23, 1847, leading the 2nd Kentucky Volunteers during the war with Mexico. Lieutenant Colonel Henry Clay, Jr., son of the venerable Whig politician, also died in that action

Korea's royal family was very weak in the nineteenth-century. Sovereigns were often minors with regents and factions vying for power. In 1849 a juvenile named Prince Chongye – renamed Cholchong – was chosen to be the 25th king of the Chosun Dynasty. He was located on Kanghwa Island, plowing a field with a red oxen, when selected for the job and whisked off to the royal palace in Seoul.

King Cholchong died at age 32 of "excesses and extravagances of the court", nineteenth-century spin for heavy drinking and carousing.

The three dowager queens each maneuvered to name a successor with Dowager Cho winning the contest and naming Kojong, 11 years old, to take the vacant throne.

King Kojong was the son of Prince Hungson, and this presented a real problem. As Kojong was the king, his father would be one of his subjects and would have to bow to his son. This would present a problem as Asians treasure seniority and venerate their elders. What to do?

The problem was solved by giving Prince Hungson the title "Taewongun" – or "Prince of the Great House." This gave him the power to rule from behind the scenes for the next decade.

The Taewongun was bitterly xenophobic, especially in dealings with the West. He was beside himself with joy when he heard of the destruction of the *General Sherman* and the defeat of the French fleet. His foreign policy could be summed up as the "Five No's":

NO Treaties
NO Trade
NO Catholics
NO West
NO Japan

Lieutenant Hugh Wilson McKee was born in Lexington, Kentucky, on April 23, 1844. He was appointed to the Naval Academy at age 17 and graduated 52nd in a class of 73 on June 12, 1866, too late to take part in the American Civil War. As was the protocol in that era, he served two years as a midshipman before being commissioned an ensign in 1868. He was promoted to lieutenant (equivalent to an army captain) in 1870 and served with the North Atlantic Squadron, the European Squadron, and on the Great Lakes before being assigned to the Asiatic Fleet.

Though he lived only 27 years, the young lieutenant has three notable "firsts" to his credit:

Leading Company D, he was the first American officer to enter the citadel, Kwangsungbo.

He was the first American officer to die in Korea, having been struck down as soon as he was inside the perimeter of Kwangsungbo.

He was the first American to have a fort in Asia named after him, as Kwangsungbo was renamed Fort McKee in his honor when the battle was won.

Setting the Table

Kanghwa is a large island and its forts were the key installations guarding Korea's capital city of Seoul. To sail to Seoul, ships had to pass by the forts to get into the Han River with Seoul being some 30 miles upstream. So it should come as no surprise that the cream of the Korean Army of 1871 was stationed on Kanghwa. Local legend said that every member of the garrison had personally killed a tiger. That was highly unlikely as tigers were not that plentiful in Korea.

One of Korea's top military leaders, Lieutenant General Oh Chae-yon, was in command on Kanghwa Island. The garrison knew that if it allowed foreign ships to pass not only the soldiers, but also their families, might be executed.

The United States was still smarting from the loss of the *General Sherman* five years earlier at the hands of those most Americans considered to be "barbarians." The Grant administration ordered the navy to return to Korea.

The American Asiatic Fleet, Admiral John Rodgers commanding, numbered seven "ships of the line" and a number of smaller steam launches and landing craft. The fleet that would be sent to Korea consisted of its flagship, the *Colorado*, the *Alaska*, the *Benicia*, and the gunboats the *Monocacy* and *Palos*. The *Idaho* and the *Ashuelot* were left behind.

The Americans had three goals in mind in planning the trip to Korea: (1) To finally settle the matter of what happened to the crew of the *General Sherman*, (2) to negotiate the long-sought treaty safeguarding the rights of sailors who were found on Korea's shores and (3) to obtain a trade treaty with the Hermit Kingdom.

Korea's king, the Taewongun, and the ruling court considered none of these reasons to be valid.

The Korean government's position was that the crew of the *General Sherman* had been killed by an angry civilian mob, with the Korean government playing no part. As far as the Koreans were concerned, the matter was closed.

Korea claimed that wayward sailors had always been treated well and that a treaty would be redundant. And the Koreans felt they had survived for 5,000 years without a trade treaty with the West and that they could do the same for another 5,000.

Just what was known about, as they were called in those days, the "Coreans?"

Scuttlebutt around the ports of call in Asia, as reported by Rear Admiral Winfield Scott Schley in his book *Forty-five Years Under the Flag*, was that they were ferocious giants armed with needle guns and Krupp artillery. They were reported to skin and pickle slain enemy soldiers.

Speer, in *Corea, What Shall We Do With Her?* reported that "The Coreans were taller and stronger than the Chinese, more imaginative, more humorous, more musical, less patient, less moral, less commercial. They are more tender with criminals, and rarely inflict capital punishment; banishment from home and kindred to the bleak islands along the coast being considered equal to death. And a special trait of their character is their honesty in money matters."

In truth almost nothing was really known of the people of this land who had been locked away for so many centuries.

The primary mission of the Asiatic Squadron was to take the American Minister to China, Frederick F. Low, to Korea to investigate the sinking of the *General Sherman* and to negotiate the desired treaty.

While in China, Low, and Counsel General George Seward, tried in vain to have the Chinese government intercede with that of Korea. The Chinese refused, insisting that Korea was a sovereign nation over which China had no control. The Americans would be on their own.

The American diplomatic mission consisted of Minister Low (the term ambassador would not be used until later in the century), E.B. Drew, assistant secretary of the legation, John B. Cowles, acting secretary of the legation (skilled in the Chinese language) and two Chinese interpreters who spoke some Korean. On May 16, 1871 the fleet pulled up anchor in Nagasaki, Japan, and headed north.

Admiral Perry pried open Japan in 1854 with a show of force in Tokyo Bay. For Minister Low and Admiral Rodgers to intimidate the Koreans into signing a treaty they did not want, the Asiatic Squadron would have to make a similar show of force in Seoul, the ancient capital of the "Land of the Morning Calm." Gunboat diplomacy in the drab city of Inchon, the port city serving Seoul, would impress no one. The fact that Seoul, unlike Tokyo, was inland, would be a critical factor in sparking the *6/11 Incident*.

Misunderstandings

Two of the misunderstandings that triggered the *6/11 Incident* stemmed from the differences in Eastern and Western cultures. The first was "no objection" and the second, and more critical, was "apology."

Unfamiliarity with the tides and river depths along Korea's West Coast had caused the stranding and destruction of the *General Sherman* five years before.

To preclude sharing the fate of the crew of the *General Sherman*, Admiral Rodgers and his staff determined it would be necessary to take soundings of the channel between Kanghwa and the mainland and eventually the Han River to determine which ships could safely sail to the capital of Seoul. Several small boats were sent up the channel, which the U.S. Navy called the Salee (or Salt) River, to begin the task of taking the soundings.

Notwithstanding that Korea's policy was "no foreign ships" in the channel or the Han River, American reports state repeatedly that the Koreans had "no objection" to the American ships and their mission of testing the depths of the waterways.

More correctly, the Koreans "voiced" no objections, a subtle but critical difference.

To say no to a guest, even an unwelcome one, would have been rude on the part of the Koreans. So the Korean delegation probably nodded but remained mute. To the Americans this meant "no objections" – to the Koreans it meant "no approval."

So the *6/11 Incident* began on June 1, 1871 when the *USS Monocacy* and the *USS Palos*, together with some steam launches, began their measuring mission.

As the small fleet reached the lower end of Kanghwa Island, Korean shore batteries opened fire. Better armed, the American vessels silenced the Korean guns and retreated back to where the fleet was anchored.

Admiral Rodgers and his commanders agreed that the "barbarians" would have to be punished for firing at an American naval craft. By 1871, even the American government was willing to forget about the *General Sherman* incident as the merchant ship was more than likely trespassing, but firing at the U.S. Navy! – *that* was another matter!

As Dan Kurzman points out in *Day of the Bomb*, Japanese warriors eight years earlier had bombarded American ships plying the waters between the islands of Kyushu and Honshu. The American ships reduced the shore installations from boulders and mortar to pebbles and dust and then sailed on.

Minister Low and Admiral Rodgers agreed that the Korean government would be given ten days to "apologize." To facilitate this, a communication system worthy of a grade B Hollywood movie was devised.

The Americans would fasten a note to a pole well above high tide. Overnight the Koreans would fetch the note and, in a day or two, leave a reply.

Again, the differences between East and West surfaced over the "apology."

To a Westerner, an apology is "sorry, won't do it again, case closed." Not so in the Orient.

Two trains collide. The Minister of Transportation apologizes to the nation and resigns. Crops fail and the Minister of Agriculture is sacked, but not before he begs forgiveness. A star athlete in Japan smuggles an illegal gun into the country. He is forced to apologize on national television. His star status goes into eclipse.

In the movie the *Bridge on the River Kwai* Colonel Saito, commander of the camp housing the British prisoners building the bridge, confesses that if the bridge would not be done on time he would have to apologize to his emperor. And to show he was sincere, he then would have to commit suicide. Had Union General George B. McClellan been Japanese he would have been expected to self-destruct after being fired twice as head of the Northern Army in the Civil War. Instead he ran for president in 1864 against Abraham Lincoln, the man who twice stripped him of his command.

Still in all, Minister Low and Admiral Rodgers expected King Kojong to apologize for his army protecting the sovereignty of his country.

An analogy would have been Emperor Hirohito demanding that President Franklin Roosevelt apologize for American forces trying to shoot down Japanese Zeros as they rained bombs on Pearl Harbor!

Ten days went by, the communications post was yanked out of the ground, and the "war" was about to begin.

The 6/11 Incident Explodes

(The best narration of the two days of combat, related by Marine Major C.F. Runyan, was printed as a two-part series in the *Marine Corps Gazette* of February and March of 1958, entitled *Capt. McLane Tilton and the Korean Incident of 1871*. Excerpts of the March issue are offered here with permission of the *Marine Corps Gazette* to which this author is indebted.)

After Commander H.C. Blake's surveying party returned from upstream and the decision was tentatively made to attack the forts, Captain Edward Nichols, Fleet Captain and Chief of Staff to Admiral Rodgers, began work on a landing order for the Fleet Landing Force. To assist him, he enlisted the aid of Lieutenant Commander Winfield Scott Schley, a hard-working, aggressive young officer who was to act as Adjutant General of the Force.

On the fifth of June, the order was published as a Fleet General Order.

Commander Blake, with his knowledge of the river, and the location of the forts, was to command the Expeditionary Force. Lieutenant Commander Silas Casey, Executive Officer of the *Colorado*, was to command the infantry and Lieutenant Commander Douglass Cassel was to command the artillery. Captain McLane Tilton, of course, was to command the Marines of the *Colorado, Alaska,* and *Benicia.* The Marines were to act as advance guard and to provide protection for the front and flanks of the force; placed in this position because of their 'steadiness and discipline' and looked to with confidence in case of difficulty.

Besides providing the tactical formation for the landing (which was not followed), and the general order of march while ashore (which was followed), the order also contained necessary administrative details.

All hands were to carry blankets, done up in a roll, strapped over their shoulders. Each man was to carry his pot slung to his belt along with two days cooked rations. Sixty rounds of ammunition would be carried by the infantry, and the artillery were to carry cutlasses and pistols, their customary arms at battle stations.

Now that it was almost a certainty that the 10th of June would see the Landing Force landed, exercise and training of the companies, batteries, and boat crews was accelerated. All ships of the squadron were exercised at clearing the ship for action, the launches and cutter crews drilled at manning the howitzers, and bluejackets and Marines instructed in bugle calls and drum rolls for land operations.

The large ships were exercised at getting up yards, stays, and water whips for loading howitzers and provisions into smaller craft. The seamen of the Landing Force were exercised at the manual of arms and instructed in loading, aiming and unloading the new Remington breech-loading carbines with which they would be armed. Finally, in full dress review, the admiral ordered all the 'companies of infantry, the field batteries of artillery, and the pioneers, sappers and miners and hospital corps be assembled, and pass in review.'

On the 9th of June, the *Monocacy* edged alongside the *Colorado* and two 9-inch guns of the *Colorado's* quarter-deck battery, 30 rounds of 9-inch grape, 30 rounds of 9-inch shrapnel and 10 rounds of canister were loaded aboard her. The preparations for moving up the river were complete.

Saturday, June 10, 1871

At 10 a.m. the 10th of June, the Gunboat *Monocacy* weighed anchor, and in the company of two steam launches, steamed north toward the mouth of the Salee River to act as the Expeditionary fire-support ship. The mission of the *Monocacy* was to drive the Koreans from the fort and its redoubt before the Landing Force landed.

At 10:30 the *Palos*, towing 22 launches, cutters, and boats with 546 naval officers and men, four Marine officers and 105 Marines embarked, started up the channel in the wake of the *Monocacy*.

Just before noon, the *Monocacy* reached a point in the river about 800 yards below the fort and began lobbing shots into it. As the *Monocacy* continued to steam toward the fort, the narrowness of the river channel directly abreast the walls forced the ship to pass within 300 yards of the defenders' guns. At this point, the Koreans began returning American fire, but as with the engagement of the surveying party ten days before, the Asians' fire was inaccurate and ineffective. The standing rigging of the *Monocacy* was cut by some round passing overhead, and a few balls lodged in the hammock-nettings, but no casualties were suffered.

The gunboat continued up the river past the bottleneck at the fort and Commander E. P. McCrea ordered the anchor dropped at a spot about 500 yards above the fort and redoubt bearing south, southwest. Commander McCrea poured a withering fire into the fort, demolishing the north and river faces of the redoubt that extended 100 yards from the river edge from the fort proper. At 12:30, about one-half hour after firing on the fort began, all firing from the fort ceased.

By the time the *Palos*, looking like a mother hen with a large family, hove into view with her 22 boats strung out behind her and anchored a few hundred yards below the fort, and about a thousand yards below the *Monocacy* whose guns were still thundering at the now silent fort. The original plan had envisioned a landing supported by overhead or slightly angled fire from the fire-support ship but Commander Blake was influenced by the advice of Lieutenant Commander H. F. Picking, who was commanding all of the steam-launches. Commander Picking had come along side the *Palos* with the information that a spot below the fort looked like the best beach for the landing.

Commander Blake, squinting through his glasses at the distant beach, immediately agreed and at 12:43 gave the order to land the Landing Force. Two minutes later the first boats touched the 'beach.' This change in plans was perhaps the only bad tactical decision of the entire operation.

The first and most obvious criticism was that it threw the Landing Force into the line of fire of the *Monocacy*. Granted that the fort itself was generally between the Landing Force and fire-support ship, it was still a lucky chance that ricochets and long rounds did not fall among the boats and troops. Fortunately, no casualties did occur.

The second fault was the landing area that Lieutenant Commander Picking had chosen, and this was one of major proportion as the 'beach' was no beach at all, it was a mud flat!

As the first men leaped from the boats and landed in the soft, tenacious mud, curses and yells filled the air. The nearest solid ground was over 400 yards away and guns, ammunition, caissons and provisions had to be hauled through the grayish-brown morass. As the howitzers were rolled over the gunwales of the launchers and dropped into the mud, they sank down until their axles disappeared from sight. The gun crews were powerless to move the guns toward firm ground.

Commander L. A. Kimberly, standing in mud to his knees, his long, black mustachio forming weary semi-circles around his mouth, must have wished heartily that he had not been so eager to volunteer to command the Landing Force. Commander Douglass Cassel, whose artillery was now immobilized, asked Commander Kimberly for additional men to help the sweating crews straining at the gun wheels and carriages. If he didn't get help the batteries would stay where they were. Commander Kimberly wasted no time in sending the pioneers and several infantry companies to Commander Cassel's aid.

As the artillerymen struggled with their guns, Captain McLean Tilton formed his Marines into two long skirmish lines with the right flanks on the river and the left flanks extending toward solid ground several hundred yards away. The main body of infantry seamen formed into ragged line behind the Marines. The advance began with rifles loaded and at the ready.

There was still no firing from the fort, though black heads could be seen peering over the escarpments at the advancing troops and ducking down when a shell from the slowly-firing *Monocacy* struck in and around the fort.

Finally, the combination of shelling, and the plodding, inexorable advance of the Marines, proved too much for the remaining defenders. With frustrated yells of defiance, white-clothed figures began pouring over the walls and scurried to the west and north, firing a few futile shots as they ran. A signal went up for the *Palos* and the *Monocacy* to ceased firing. In a few minutes, the Marines poured into the fort to find it occupied only by dead bodies. Captain Tilton threw up his own defenses inside and around the fort and held there awaiting the arrival of the main body.

Commander McCrea, when he saw the signal from the *Palos* to lift his fire, wiped the sweat pouring down his face from his bald head, and turned his attentions to next fort up the river about 900 yards. The *Monocacy* weighed anchor and steamed slowly toward the second fortification that lay on a projection of land at the height of about 50 feet above the river. When he was within 500 yards of the place Commander McCrea ordered the anchor dropped and the guns of he American ship began a systematic destruction of the walls and occupants. The fort, an apparently well-constructed rock and mortar edifice of about 100 feet to a side, returned fire for a considerable while but the notorious inaccuracy of the Korean batteries saved the *Monocacy* from damage. The fire-support ship silenced the fort and except for an occasional shell thrown at targets of opportunity appearing on shore, the *Monocacy* remained quiet throughout the night.

Back at the first fort, called the *Marine Redoubt* in honor of the Marines, the artillery batteries finally struggled to firm ground about 4:30.   Hot, disheveled and exhausted, the artillerymen glared at the Marines and bluejacket infantry who for the past three hours had stood a relaxed guard to the north and west. The gumbo had been so tenacious that the sailors lost shoes, gaiters, and even part of their trousers in the mud. Most of the Landing Force looked as though it had been campaigning for weeks instead of hours.

Taking the weariness of the artillerymen into account, Commander Kimberly decided to go no further that night and to bivouac the Landing Force near the site of the fort. For purposes of security, Captain Tilton was ordered to reconnoiter ahead through the small village and fields just to the north. The Marines moved out along the narrow road running from the fort through the village and meandering across the rice paddies in a generally northwesterly direction.   Finding no Koreans during his reconnaissance, Tilton decided to establish his camp for the night on a small hill about one-third of a mile to the north of the main body.

The hill was found to be a Korean burial ground. From this point he put out pickets, divided his command into three reliefs, one to be on the alert at all times, and turned in among the graves of the long-dead for his first night's sleep on Korean soil.

The main body, bivouacked on a slightly raised plateau just behind the newly razed Marine redoubt, also turned in for the night after establishing local security. Both the Marines and the bluejackets were to discover, as many of their great-grandsons eighty years later were to discover, that the Korean soldier stayed up late. About midnight, screams and howls, intermixed with the firing of small arms were heard from a short distance inland. Commander Silas Casey, the infantry commander, ordered the drummers to beat a long-roll and the men fell in quickly, prepared to fight a night battle.   Commander Cassel's artillery was unlimbered and fired a few rounds in the direction of the noise which served to quiet the restless Orientals, and a few minutes later, retreat was sounded and the men returned to their blankets.

Sunday, June 11, 1871 – The Assault

At 4 a.m. as the first grey light of the false dawn came stealing over the mainland, the bugler's reveille echoed across the glassy rice-paddies and down through the still, dark ravines to the north of the American positions. Stiff and tired from their unaccustomed exertions of yesterday and the poor substitute of rocky soil for restful hammocks, sailors and Marines began stirring about, putting on their shoes and gaiters, rolling blanket rolls and starting little fires to heat their tea and coffee.

After breakfast, Company C, under Lieutenant G. M. Totten, along with the pioneers under Mate Quinn, were sent back into the redoubt to complete the destruction of the walls, buildings and guns. Quantities of rice and dried fish were destroyed and such huts and buildings what were obviously being used for military purposes were burned.

At 7:30 Commander Silas Casey directed Captain Tilton to push his Marines across the flat land toward the higher ground to the north, on which the second fort stood. The narrow path, which led from the first night's encampment, was suitable for Captain Tilton's purpose. It angled away from the river, leading generally toward the rear of the second fortification and gave dry footing for the Marines and solid ground for the advance of the artillery, running between the rice paddies on the left and the mud banks of the river on the right.

Upon reaching the line of low wooded hills without opposition, Captain Tilton changed his formation from a column to a skirmish line that he extended across the small peninsula upon which the fort stood, and in the rear of it.

Moving cautiously toward the silent fortification, the Marines advanced until the landward wall could be observed from their positions in a wooded area raised slightly above the level of the fort.

There were no signs of life on the walls, but brass cannon could be seen, trained toward the river. Holding two-thirds of his force in concealment as a base of fire, Captain Tilton sent his remaining Marines forward. They moved stealthily down out of the woods toward the fort, keeping well dispersed and momentarily expecting a hail of bullets from the hidden defenders. As they reached the walls, the Marines quickly moved through the ominously dark entrance cut into the stone walls, disappearing from view for a few seconds, and then reappeared waving the rest of the force on. The fort was deserted, mute evidence that the sharp-shooting crew of the *Monocacy* had done their work well the afternoon before. It was just 8 o'clock, Sunday morning.

While waiting for the main body to move up, the Marines started to dismantle the fort, tearing down the stone parapet to the level of the banquette on the side facing the river. About 30 cannon, some of which were still loaded 32-pounders, were thrown over the wall facing the river and Marine Bugler English jumped down off the 12-foot wall of the fort to roll the cannon off the precipice into the river. Master John Pillsbury soon arrived with his company and gave the Marines a hand in the destruction of the walls and destroying military stores. (Ranked between ensign and lieutenant, the title of "master" was changed to lieutenant junior grade in 1883).

Before the destruction was complete, Commander Kimberly ordered Captain Tilton to take the lead again and scout the route leading to the main fortification, called the *Citadel* by the Americans, about a mile and half distant. Captain Tilton put flankers out on both sides of the route of advance, scouring the scrubby woods and fields of grain, occasionally stirring up unarmed natives whom the Marines permitted to scamper off unmolested. The main body followed in four roughly aligned columns with two pieces of artillery at the head of the column, three pieces near the center and the remaining two bringing up the rear.

As the terrain became more deeply cleft with ravines and crossed with sharp ridges, all semblance of a road disappeared. The sun was now blazing down on the dense undergrowth that threw it back in shimmering heat waves through which the blue-clad column slowly advanced. It was rough going for the infantry, particularly the Marine skirmishers flanking the column, but it was sheer back breaking torment for the artillerymen as they pulled and shoved the heavy howitzers and their caissons up and down the tortuous route. Time after time, companies of infantry had to be detailed to aid the exhausted cannoneers manhandle the guns forward.

After advancing about a half mile from the second fort, named *Fort Monocacy* in just tribute to the accuracy of the gunboat's batteries, the Landing Force was hit by small arms fire. The firing, in ragged volleys, was being directed at the column from a high ridge to the front and left of the Force. The left flankers, on Captain Tilton's orders, wheeled and struggled upward toward the Koreans, who retreated to the next ridge parallel to the route of march.

There they continued firing their muskets and jingalls (a crude, unrifled musket usually fired from a rest, though sometimes a team of two men fired the piece with one man holding the muzzle on his shoulder) at the main body, but poor marksmanship and distance combined to spare the Americans any casualties. To save diverting the flankers further, an artillery piece was brought up by Commander Cassel and his men, through superhuman effort, and a few shells were thrown at the Koreans, dispersing them, and the Landing Force pushed on.

It was the middle of the morning now, and as the sun-baked column slogged painfully on, the officers became aware of a menacing and dangerous situation developing to the left of the column.

Where earlier there had been just a hundred of so white-clad hostiles on the ridges, there now were thousands. As the 655 sailors and Marines toiled along the ravines and over the ridges, the enemy multitude stayed abreast, keeping the American column between themselves and the river. In another half hour the force would arrive at the land end of the peninsula upon which the *Citadel* stood. There the Americans would have to change directions to attack the final line of fortifications that the *Citadel* dominated.

This change of direction would place the Koreans, now on the left, directly in the rear of their column. Kimberly and Casey recognized the precariousness of their position and Tilton was particularly concerned over the possibility of a trap. The abandonment of *Fort Monocacy*, the overwhelming numbers of Koreans paralleling the Landing Force, the powerful stronghold ahead could indicate that the Koreans planned to wait until the Americans attacked the *Citadel*, then launch their main effort from the American rear, smashing them in a classic pincer movement.

Improvising as the column struggled forward, Commander Kimberly sent Commander Oscar Heyerman with A Company, Master John Pillsbury with F Company and Lieutenant A. S. Snow with his section of artillery to the crest of a hill overlooking the route of march to protect the rear of the force. He then ordered his Second in Command, Lieutenant Commander W. K. Wheeler, who commanded the Landing Force Reserve, to the top of another hill a quarter mile further along toward the *Citadel*. Commander Wheeler took Master F. J. Drake with B Company and three pieces of artillery under the command of Lieutenant W.W. Mead to the crest of the hill with him. With the heights above them commanded by the far-shooting and accurate artillery, the members of the Landing Party felt safe.

The Force now moved on with all the rapidity the heat-debilitated men could muster, with red-faced and sweating Marines searching anxiously for the outer works of the fortifications they knew lay somewhere ahead in this incredibly chopped up terrain

At last, Captain Tilton called a halt, judging that his skirmishers had reached a point about one-third of a mile from the *Citadel*. The men were exhausted and a number had fallen from the heat. It was necessary to rest them even though several thousand Koreans were pressing in from the rear. The all-important question was: Could Commanders Heyerman and Wheeler with three companies of infantry and five pieces of artillery effectively block the movement of the Koreans against the rear of the Landing Force?

As soon as the men had rested momentarily, Captain Tilton ordered his skirmishers to push on cautiously until the Marines reached a ridge just separated from the conical hill upon which the *Citadel* stood. In order to get to the last ridge it was necessary for the Marines to cross about 30 yards of open ground. Just to the right and front of the Marines' position stood a line of Korean banners planted on a path leading to the *Citadel*.

Captain Tilton assumed that these banners were placed in that position to decoy the American force and decided to use them to his own advantage.

The Marine captain, with several of his men, bravely rushed to the row of pennants and pulled down about fifteen of them before the defenders in the *Citadel* loosed a tremendous hail of bullets. The Marines' action had evidently been too sudden for the Koreans, for none of the Marine decoys were hit, and as soon as the firing slacked off, Tilton gave the order to rush for the next ridge. Most of the muskets of the Koreans in the fort being empty, the Marines made it across the open ground to the final ridge with only one casualty, Private Dennis Hanrahan of the *Alaska* who fell dead from a Korean bullet.

Now the Marines had some cover from the firing from the fort, and by lying in concealment in the grasses and undergrowth of the ridge, they could place deadly fire from their own long rifles into the fort now about 125 yards away.

The *Citadel* itself was a circular redoubt with walls of earth, stone, mortar and mud sitting atop a cone-shaped hill. Its interior diameter didn't exceed 60 feet, and it was used, because of its height, as a command post for the complex of forts on the lower reaches of the river. It was occupied now by Oh Chae-yon,

Lieutenant General of the fortified island of Kanghwa-do, and his bravest and most trusted officers and men. The side of the hill toward the American positions formed a steep slope starting from the bottom of the ravine and connected with the wall of the fort so closely that it was difficult to tell where the slope of the hill ended and the fortification began.

Below the *Citadel* on the same land projection, were two more fortifications: One of which was constructed on a projection of rock on the south side of the peninsula, the other at the waterline on the north side of the peninsula, both being armed with cannon of a wide range of age and caliber. (It is entirely probable that the sailors and Marines of the Asiatic Fleet enjoyed the dubious distinction of having been fired upon by the oldest artillery still in use in the world. A close study of the five bronze cannon captured by the Landing Force and brought back to the U.S. revealed that two had been cast in 1313 A.D., one in 1607, one in 1665 and one in 1680.)

As the main body found firing positions on the ridge and began sniping at the defenders in the *Citadel*, the crashing roar of large guns from the rear told of the fight that Commanders Heyerman and Wheeler and their artillery were making against the large forces attacking the rear. A few minutes before, hundreds of heads began appearing over the crest of a hill about 500 yards to west of Commander Wheeler's position, and balls from muskets and jingalls started zinging around the sailors.

Twice waves of white-garbed figures surged over the top of the hill and headed down the slopes toward the American rear guard, and twice the roar of the five pieces of artillery and the crack of the sailors' carbines drove the Koreans back with heavy losses. The grape shot, canister and explosive shells terrorized the Asians. The American rear seemed to be safe.

The fight at the *Citadel* had increased in intensity. The shells from the *Monocacy* exploding over and in the walls of the *Citadel* and the water forts, had killed many of the defenders and the rifles and carbines of the Marines and sailors firing from 100 yards away were killing many more. The Koreans, tough fatalistic fighters, must have known that they had little chance for survival. They began to expose themselves recklessly over the parapet of the fort from the waist up, and from inside the walls came a dirge-like death chant that chilled the American fighters.

At exactly 11, Commander Kimberly ordered the Signal Officer, Mr. Houston, to signal the *Monocacy* to cease firing. At 11:15 Commander Silas Casey gave the order for the assault, and the entire line of 350 sailors and Marines rose up with a thunderous yell and started down into the ravine separating the two hills. Captain Tilton and his Marines were on the extreme right, and Lieutenant Hugh McKee, with Company D and Master T. C. McLean with Company G were on the extreme left.

The Americans plunged down the slope, some loosing their footing and falling headlong down the steep incline, others stopping momentarily to get off a hurriedly-aimed shot at the walls looming above them. The defenders were now standing in full view on the parapet, discharging their muskets down on the attackers. Jingall 'teams' would mount the wall, the man carrying the muzzle kneeling down to depress the musket's aim into the ravine below, while the 'shooter' would touch off the piece while it rested on his shoulder. Their muskets and jingalls empty, the Koreans picked up rocks and pieces of debris and flung them down on the force struggling up the hill. But although the Koreans in the *Citadel* matched in numbers the sailors and Marines fighting their way up the side of the fort, nothing seemed to slow the Americans. On they came with dirty, bearded faces streaked with sweat, their mouths open as they gasped for breath, their teeth gleaming in sun-reddened faces.

Private Michael Owens of the *Colorado*, clambering up the hill a few years ahead of the rest, was only 40 feet from the wall when he fell with a bullet in his groin. Landsman Seth Allen, from the *Colorado* was well ahead of the charging attackers and almost to the walls of the fort then he was struck and killed by a crude ball. The ranks kept coming, up to the stone walls, broken in places by the shelling of the *Monocacy*, and over the parapet and into the fort itself, locking hand-to-hand with the crazed defenders.

Elsewhere within the fort the fight raged on with savage intensity, the Koreans using spears, swords, knives, stones and even throwing dust in the faces of the Americans. The sailors fought on, after their guns were empty, with cutlasses and carbines used as clubs. The Marines countered the spears of the tiger-hunters with bayonets on the end of the long rifles, then reversed the weapons and crushed heads with the rifle butts.

Private Michael McNamara of the *Benicia* closed with a stocky Korean, wrenched the matchlock from his hands and clubbed him to death with it. Private John Coleman of the *Colorado* plunged into a group of Koreans surrounding Alexander McKenzie and dispersed the Koreans, saving the wounded McKenzie's life. Private James Dougherty of the *Benicia*, spotting a soldier distinguished from the others by his hat adornments of peacock feathers and horsehair dyed red and yellow, correctly assumed this was the Korean commander. Dougherty fought his way to the side of the yelling, gesticulating commander and killed Oh Chae-yon, Lieutenant General of the Kanghwa-do forts.

The focus of the fighting, after the main body of the Americans entered the fort, centered around the huge yellow standard of the fallen Korean commander. Captain Tilton, with Corporal Charles Brown of the *Colorado* at his side, charged for the flag to rip it from its pole. Seconds before they reached it, the wiry figure of Private Hugh Purvis of the *Alaska* was at the standard, unknotting the halyards. Captain Tilton and Corporal Brown, ignoring the halyards, lunged at the flag and tore it from its lashings. Far below, cheers rang out from the *Monocacy* and *Palos* as the crews saw the first indication of how the fight inside the fort was going.

Now that the flag was down and their commander killed, the remaining Koreans lost heart and began to retreat from the *Citadel* to the forts below. Captain Tilton spotted the retreat and ordered one of his companies to cut them off. The Marines caught and killed many as they were scaling the parapet. Some who escaped the fort were shot down as they ran down the ridge toward the water fort on the south of the peninsula.

Commander Cassel's batteries on the ridge were quick to spot the fleeing Koreans, mowing them down in swaths with canister. Moving at full speed, the white-garbed figures tumbled head over heels as they were hit by rifle balls and exploding howitzer shells, rolling down the ridge into the water. A few, escaping the fire of the Americans, were seen to jump into the river where they were dragged under by their water-soaked clothing. Some sat on the riverbank and methodically cut their own throats.

At 11:20 the battle was over. The American flag flew from the east parapet of the *Citadel*, overlooking the river where all could see. Two hundred forty-three corpses were strewn in and around the fort. On some the thick layers of clothing smoldered and burned from the exploding powder of cannon shells and the sickening stench of roast flesh filled the air. At least 100 bodies were floating on or sank in the river, which ran in crimson streaks here and there. Only twenty prisoners, all wounded, had been taken of the estimated 350-400 Koreans defending the works.

The American losses were three killed and nine wounded, three severely.

The Landing Force re-embarked the next morning at daybreak, with the Marines holding the beachhead against a possible counterattack, which never materialized.

The Death of Lieutenant Hugh Wilson McKee

Lieutenant Hugh McKee, for whom the *Citadel* was named, was a respected naval officer, popular with his fellow sailors. The account of his death is best chronicled by his friend, Lieutenant Bloomfield McIlvaine, in a letter Lieutenant McIlvaine wrote to his (McIlvaine's) mother from Korea on June 22, 1871. The letter was printed in the November 18, 1900 issue of the Lexington (Kentucky) *Morning Herald*:

As the Admiral, I think, intends to send a telephonic dispatch, you will undoubtedly see in the papers before you get this, that our expedition against the Coreans, of which I spoke in my last letter, has been successful.

We defeated the enemy and accomplished everything that we attempted, but it was done at a fearful cost. It cost the Navy one of its finest officers, the country one of the noblest and bravest men it has ever produced, and me, the dearest and most intimate friend I had on earth – Lieutenant Hugh McKee, glorious, splendid fellow!

If a high and noble life will take a man there, he must now undoubtedly be in Heaven. I cannot tell you, dear mother, what a loss and what a friend he has been to me. I could not have loved him more had he been my brother ... He was several years older and had a great deal of experience in the world. As for bravery, from the day he entered the Naval Academy, everybody has known that nothing on earth could daunt him. I have written to his mother. It was the most painful experience in the world. His mother was completely wrapped up in him. His body was prepared to send home. He and I, when we first left the United States, entered into an agreement to do that in case of the death of the other. Poor fellow, I think he felt some premonition that he was going to be killed in the fight. I found in his desk a letter addressed to me giving explicit directions in regard to everything, written the evening before he left the ship on the expedition.

After he received the wound he said, "There never was a McKee who went into battle who was not killed." His conduct in the fight was absolutely heroic. I have never heard in the history of our country a more beautiful instance of noble intrepidity. His father was killed in exactly the same way, while gallantly leading his men in the battle of Buena Vista.

I will now give a short account of our operations on shore: Our force consisted of a battalion, or regiment of ten companies and seven pieces of field artillery. I had command of a company, as had also McKee...the enemy retreated from their fortifications as we approached. We destroyed their guns, etc. and kept on.

At last they took refuge in a fort or citadel on the very peak of a high hill. Their position seemed impregnable and they had no doubt but that they would defeat us badly if we attempted to dislodge them ...we advanced and came in plain view of the citadel; the ramparts were decked with quantities of flags and streamers. The enemy, seeing it was our intention to attack, commenced cheering, that is, I suppose it was intended to be that, but the noise they made sounded more like the howling of dogs at midnight than anything else – a painful, dismal thing to listen to.

McKee turned to me and said, "Mac, we must capture one of those flags." We did it too. His company and mine captured two of the largest.

We arrived on the brow of the hill and got our companies stationed for the charge. At last the order was given and away we went. Our gallant sailor/soldiers, although ready to drop with fatigue, followed us and made for the citadel with a yell.

McKee got the start on all of us in the commencement of the charge and kept it. I think his heart was set on being the first man into the fort. I was with my company, close behind and a little to his left. My men did their best but we could not overtake him. When we got about half way up to the citadel, the enemy jumped up on the parapets and commenced throwing rocks and stones down at us, which we dodged as best we could, and shot them for their reward.

At last McKee arrived at the head of his company at the foot of the parapet. He was very conspicuously dressed as an officer, but without an instant's hesitation, and when he knew it was almost certain death, he clamored to the top, revolver in one hand and sword in the other. He stood for an instant facing the enemy, fired twice, and leaped in, the first and foremost, followed by his men.

My men then made a rush and I got on the parapet a few seconds after McKee. I jumped down inside, and such a fight was going on there I suppose I shall never see.

The Coreans fought desperately, but our men rushed upon them with the most irresistible force. The former fired everything they had loaded at us, then threw them down and took their long spears. Our men went at them with carbines, pistols, bayonets and cutlasses. In less time that it takes me to write it, we had killed or driven every one from the citadel and victory was ours.

Just before the fighting was over, and I was advancing in the fort, I looked down at my feet among the dead and saw McKee lying there. He looked up at me and said in the cool, calm way: "Mac, I am mortally wounded." With the assistance of two or three of his men, I carried him a little aside and looked at his wound. It was in the stomach from a bullet. I could not and would not believe it was serious and told him so...the doctor soon came up from the rear and said he ought to be taken aboard the *Monocacy*. I obtained permission to go with him, the fighting being over, but was told to come back immediately. All the way he talked very little, but lay perfectly quiet with the eyes closed. When we arrived aboard the *Monocacy*, I gave him over to the care of the surgeons and then I said, "Now Mac, you know I must go back to my company." He held out his hand, smiled and said, "Well, good-bye Mac, if I don't see you again ..." at about 6 o'clock in the afternoon the boat came in from the *Monocacy* and an officer came up to inform me that McKee had died. His last words were, "Tell the dear beloved ones at home that my last prayer was for them."

For the present our fighting was over. We were victorious, but I cannot see that the object for which we came here is one bit advanced. And in about a week we will leave without having accomplished this objective. It is true that we have done everything that could have been done. The Coreans will resist and are evidently determined to resist, and as we have not force enough to march through their country, which is the only way to bring them to terms, there is northing for us to do but to leave ... I think it is our intention to leave here in about a week for Chefoo. From there we will go immediately to Yokohama.

Your affectionate son
Bloomfield McIlvaine

Small War – Large Rewards

During the Korean War of June 25, 1950 to July 27, 1953, more than 1.7 million Americans served in that theater. During the Weekend War, slightly more than 1,200 sailors and Marines took part, counting those who stayed on the ships during the action.

Medals of Honor were awarded to 131 American service personnel during the Korean War; 15 medals were won during the Weekend War. In perspective, one of each 13,600 men serving won the country's highest military decoration during the Korean War, while Medals of Honor were won by one of every 80 who were in the Kanghwa area during June 1871. The decorations of 1871 marked the first time that medals were awarded for action in a foreign country.

An anomaly would seem that of the 15 MOH's awarded, none went to Lieutenant McKee. This was according to protocol as only enlisted navy and Marine personnel were eligible for the award in 1871.

U.S. Naval Personnel Awarded Medals of Honor

Name	Assigned to	Born
Ordinary Seaman John Andrews	USS Benicia	Maryland
Quartermaster Frederick Franklin	USS Colorado	New Hampshire
Chief Quartermaster Patrick Grace	USS Benicia	Ireland
Carpenter Cyrus Hayden	USS Colorado	Maine
Landsman William Lukes	Company D	Bohemia
Boatswain's Mate Alexander McKenzie	USS Colorado	Scotland
Landsman James Merton	Company D	England
Quartermaster Samuel Rogers	USS Colorado	New York
Ordinary Seaman William Troy	USS Colorado	Massachusetts

U.S. Marines Awarded Medals of Honor

Name	Assigned to	Born
Corporal Charles Brown	USS Colorado	New York
Private John Coleman	USS Colorado	Ireland
Private James Dougherty	USS Carondelet	Ireland
Private Michael McNamara	USS Benicia	Ireland
Private Michael Owens	USS Colorado	New York
Private Hugh Purvis	USS Alaska	Pennsylvania

The Rest of the Story

The American commander tried one more tactic to try to win the treaty – a trade.

A number of Korean soldiers had been captured and were aboard the American warships. A trade was proposed – sign the treaty and the captives would be returned.

The Koreans gave a tart reply. The captives had disgraced themselves and their ancestors by falling into enemy hands. If returned they would be executed. The final American blue chip had faded.

The body of Lieutenant McKee was embalmed and sent back to Kentucky for burial in the Lexington Cemetery beneath an appropriate marker. He received a hero's welcome in his hometown.

Newspaper accounts from the *Kentucky Statesman* reported that the coffin was taken to the Second Presbyterian Church where a detail from Company A, Fourth U.S. Infantry stood guard.

A number of Lieutenant McKee's artifacts have been donated to the library of Transylvania University in Lexington, Kentucky, where they are on display.

The Taewongun was eased out of power two years after the *6/11 Incident* by King Kojong who had reached his majority but not before he ordered a number of stone tables scattered around Korea that read:

The Barbarians from beyond the seas have violated our borders and invaded our land. If we do not fight we must make treaties with them. Those who favor the making of a treaty sell their country. Let this be a warning to ten thousand generations.

Little by little the "Five No's" of the Taewongun were dismantled as Korea moved, slowly and not always willingly, toward modernization. His stone tables were largely ignored.

The Reverend Thomas, of the *General Sherman* incident, is usually considered to be the first Protestant martyr to die in Korea trying to spread his version of the gospel. Thought it is usually believed that he was decapitated just after giving his Bible to his executioner, his efforts were not entirely in vain.

Thirteen years after the *6/11 Incident*, Methodist and Presbyterian missionaries arrived in the Korea and Protestantism has been growing steadily since.

According to the *Korea Overseas Information Service*, while only two percent of the Asian population is Christian, a full

33 percent of South Koreans confess that faith. There are 11 million Protestants and three million Catholics out of a population of some 42 million. Korea today is second only to the United States in sending Christian missionaries around the globe.

The highly sought – by the Americans – treaty of commerce and friendship was negotiated in 1882. To say the treaty was *negotiated* would be to overstate the case. It was *agreed* upon by the U.S. Navy Commodore Robert W. Shufeldt and Chinese diplomat Li Hung-chang, supposedly representing Korea.

The treaty was comprehensive, including designing the flag still used by South Korea. More importantly, the United States got extraterritorial rights for its citizens, consular representation, fixed tariffs, and port concessions, among other benefits. The United Kingdom and Germany signed similar treaties within weeks. Korea received little in return.

Korea slowly slipped out of consciousness in America. China, Japan and Russia were jockeying for supremacy on the peninsula with Japan "winning" the right to control Korean affairs as a result of defeating Russia in the Russo-Japanese War of 1904-05. The maxim "when the whales fight, the shrimp are crushed" again proved to be true. Korea was annexed by Japan in 1910 as the international community looked on.

Winners and Losers

Like the proverbial baseball trade that helps both teams, both sides could claim victory in the *6/11 Incident.*

The U.S. Navy had proven that no country could fire at its naval vessels with impunity. The "lesson" taught the Koreans also took some of the sting out of the burning of the *General Sherman.*

The Koreans could also claim victory. True, some 300 soldiers were reportedly killed and loads of military stores were destroyed, dumped into the sea, or carried back to the United States by the U.S. Navy. But the foreign ships soon disappeared over the horizon and left no mark.

Both sides were also a little embarrassed by the *6/11 Incident.*

It took more than 125 years before a suitable marker was dedicated to General Oh and the "martyrs" who died on Kanghwa Island. Considering how easily their countrymen had routed the French five years earlier, the *6/11* fighting was not the Korean Army's finest hour.

The American press played up the American victory over the "barbarians" for a few days but few people seemed to care.

The New York *Times* ran a page one, full column, story on August 23, 1871, under its familiar stacked headlines:

THE COREAN WAR

Full Details of the Recent Operations

Interesting Description of the Second Engagement

Origin of the Difficulty and the Final Result

The Movements of the Exploring Expedition

Complete Success of the Attack on the Forts

Admiral Rodgers' Congratulatory Order

The Origin, Purpose and Result of the Expedition – Future Action of Civilized Powers Foreshadowed

Special Dispatch to the New York Times

WASHINGTON, Aug 21. – The Eastern mails have been received. They bring full reports of the Corean expedition, both to the Navy and State Departments. The expedition was undertaken with the purpose of securing a treaty with the Coreans that would assure safety to any of our sailors who might hereafter be shipwrecked on the Corean coast. It seems that when the fleet arrived at the mouth of the Salt (Salee) River, the last of May, communication was opened with the local authorities or magistrates with the dispatches style perfects, and they made known that they were willing to negotiate for a treaty, and in reply to a request, gave our fleet permission to make a survey of the river.

The beginning had such a seemingly propitious fortune, but it turned out that when the survey was undertaken on June 1, as the party came to a bend in the river an attack had been arranged beforehand, which was made from forts on the shore, with results which have been pretty fully published.

The Coreans had treacherously lured the surveying party where they expected they would easily destroy it. After the return of the party which had thus been fired upon to the anchorage of the fleet, a dispatch was sent by Minister Low to the Corean officials demanding an explanation and an apology for the incident and expressing the determination of the United States forces, in

44

case proper reparations were not made, to redress the injury occasioned by the perfidy. Every effort was made to have the wrong acknowledged and redressed but they failed, the Coreans refused in an insulting manner to make any amends.

The *Times'* story went on to recount the battle at the forts and then printed a "victory lap" from the pen of Admiral Rodgers.

THE COREA.

Conclusion of Admiral Rodgers' Report –
Gallantry of the Attacking Force –
The Iroquois to Reinforce the Asiatic Squadron

WASHINGTON, Aug. 22. The following is the report of Admiral Rodgers: "We captured and destroyed five forts – those of Point du Coude and Fort McKee being probably among the principal and the strongest in the Kingdom, fifty flags were taken, including those of the Generalissimo; 481 pieces of ordnance fell into our hands, besides very many gingals; 243 dead Coreans were counted in the works; a few prisoners were taken, not above twenty, and most of these were wounded. These last were treated with all the attention possible and finally released. Thus was the treacherous attack upon our people and the insult to our flag redressed. It was not deemed desirable to hold the position, as our purpose was not to enter upon extended operations; and on account of the exceeding danger and difficulties of holding the vessels in position, exposed to the furious and uncertain currents of the river, it was deemed best to withdraw the entire force upon the following morning, the 12th of June. It gives me the greatest of satisfaction to say that in this expedition our officers and men encountered difficulties that were surmounted only by the most arduous labor, and defeated a determined enemy in a desperate fight, with courage the most admirable. The victory is one of which the navy may well feel proud."

Little by little the American public began to get the queasy feeling of having cheered while the football captain beat up the band's piccolo player.

One of those who did not join in the cheering was long-time editor of the New York *Tribune* Horace Greeley.

Greeley was opposed to the administration of President Ulysses S. Grant, and carried on a running feud with the Republican-leaning (at that time) New York *Times*.

In the *Tribune* of July 17, 1871, Greeley reprimanded the expansionist policies of the Republicans by writing:

The American Minister has plausibly urged upon the Coreans the policy of making a treaty; but his smooth speeches, strained through Chinese interpreters, availed naught to the suspicious people, especially as the frowning sides of the men-of-war and their black-muzzled batteries were threateningly held behind the oily utterance of the Minister's opening overture. The surveying party went to work 'in the interests of civilization.' For though the massacre of the crew of the *General Sherman* was one of the original excuses for the expedition, that grievance seems to have disappeared before the overpowering necessity of mapping the Corean coast and inviting the people to partake of the sweets of American civilization.

Greeley ended his piece with words that resonate to the current decade: "What right have we in Corean waters, what are we to gain by killing these people, how many more are to be killed and where is this fierce diplomacy to land us – all these questions will become interesting *as we find how much easier it is to go to war than to get out of it.*" (emphasis added)

Perhaps the final lines of the Pete Seeger protest song of the 1960s were more prophetic than poetic ...

"When will they ever learn?
"When will they ev – er learn?"

Even the New York *Times* eventually lost its zest for the war. As quoted in the New York *Tribune* of November 18, 1871, the *Times* is reported to have written:

Advises from Shanghai of Oct. 12 contain the curt announcement 'The Corean expedition seems to have been given up.' If this statement turns out to be correct, it is one that the country will not hear with much satisfaction. Having gotten into a vexatious squabble with a parcel of semi-barbarous Orientals, it was highly desirable that we should at least extricate ourselves from it with dignity. We have simply succeeded in making the Coreans our lasting enemies and have allowed them to form a mistaken idea of our weakness.

To obtain any sort of consideration in the East, a nation must have some intelligible policy. It must either abstain from the employment of force to protect its subjects, whatever be the outrages to which they have been subjected; or if it is to employ powder and shot in the interests of commerce and civilization, it must see that dose is strong enough to produce the desired effect or better behavior in the future. In Corea, we have blundered between the two policies, and have retired without either glory or satisfaction.

The *Tribune* maintained its anti-imperialist stance in the same article by writing:

To "dose" them with more shell and grape, in view of the known facts, would be wanton, inexcusable murder. Such a "dose" might be ever so strong without inducing other sentiments in the breasts of the victims than those of grief, indignation, and hatred. Let us try instead one "dose" of apology and reparation; for this need not be "strong" to secure the desired results.

Speaking in the Senate in 1878, and alluding to relations with Corea and the *6/11 Incident*, California lawmaker Aaron Sargent sided with the *Tribune* and asked rhetorically what would happen if a foreign power, uninvited, decided to sail up the James River toward Richmond, Virginia?

In the American Heritage publication *The Confident Years,* the *6/11 Incident* is dismissed in 62 words as a punitive expedition to "chastise hostile Koreans" for firing on and sinking an American trading vessel and killing the crew. Though not mentioned by name, the reference was to the *General Sherman* incident.

Korea and the United States next met in 1945 when American forces accepted the Japanese surrender south of the 38th Parallel at the end of World War II.

Five years later the Forgotten War began, overshadowing by a thousand fold the Unknown War of 1871.

Loose Ends

Two "loose ends" bear some discussion.

A group of Americans living in Korea are working to have the United States return the "Generalissimo Flag", currently at the U. S. Naval Academy, to Korea. The United States and South Korea have been allies for more than 50 years and the Weekend War happened more than 130 years ago. Returning the flag would be a good will gesture. This same group would like the North Koreans to return the *USS Pueblo*. Chances of this happening are pretty slim.

The second loose end is how accurate are the casualty figurers?

Can a ratio of 100 to one deaths be realistic? A comparison with a similar battle in the American Civil War just eight years earlier should shed some light on the situation.

At Fredericksburg, Virginia, the Confederate Armies of Generals Robert E. Lee, James Longstreet and Stonewall Jackson occupied the high ground and used as fortifications a stone fence, parapets, and a sunken road. The Confederates fought on the defensive.

Union General Ambrose Burnside's Army was about twice as large as the Confederate force. But Burnside's men were on the offensive, and charged, uphill, over open ground, again and again.

When the last musket misfired, and the smoke finally cleared, the Union forces had suffered more than double the casualties as the defenders.

The same story was repeated, only more so, at the battle of Kennesaw Mountain in Georgia in 1864.

The battle-tested soldiers of Union General William T. Sherman attacked the Confederate defenders under General Joseph Johnston three times, charging uphill into the Confederate fortifications. The toll this time was almost 2,000 killed and wounded Union soldiers as opposed to less than 300 Confederate casualties.

To summarize the fighting on Kanghwa, the American forces had many advantages. They had the support of massive naval batteries that battered the Korean defenses. The bluejackets had breech-loading Remington rifles. The sailors and Marines had superior leadership and were supported by field artillery. The American sailors and Marines fought with great courage and won the battles easily. It was basically a battle between nineteenth-century armed Americans fighting Koreans equipped with sixteenth-century weapons.

On the other hand, the Koreans, knowing that their lives and those of their families were on the firing line, fought like "tigers." They were more familiar with the terrain. Most importantly, they held the high ground and were within fortifications.

Were the Korean defenders the worse marksmen ever to hold a musket? Or is the casualty count a nineteenth-century rendition of classic military "spin?"

Could the American force have undercounted its dead? Considering that almost half of the Medal of Honor winners were born outside the United States, it is logical to assume that a large percentage of foreign-born were part of the Asiatic Fleet. These men probably had few ties in the United States and their deaths could possibly have been under-reported with no one noticing.

Consider a letter from an anonymous officer aboard the *USS Colorado* published in the New York *Times* of August 25, 1871 under the headline:

LETTER FROM KOREA
Interesting Description of the Expedition
As a Narrative of Events – Details of
the engagement and the Probable Results

The following private letter, written to a friend by an officer of the United States Asiatic Fleet, under command of Admiral Rodgers, will be read with interest, as it affords information not otherwise to be obtained, and is reliable in all its details.

UNITED STATESHIP COLORADO
Boosee Anchorage, Corea
Thursday, June 29, 1871

I sent you a letter by last mail from here (per United States Ship *Palos*, to Chefoo and Shanghai) on June 3, though I am afraid it was short and scrappy. The *Palos* returned from Chefoo on the 8th, bringing our mail with dates to April 30, and among my letters was the thick one from you of April 4. Very glad indeed, was I to get it too, old friend, especially as I don't know but that these Coreans might knock me over in the fight so soon to come off, and so I wouldn't get any more letters from you.

I suppose that long before this reached you, you will have seen the Admiral's telegram to the Department, with the account of the two days fight, and how we whipped the Coreans. I was ordered to the *Monocacy* and did duty on board her and the hospital boat bringing off the wounded; we had three killed and nine wounded in all – two men killed outright. One of our landsmen and one marine of the *Benicia* and Lieut. McKee of our ship, a brave generous fellow, who died just six hours after being hit, shot through the abdomen; the father, an army officer, went down the same way at Buena Vista. Our wounded are all doing well.

The Coreans, at every fight except the citadel, dragged off the dead and wounded, and there they hadn't any left to do it; I suppose that their loss in all could not have been less than eight hundred killed and wounded; they fought like wild beasts, and with immense pluck, but their arms and powder are very bad. They have for firearms, old-fashioned gingals, match-locks, and wall

49

pieces, and a kind of breech-loading six-pounder, with some larger pieces.

They lash their guns to big logs and train them on mid-channel, then they can't alter the range. In both fights, the attack of June 1 and also on June 10 and 11, their shot flew like hail. Capt. Blake said he never saw shot come so thick, but their aim was awful poor.

How our loss was so few I can't fancy, except for the poor aim. Their chief stronghold, the citadel, which commands the river and the way to the capital "Saoul" (sic), is on a point stretching out into the river. The river thereabouts is full of rocks and the current runs like a millrace.

Our lads had to march that morning about eight miles, fighting as they went, and just at noon, charged, and took the citadel in the flank; the beggars evidently did not expect any enemy would attack the front, so we wiped them out.

I am afraid that the Chinese will circulate the report that we were driven off here. Anyway, I am afraid that the whole thing will adversely affect out interest in China.

I don't think the lives we lost could be made up by any gain we could ever get out of Corea (emphasis added).

Two points are made in this letter that are of interest: First, the writer reported that the Coreans rained shots down "like hail" and that Captain Blake had "never seen shots so thick." Firing from behind fortifications, into an enemy charging uphill in daylight, is it logical that so few of the bullets hit home?

And secondly, the writer understood the futility of the action saying nothing had been gained which was worth the lives of the Americans who had died.

The return of the generalissimo flag and the *USS Pueblo* may take place some day tying up one loose end.

More than 130 years after the fact, the accuracy of the casualties during the Weekend War will have to remain an academic question.

And while the name Hugh Wilson McKee may not resonate outside a small circle in Lexington, Kentucky, he has been memorialized four times by the U.S. Navy.

Three ships have been named the USS McKee, a Dahlgren-class torpedo boat in the Spanish-American War era, a Wickes-class destroyer during World War I, and a Fletcher-class destroyer carried the name during World War II.

A three by five foot marble plaque in the Chapel of the U.S. Naval Academy bears this inscription: "Lieutenant Hugh W. McKee, born April 23, 1844; died June 11, 1871; from wounds received the same day on the parapet of the *Citadel*, Kanghoa Island, Corea; while leading heroically the assault of the naval battalion of the U.S. Asiatic Fleet. Erected by his brother officers on the squadron."

A lasting tribute from the men with whom he fought and died.

PRIMARY SOURCES

K. Jack Bauer, *The Korean Expedition of 1871*, United States Naval Institute Proceedings, February, 1948

Max Boot, *War Made New, Technology, Warfare, and the Course of History 1500 to Today*, Gotham Books, 2006

Albert Castel and Andrew Nahne, *Our Little War with the Heathen*, American Heritage Magazine, 1968

Gordon H. Chang, *Whose "Barbarism"? Whose "Treachery"? Race and Civilization in the Unknown United States-Korea War of 1871*, The Journal of American History, 2003

Dr. Bruce Cumings, *Korea's Place in the Sun, A Modern History*, W. W. Norton, 1997

John S.D. Eisenhower, *So Far from God: the United States War with Mexico, Random House*, 1989

Charles Flood, *Grant and Sherman, the Friendship Which Won the Civil War*, Farrar, Straus and Giroux, 2005

J.S. Gale, *The Fate of the General Sherman from an Eyewitness*, Korean Repository, 1895

David Halberstam, *The Coldest Winter, America and the Korean War*, Hyperion, 2007

Richard, Holmes, *Battlefield, Decisive Conflicts in History*, Oxford University Press, 2006

Yogkoo Kim, *The Five Years' Crisis 1866-1871, Korea in the Maelstrom of Western Imperialism*, Circle, 2001

Dan Kurzman, *Day of the Bomb*, McGraw-Hill, 1986

Clyde H. Metcalf, *A History of the United States Marines*, G.P. Putnam's Sons, 1939

Allan Millett, *The War for Korea*, University of Kansas Press, 2005

James B. Palais, *Politics and Policy in Traditional Korea*, Harvard University Press, 1975

James S. Robbins, *Last in their Class, Custer, Pickett and the Goats of West Point*, Encounter Books, 2006

Major C.F. Runyan, *Capt. McLane Tilton and the Korean Incident of 1871. Marine Corps Gazette*, March, 1958

Winfield Scott Schley, Rear Adm. U.S. Navy, *Forty-Five Years Under the Flag*, D. Appleton and Company, 1904

-----------------, *Scott Standard Postage Stamp Catalog, Countries J-L*, 2006

Otis A. Singleton, *The Mexican War*, University of Chicago Press, 1960

William Speer, *Corea: What Shall We Do With Her?*, Galaxy Magazine 1872

Robert Swartout, *Cultural Conflict and Gunboat Diplomacy: The Development of the 1871 Korean-American Incident*, Journal of Social Sciences and Humanities, 1976

Glyndon G. Van Deusen, *Horace Greeley, Nineteenth Century Crusader*, University of Pennsylvania Press, 1958

John E. Weems, *To Conquer a Peace*, Texas A&M University Press, 1974

SECONDARY SOURCES

Answers.com
Earthlink.com
Globalsecurity.com
Han Gyu Mu
Kim Young Sik
Lee Whoe Rang
Samurai-achieves
Shinmuyangyo.homeofheroes.com
Shipsonstamps

MEDIA SOURCES

Kentucky *Statesman*
Korea Overseas Information Service
Lexington (KY) *Herald-Leader*
Louisville (KY) *Courier-Journal*
New York *Times*
New York *Tribune*

Bayonet Decides

Doughboys in the Deep Freeze

"People do stupid things" is the tag line of a television ad campaign. The video shows a man cutting down a tree with a chain saw – and the tree falls on his car. In another version, a young baseball player swings his bat in the backyard. He loses the bat and it crashes through the patio window. The accompanying audio says people do dumb things like paying too much for the products of a competitor.

Companies are not immune. Decades ago the maker of the world's most successful soft drink decided to reformulate its product. The new product failed and the company went back to the all-time favorite. Some 60 years ago, a meat packer brought out a sure winner – the round hot dog. The circular wiener took a very small bite out of the frankfurter business. Little more successful was chlorophyll toothpaste that did little to fight cavities but was very successful in turning tongues green.

More serious are government initiatives which, when they are completed, leave people shaking their heads and asking: "What was that all about?"

A half-century ago the French were fighting a losing battle in Vietnam. The French knew they were going to withdraw but decided to make one last stand at a place called Dien Bien Phu.

Anyone who has ever studied Military Science 101 knows the high ground is never surrendered to the enemy. Nobody told the French. They pulled their forces into a bowl and were ready to fight to the end.

The Viet Minh circled the bowl-shaped valley and poured shells into Dien Bein Phu. And though the French knew they would soon sue for peace and leave Vietnam, fresh paratroopers were dropped to almost certain death inside the perimeter. "What were they thinking of?" mused the French population.

Almost a quarter-century ago American forces were stationed at an airport in Beirut, Lebanon. As Thomas Friedman pointed out in his book *From Beirut to Jerusalem*, the Marines and their counterparts had been dropped into the middle of an eight-sided civil war. Finally, in October 1983, a Hezbollah suicide bomber drove a truck packed with explosives into the building housing the Americans; the count of dead Marines and other servicemen totaled 241. The remaining force pulled out. No one has ever given a clear explanation of what the Americans had *hoped* to accomplish.

All of the above certainly fall into the category of people doing dumb things.

But it would be hard to find a more inexplicable government initiative than sending thousands of American soldiers into northern Russia in 1918 at cross purposes with their allies, in weather so cold that blood from a gunshot wound would almost instantaneously freeze. Again, no one seemed to have an answer when the Doughboys asked: "What are we doing here?"

The story unfolded like this: Europe had not fought a major war in almost a century. But by the 1910s the war clouds were gathering and the European powers were choosing up sides and signing alliances. The United States was watching from a safe haven across the Atlantic.

World War I in Capsule

The trigger for World War I was the June 28, 1914 assassination in Sarajevo, Serbia, of Austrian Crown Prince Francis Ferdinand and his wife by Gavrilo Princip of the terror group the "Black Hand." One month later Austria-Hungary declared war on diminutive Serbia and diplomats almost fell over each other to get their war declarations on the table and into the newspapers. Four days later Germany declared war on Russia. Three days after that Great Britain declared war on Germany – and so it went.

When the fighting was over some four years and three months later, more than eight and a half million graves had been filled by service members of all sides, with Russia and Germany making the largest contributions, more than a million and three-quarters each. All told, more than 37 million casualties were recorded, almost 60 percent of those taking part in the war ended up dead, wounded or missing.

As would also be the case in World War II, Russia had enormous human resources to pour into the fight but only a small industrial base. To ensure that Russia could remain in World War I, thus causing Germany and Austria-Hungary to fight a two-front battle, the Allies poured mountains of supplies into Murmansk and Archangel in the Arctic north and Vladivostok on the far eastern frontier of Russia.

And though little thought was given to Allied intervention in Russia in the early days of the war, the supplies stockpiled in and around the Arctic ports would be the catalyst for American troops fighting in Arctic Russia well *after* the Armistice of November 11, 1918.

Three major events in 1917 drastically changed the complexion of the war:

On February 1st Germany declared that it would initiate unrestricted submarine warfare;

On March 15th Tsar Nicholas II of Russia abdicated his throne;

On April 6th the U.S. House of Representatives, by a vote of 373 to 50, and the Senate, by a tally of 82-6, opted for war with Germany, primarily due to the doctrine of unrestricted submarine warfare.

By October of 1917 the Bolsheviks had brushed aside the provisional government of Alexander Kerensky and had seized power in Russia. High on their agenda was concluding the war with the Central Powers (Germany and Austria-Hungary) as quickly as possible, and on as favorable terms as could be obtained.

The terms offered were harsh, but the Bolsheviks accepted and Russia was out of the war by March 1918. This separate peace allowed Germany and Austria-Hungary to move tens of thousands of men to the Western Front in France and the outcome of the war was once again very much in doubt.

Russian and Allied Concerns

Both the Russians and Allied Forces had serious concerns in European Russia, from the Arctic Circle to Moscow and beyond.

The Bolsheviks, also known as the "Bolos" or the "Red" Russians, were now fighting a civil war with the "White" Russians, made up of anti-Communists, Social Democrats, tsarists, royalists, and other splinter factions. The Reds feared that the Whites were being helped by Germany and would be willing to allow German forces into Russia proper to fight the Bolsheviks.

Finland, which shares a long border with Russia, was also split Red-White and the concern was that the White Finns would join the Germans in a drive on St. Petersburg and possibly Moscow.

The Allies main dilemma was that the Germans might move into the Murmansk/Archangel areas and help themselves to the acres and acres of war machines and supplies basically there for the taking. If not taken by the Germans, there was no way to ensure that the supplies would be safeguarded by the Bolos, or paid for, if used.

Based primarily on the desire to secure these war supplies, an Allied plan was hatched to move forces into Arctic Russia. At least that is what the American government believed. The motives of Great Britain and France were more complex and expansive.

George F. Keenan, America's foremost authority on the Soviet Union, in his book *Soviet-American Relations 1917-1920, The Decision to Intervene*, makes it clear on numerous occasions that American President Woodrow Wilson was a passive participant in the Allied plans to occupy Arctic Russia. President Wilson was willing to go as far as sending in limited naval and ground forces to be used *only* to safeguard the war supplies.

The British, and to some degree the French, had a more ambitious agenda.

In 1918 no one could be certain which side would win the Red-White Civil War in Russia. By 1918, the British and French had suffered catastrophic casualties and were desperate to do anything to get Russia back into the contest to force the Central Powers to again fight on two fronts. As such, the British were the leading exponents of smothering the Bolshevik "baby" in the cradle and would work with any faction to restart the war.

The French were primarily interested in finding a way to transport the Czech Legion from inside Russia to the Western Front. If that meant smothering the baby, so be it.

The American government was split on the future political course for Russia – some favoring working with the Bolsheviks, others not. As this was going on, President Wilson's policy remained to commit limited forces only to safeguard the supplies.

The first Allied troops to arrive in Arctic Russia were British Marines who landed at Murmansk in March 1918.

The Bolsheviks had established a Communist government, known as a "Soviet," in Murmansk. Separated from the central Red government by hundreds of miles, and fearing an invasion from Germany, that government actually joined with the Allied forces in governing the area. This strategy was endorsed by Leon Trotsky as evidenced in a telegram to the Murmansk Soviet which noted, that because the peace negotiations with Germany were thought to be breaking down, drastic action was necessary.

The Soviet was advised that: "It is your duty to do everything to protect the Murmansk Railway. Whoever abandons his post without a fight is a traitor. The Germans are advancing in small detachments. Resistance is possible and obligatory. Abandon nothing to the enemy. Evacuate everything that has any value; if this is impossible, destroy it. You must *accept any and all assistance from the Allied mission* (emphasis added) and use every means to obstruct the advance of the plunderers..."

Perhaps the thinking on the part of the Soviets was that the democratic Allies would be less of a long term threat that the totalitarian Germans. An agreement was reached vesting supreme military power in Arctic Russia among the Soviet and representatives of Great Britain and France. The United States at this point was not involved.

Both to strengthen their hand against the Germans, and to counterbalance British and French influence in Arctic Russia, the Soviet actively sought to have an American ship join the Allied force.

President Wilson, showed no great enthusiasm for the project, but ultimately agreed to send a ship to Murmansk, provided one could be found in the general area. His guidance to its captain was "not to be drawn in further than the present action there without first seeking and obtaining instructions from home."

The *USS Olympia,* the aging flagship of Admiral George Dewey's victory in the Spanish-American War, was sent to Russia in late April.

Two provisos were made which would impact on the American forces to be sent to Arctic Russia later in the year: (1)

The force would be subject to British command, and (2) American forces were to safeguard the military stores but not to take part in land operations away from the ports.

By the summer of 1918, the British and French had determined that the Czech Legion forces still in European Russia should move to the Murmansk/Archangel area to assist in the Allied defense of their perimeter in Arctic Russia.

During the summer months, the American government came under increasing pressure from Britain and France to commit ground forces to Arctic Russia. President Wilson remained cool to the request, feeling that every soldier sent to Arctic Russia was one less who could fight in France. The American government recognized the need to safeguard the military supplies and finally agreed that a ground force of up to a thousand could be committed to the plan. The American contribution began in June 1918 when some 150 Marines were landed in Murmansk

British and French pressure continued and finally on July 17, 1918, the United States government informed its allies that it was now willing to expand its support of the effort to guard military stores but to do nothing greater. It was stipulated that should the forces be put to use other than to guard the military stores, they would be withdrawn and dispatched to the Western Front. Notwithstanding these misgivings and caveats, the fate of the U.S. ground force that would come to be known as the "Polar Bears" was sealed on July 17.

George Kennan offers a very unflattering assessment of British motives. He noted that, "The Americans were regarding by many of the British, throughout this episode, not as partners with whom a real and intimate understanding was to be sought, but rather as stupid children to be 'gotten around' in one way or another – to be wheedled into doing things they were not expected either to desire or to understand... that it was not important that the Americans really understood what they were doing; what was important was they should be coaxed and cajoled into doing these things, whether they understood them or not."

Thus, some 4,500 young Americans were turned over to British command with official Washington paying little attention to their ultimate fate.

The Russian Tundra

Zero weather and knee-deep snow was nothing unusual for the Midwesterners who populated the 85th Division, parent unit of the soon-to-be nicknamed Polar Bears. But few were prepared for what they would find upon landing at Archangel.

The area in which the Polar Bears would live and die is usually called the Murmansk section of northern Russia. Murmansk today is a city of almost a million people and a major Russian naval installation. But that is now; life was much different in the twilight of World War I.

The Russian Arctic the young Midwesterners found was rock-hard in the winter, with snow covering everything. Pale sunlight could be seen, on a good day, for some four hours. Temperatures of 40 and 50 below zero and more were common. As foreboding as the Arctic was in winter, it could be even worse in the short summer.

When the tundra melted, it became a squishy swamp and marsh, with the mud pulling at the soldiers' boots as they tried to trudge along. The area was heavily forested, an ideal place to become lost with no trace ever to be found. And in the summer, the bogs and marshes were the home of millions of mosquitoes.

The Russian tundra would be like nothing the Midwest farm boys had seen at home. American farmsteads are surrounded by acres and acres of crop land, meadows and woods. The next farmstead was a quarter of a mile, or more, down the road. Not so in Arctic Russia.

The homes of the peasants – the *moujiks* – of Arctic Russia were clustered together like the nuts in peanut brittle. Surrounding the villages were the fields where the peasants were expected to coax a crop of rye (the staple of black bread), other grains for the family and the animals, vegetables and maybe a little flax for clothing and sale. A few chickens, wild game, and fish rounded out their simple diet.

The growing season was both short and long.

Short in that only a few weeks separated the spring thaw and the first frosts of fall. And long in that, with the Northern Hemisphere tipped toward the sun, the Arctic was in almost perpetual daylight. These long days gave the peasant family, women and well as men, time to sow the crops, tend to them, and reap the harvest before the snow would fly. The *moujik* way of life had changed little for centuries.

The homes themselves were crude but efficient. They looked somewhat like overgrown Lincoln Log buildings, with interlocking beams keeping out the frigid winter weather. Heavy roofs were necessary to hold the accumulation of snow and double windows were the norm.

The house doubled as a stable for the livestock, a granary to store the crops, and an outhouse, under which a pit would be dug to collect the waste that would be spread on the fields in the spring. With no chemical fertilizer, the *moujiks* improvised – using wood ashes to boost productivity.

The portion of the building used by the family featured a centuries-old stove design that was used for cooking, heat, and was the choice sleeping area, reserved for the elderly and small children. The design was so efficient that a small armful of wood would heat the house for a full day.

Many of the Polar Bears would spend part of the winter bunking in with *moujik* families. The peasants were usually not politically active and treated the Americans well, considering that on more than one occasion the Doughboys put the torch to peasant villages to deny use of the buildings to the Bolos. The Russian peasants also appreciated that the Americans were willing to treat them with respect, something the British never learned to do.

With time on their hands during the winter, some of the Russians would help the American engineers fell trees and build blockhouses and barracks, probably one of the few times they had ever been paid for the work they did. Others acted as cart or sled drivers and scouts.

The Americans would share what food they had with the *moujiks*, and even more importantly, would offer genuine American cigarettes, which would be accepted by the men with great relish.

From Fort Custer to the Tundra

When the bombs began bursting in Europe in August 1914, the United States could only muster some 98,000 Regular Army soldiers backed up by some 27,000 in the National Guard. The U.S. was not in the top ten among armies in the world with the forces of Russia, Italy, Germany, Austria-Hungary and France numbering in the millions and Great Britain and Japan almost that large. Indeed, the American Army was smaller than that of Greece, Turkey, Romania and even Bulgaria.

As war clouds gathered, the U.S. War Department drew up plans to expand the Army to 38 divisions, six being Regular Army, 16 National Guard and 16 in a new category known as the "National Army." The National Army was to draw its officers from the regular force and fill its ranks from among the four million draftees called to arms in the "War to End All Wars."

One of the National Army units was the 85th Division, to be trained at Camp Custer, near Battle Creek, Michigan. The camp was named for General George Armstrong Custer, who commanded Michigan cavalry regiments in the American Civil War. Famed as the youngest general officer of the war, he earned his star at age 23. He earned a second star just three years later.

General Custer called his brigade the "Wolverines," and they became known for their spirit and devotion to their leader.

Camp Custer had none of the dash of its namesake.

The camp is described in contemporary accounts as being built on a sand pile with the only living foliage being around the officers' quarters. Blowing sand "flavored" the soldiers' food. Living quarters consisted of hastily built, unpainted barracks, the only furniture being steel bunks. Still, the 85th was better off than its southern counterparts who lived in tent cities because of the warmer climates.

The division was organized at Camp Custer on August 25, 1917. Troops began to pour in, primarily from Michigan and Wisconsin, with a smattering from other states. Training was that of a regular infantry division.

On July 22, 1918, exactly 113 days before the armistice would be signed, the 85th Division was loaded on a troop convoy of primarily converted merchant ships and began to zigzag its way toward England.

The men of the 85th generally felt that the war was coming to an end. They thought they would spend a few weeks in England and then ship over to France to help put an end to the war-making machine of the Central Powers, perhaps spend a few days in Paris, and then return home to victory parades with bands playing.

Things didn't turn out that way.

By August, the 85th Division had arrived in England. But the island did not prove to be a way station en route to France. Instead, the division was recast as a "depot" unit, basically a replacement pool for units already in France. And to fulfill the pledge of President Wilson to send an American force to Arctic Russia, four units of the 85th – the 339th Infantry, the 1st Battalion of the 310th Engineers, the 337th Field Hospital and the 337th Ambulance Company – drew the short straws and ended up being the Polar Bears.

Perhaps the men of the Custer Division were selected for the assignment to Russia because, being from the Midwest, they were considered best able to handle the weather conditions. Perhaps they were selected just because they were there.

Whatever the case, the Polar Bears, all 4,477 of them, after less than a month in England, were at sea again, this time zigzagging their way through the North Sea.

The men had no special cold weather training. They were outfitted with some warm clothing but this concession was more than offset by having to surrender their British-made Enfield rifles for the Mosin-Nagant type being used by the Russians. The reason given was that among the mounds of equipment at Archangel and Murmansk were millions of cartridges for the weapons being used by the Russians. The fact that the weapons were awkward to use, and not very accurate, didn't seem to make a difference.

The British had arrived a month earlier and had pitched their tents at Murmansk, a relatively safe place with a pro-Allied population. The 85th expected to join their British cousins there.

Again they drew the short straw.

The little convoy sailed past Murmansk and dropped anchor September 4 at Archangel, some 400 miles to the south and east, considered to be more pro-Communist.

Still, with the assignment of only guarding the supply dumps, how dangerous could the duty be? The young Americans were soon to find out.

Early Combat

"Mission creep" began almost before the first of the Polar Bears – now members of the American North Russia Expeditionary Force (ANREF) – stumbled down the gangplank into the ancient city of Archangel to join the "Coalition of the Confused." That group included the French, Italians, Polish, Lithuanians, Serbians, Chinese, Czechs, and, of course, the anti-Soviet Russians. No one seemed to be able to quite explain what was the mission.

Archangel is a port city founded in the sixteenth-century by Tsar Ivan the Terrible to give Russia access to the sea should enemies close off the route to the Baltic.

With the harbor frozen over for half the year, poverty was rampant in the city that served as a trading post for British merchants dealing in timber, furs and flax. Most of the Polar Bears described the city as dark, dirty, and foul smelling.

Archangel's water had to be boiled before drinking, the city had one of the highest rates of venereal disease in the world and the kindly Russians who sold the eggs and vegetables to the Doughboys during the day were likely to be Bolshevik sympathizers who would try to kill them at night. This was the situation under which the draftees from Michigan and Wisconsin began their service.

Like the French admiral half a century earlier who felt he could depose the king of Korea with a force of 600 men (see chapter one), the British commander greatly overestimated the multiplier effect of the Allied soldier. General F.C. Poole assured his superiors in London that with a force of only 12,000 men, he could send five separate spearheads down into Russia from the Arctic north and capture St. Petersburg and possibly Moscow. With this would come the death of the Bolshevik Revolution. The Polar Bears were to be about half of his strike force.

With the arrogance that only the British can muster, Brigadier Poole was quoted as saying that it was to be impressed upon all ranks that the mission was to fight an *offensive* war, not a *defensive* one.

Four days after arriving in Archangel, hardly time enough to get their land legs beneath them, a battalion of Polar Bears was packed aboard coal barges for a trip down the Dvina River. The men of the 339th fought in a perimeter that never advanced more than 200 miles south of Archangel. In this wedge of land, some 200 miles long by 100 miles wide, operations for the supposedly non-combat troops continued – off and on – for some nine months. Most of the action took place along the Dvina River and the Archangel-Vologda Railroad connecting Archangel and Moscow.

The first of the Polar Bears to die in combat were Privates Anthony Soczkoski and Ignacy Kwasniewski of Detroit and Philip Sokol of Pittsburgh. Soczkoski and Kwasniewski were with Company I, 339th Infantry, while Sokol was with Company L. They lost their lives on September 17, 1918, when the Bolos counterattacked an ANREF detachment holding a bridge along the Vologda Railroad Front.

Were it not for the fact that American Doughboys were freezing, being killed by the Bolos, and existing on sub-par rations, the situation back in Archangel would have been grist for a bad Hollywood B-movie.

According to the "Chronicler," in his 1924 book *Archangel, The American Civil War With Russia:*

... A well-fed Supply Company watched over mountains of rations and supplies brought all the way from as far off as America: supplies and little good things and comforts that would have heartened and brought new life and hope to the lonely, abandoned men along the front lines in the snow...British G.H.Q. brought six hundred surplus officers and forty thousand cases of good Scotch whiskey...So it was that Archangel became a city of many colors, as gallant, uniformed gentlemen strode down the Trotsky Prospect, whipping the air with their walking sticks, and looking very stern and commanding, as they answered many salutes, in a bored, absent-minded way.

There were officers of the Imperial Army, weighed down with glittering, ponderous honor medals, and dark Cossacks with high gray hats, and gaudy tunics, and murderous noisy sabers. Handsome gentlemen of war from England, from Serbia, Italy, Finland, and Bohemia, and many other countries, all arrayed in brilliant plumage, and shining boots, and bright spurs, and every other kind of "eye wash." And of course, there were large numbers of batmen to shine the boots and burnish the spurs, and keep all in fine order and other batmen to look after the appointments at the officers' club, and serve the whiskey and soda.

In the afternoon there were teas, and receptions and matinees, and dances in the evening, when the band played and every one was flushed with pleasure and excitement. Such flirtations with the pretty *barishnas*, such whispered gossip and intrigue and scandal in light-hearted Archangel!

At Kodish, at Onega on the Vaga, and at Toulgas, far off across the haunting snows, sick men and broken men, men faint from lack of nutrition, and men sickened in soul were doing sentry duty through the numbing cold nights, because there were none to take their places in the blockhouses, and no supports to come to their relief, no reserves to hearten them and give them courage.

The blockhouses so far away, where men were maimed and crippled and shell shocked, and the black hopelessness that crept into men's hearts, and strangled men's hearts and overcame their soldier spirit – in the blockhouses – far, so far from gala Archangel.

The author of this account is generally believed to have been Captain John Cudahy of the Wisconsin meat packing family of the same name. He is considered to be a particularly credible witness having earned a bachelor's degree from Harvard and a law degree from the University of Wisconsin before entering the Army. After the war he served as ambassador to both Poland and Belgium and minister to Eire. He was serving in Belgium when World War II broke out.

Captain Cudahy was highly critical of the war in Arctic Russia joining many others in pointing out that no clear plan of action was ever drawn up and explained to the soldiers on the ground.

The Doughboys in Action

Compared to the one-day American Civil War battle of Antietam, Maryland on September 12, 1862, in which almost 5,000 Americans, Union and Confederate, lost their lives with another 18,000 being wounded, and D-Day with its casualty list of some 5,000, the action of the Polar Bears could best be described as skirmishes.   But to the Doughboys who died in battle or from wounds suffered, accidents or illness, or were missing and presumed dead, the causality rate for each was 100 percent.

Armed with second-rate rifles, short-range artillery, and water-cooled machine guns almost useless in sub-zero temperatures, the fight was difficult.   Their allies were a mixed bag, some willing to fight, others looking for any excuse to escape into the nearby forests.

The Italians and Polish played minor roles.   The French offered valuable artillery and machine gun support until they made a separate peace, stopped fighting, and were shipped home.

The Russian fighters were all over the lot.   Some really believed in the anti-Soviet cause and were faithful allies.   Others fought for a time and then disappeared into the tundra.   Other units defected en masse to the Red cause and turned their guns against the Allies.

True to their imperialist roots, both the French and British formed units consisting of Russian soldiers commanded by Western European officers and sergeants.

A British-led force, known as the Slavo-British Allied Legion, consisted of deserters from the Soviet forces, released convicts, and other less-than-savory characters.   Only a few thousand Russians joined the unit and served with little distinction.   When thousands more were impressed, the record was even worse.

Things were a little better with the French-Russian unit known as the French Legion.   They generally fought better and at times were able to offer real assistance to the Americans.

And then there were the British.

The Doughboys had high regard for the second British Commander, Major General Sir Edmund Ironside.

General Ironside was every bit the British officer.   Standing more than six foot, four, with a neatly clipped moustache, he could have been the prototype of the professional football tight end.   He would be serving as chief of the imperial general staff at the start of World War II.

Rather, he was a scholar who spoke a half-dozen languages and "led from the front," scurrying from outpost to outpost, usually alone, in a sled pulled by reindeer. Upon taking command, he quickly grasped the futility of the offense and had his forces, Polar Bears included, dig in and try to maintain a shield behind which the newly forming Russian Army could be trained.

General Ironside, known to his friends as "Tiny," was in his late 30s and had spent the previous decade as a staff officer prior to going to Arctic Russia. His rank was the equivalent of an American major but was given the "honorary" title of major general to make him the senior man in the theater, thus the commander. George Stewart was a Regular U. S. Army lieutenant colonel and rightly should have commanded the force. But by prior agreement, the British were to control the action. By the end of his career, Ironside had earned the *actual* rank of major general.

With the exception of General Ironside, and the enlisted Tommies, with whom the Doughboys worked quite well, most of the Americans felt the British officers and their methods of warfare were almost as much of a burden as the Bolsheviki.

The list of gripes was long.

The Americans resented Washington's decision to put the American force under British command. The American commander, Colonel Stewart was operating under a murky mandate with conflicting lines of authority. He routinely failed to support his troops in disputes with the British brass.

In case after case, British officers were given "social" pro-motions – without commensurate pay increases – to make them senior to their American counterparts.

On numerous occasions, Doughboys were sent to a village and quartered in really rank buildings. Once the smell and the filth were moved out, so were the Americans, and the British moved in.

High up on the resentment list was the Schakelford boot which was fine for standing guard duty but almost impossible for walking. With the resourcefulness of the American GI, they were quickly traded for Russian felt boots.

There was also the suspicion that the thousands of cases of Scotch whiskey that had been sent to the Arctic squeezed out the medical supplies needed to fight the Spanish flu. And then there was the food – never enough – and almost universally unpalatable.

The Americans asked repeatedly for American-style food. The British insisted that all Allied troops would get the same ration, consisting almost entirely of bully beef, hardtack, tea, and M&V.

M&V was a euphemism for "meat and vegetables" – though the type meat and the origin of the vegetables could never be determined. Living in temperatures 40 below zero and more with this type diet added to the misery of the Polar Bears.

Another gripe was tea instead of coffee and lime in place of orange juice. Barely smokeable English cigarettes were another reason for the dissatisfaction of the Doughboys.

Some things never change

In his 2006 book *The War of the World, Twentieth Century Conflict and the Decline of the West*, British author Niall Ferguson offers his panoramic view of the world from September 11, 1901 to September 11, 2001. He mentions the Allied intervention in Russia crediting the French with sending forces into Odessa and the British landing troops in Murmansk, Archangel and Vladivostok. He mentioned American forces in Vladivostok but omits any reference to the Polar Bears who did the bulk of the fighting and dying in Arctic Russia.

Through it all the Polar Bears had four best friends – the American medical staff, the 310th Engineers, the Canadian artillery and the combination of the YMCA and Red Cross.

The men of the 337th Field Hospital and the 337th Ambulance Company saved many of the 339th Infantry from death by heroic efforts under very trying conditions. Supplies were always short and the British medical officers constantly kept a thumb in the American doctors' eyes thanks to their social promotion higher rank. At times the American medics had to threaten their British counterparts with loaded guns to be able to offer the care needed to the wounded and frost-bitten Doughboys.

Equally important was the role of the 310th Engineers who constructed more than 500 blockhouses and machine gun emplacements and 400 barracks and utility buildings for the Polar Bears. They also modified railway boxcars into living quarters, complete with electricity. When not engaged with the Bolos, the infantrymen joined in the construction knowing that only shelter would get them through the punishing winter months.

These blockhouses were miniature forts made of logs or sawed wood. With loopholes for gun barrels, and interlocking fields of fire, they offered protection for the Polar Bears from everything expect direct artillery hits. Miles and miles of apron and concertina wire completed the fortifications.

As important as the blockhouses were for protection, they also gave the Doughboys shelter from the biting wind and freezing temperatures. The Americans were almost snug in their fortifications but still suffered from a lack of good food. One thing they didn't lack were the ever-present lice.

Equally as important were the Canadian artillery units fighting in the Russian Arctic.

Four hundred ninety-seven members of the 16th Brigade, Canadian Field Artillery, sailed from London for Archangel in mid-

September 1918. The unit was divided into two 6-gun batteries, the 67th and 68th Artillery. All were veteran soldiers and helped steady the draftee American forces who were seeing their first action. Knowing what to expect, the Canadians took along snowshoes and even sled dogs.

Though the Canadian artillery did not have the range of that used by the Bolos, it did have greater reach than the American guns and proved invaluable on numerous occasions of saving the Detroit Doughboys from being overrun by the Bolsheviks. General Ironside was heard to say many times that the Canadian field artillery had saved Allied units from destruction.

The Canadians fought on until June of 1919 with seven of the unit being killed outright or dying of wounds.

As the USO was founded just prior to the American entry into World War II, morale and welfare of the Doughboys and their allies was in the hands of the Red Cross and the YMCA

The American Red Cross had been active in Russia well before the Doughboys arrived in Archangel, offering aid to the long-suffering Russian peasants. When the American troops moved into the Arctic north, the Red Cross supplemented the Doughboys British-style rations with rolled oats, cocoa, genuine coffee and other much-appreciated goodies – socks, writing paper and books.

The Red Cross also facilitated the marriages of eight American soldiers and the return of their "war brides."

But probably the biggest morale boost offered by Red Cross was its sponsorship of the weekly, four-page newspaper the *American Sentinel*, distributed free to the soldiers and other English speakers in and around Archangel.

The first issue of the *Sentinel* rolled off the presses at the American Embassy building in Archangel on December 10, 1918. The paper continued through Issue Twenty-Five, printed on May 31, 1919. With the pending evacuation of the American forces, the *Sentinel* was replaced by the British publication the *Gazette of the Archangel Forces* that began on June 7.

Printed by GIs for GIs, the paper contained articles about the fighting in all parts of Russia, comments by the soldiers, speculation as to when a peace treaty might be signed, gossip, rugby and cricket scores, and dispatches from home.

Included were reports of the various contests and games in which the Doughboys took part. The marriages of the eight soldiers were carried on what passed for a society page. Requests were made for soldiers in the various units to contribute items about what was happening in their sectors of the front.

The soldiers were able to read about political happenings back home as the first issue of the paper reported that Michigan and Oklahoma had adopted women's suffrage and that Ohio, Wyoming, Florida and Nevada has voted "dry."

Like the Red Cross, the Military YMCA set up shop prior to the arrival of the Americans and other Allied Forces in the Archangel area. The "Y," also know as the "Red Triangles," provided what would now be called post exchange (PX) services.

Prior to the Americans coming ashore in Arctic Russia, members of the Y worked with Central Powers prisoners of war and later with members of the Russian military.

On June 4, 1917, what was probably the first baseball game in the country was played by Russians with members of the Y acting as instructors.

Milking stools with legs shortened and pounded into the ground served as bases; bats were homemade and resembled canoe paddles.

A "stab" was also made at introducing football to the Russian soldiers but the game had to be abandoned. Whenever a difference of opinion arose, the Russians chased each other around the field wielding their trusty sabers.

The Y began its mission of supporting the American and Allied soldiers in the Murmansk and Archangel areas in August of 1918 when two abandoned buildings were turned into YMCAs.

By January 1919, some 30 buildings, huts, and tents had been turned into Y facilities, 24 of which were in the Archangel area. In addition 14 railway cars, converted into canteens and libraries, rolled up and down the railroads serving the Allies. When all else failed, staffers would load comfort and health items into backpacks and make their way from trench to blockhouse to bring a bit of home to the soldiers serving in temperatures dipping as low as 50 degrees below zero.

In a 1922 report titled "*Service With Fighting Men – An Account of the Work of the American Young Men's Christian Associations in the World War*", the work of one traveling member was described thus:

He carries about 60 pounds of stuff along in knapsacks, and distributes from dugout to dugout and trench to trench around the entire front. Sometimes it's cigarettes, sometimes confectionery, of which we have precious little, sometimes it is sweet crackers or gum. Then once a week he holds a brief service in each of the dugouts as he visits the men; and old Major Moody, the Scotch evangelist, goes the rounds with him occasionally to make a most effective little address.

I heard one a few days ago. Here in a clearing, dotted with woodpiles, which have been broken and twisted into the weirdest heaps and lines by the breaking shells, are a few log huts that serve as base front headquarters for the men. As we finished our rounds that afternoon, the Captain called all the men who were not needed at the front line into one of these houses for a talk. Back they plodded through the snow, weighed down with rifles, cartridge belts, and steel helmets. It was an American company. As the major told some of his touching stories in his rich Scotch brogue, commenting on them briefly by way of a lesson sermon, tears ran down the cheeks of many of these rough Michigan boys.

At its busiest, some 100 Americans, Englishmen and Canadians were active at the various Y facilities in Arctic Russia. Four American workers were decorated for valor, one winning the French Croix de Guerre and three being awarded the Cross of St. George, an imperial Russian medal seldom awarded to civilians.

Members of the Y stayed with the American force until it was withdrawn in the summer of 1919. The last of the American staffers left Arctic Russia in September of that year.

Though most of the glamour has been rubbed off the product, the most sought after commodity in both World Wars I and II was a pack of American cigarettes with General of the Armies John J. Pershing once saying that next to ammunition, cigarettes were what the soldiers wanted most.

In World War II, the ration of smokes was considered so important that, according to Carlo D'Este, in his book, *Eisenhower, a Soldier's Life*, General of the Army Dwight Eisenhower insisted that his allotment of Camels and Chesterfields be no larger than that of the GI on the line. A heavy smoker, "Ike" was known to have rolled his-own when the manufactured type was gone.

The Battle for Toulgas

"Detroit's Own" Polar Bear Memorial Association lists on its web site 20 major actions in which the Polar Bears took part. The deadliest was at Toulgas, along the Dvina River front and began, ironically, on November 11, 1918, the day the Armistice was signed.

In the book *Fighting the Bolsheviki*, Captain Joel Moore and Lieutenants Harry Mead and Lewis Jahns give a narrative account of the four-day battle. Their account is excerpted here:

Toulgas was the duplicate of thousands of similar villages throughout this province (Archangel). It consisted of a group of low, dirty log houses huddled together on a hill, sloping down to a broad plain, where was located another group of houses, known as Upper Toulgas.

A small stream flowed between the two villages and nearly a mile to the rear was another group of buildings used for a hospital and where first aid was given to the wounded before evacuating them to Bereznik, forty or fifty miles down the river.

The forces engaged in the defense of this position consisted of several batteries of Canadian artillery, posted midway between the hospital and main village. In addition to this B Company of the Polar Bears, and a company of Royal Scots were scattered in and about these positions. From the upper village back to the hospital stretched a good three miles, which of course, meant that the troops in this position, numbering not more than five hundred, were considerable scattered and separated. This detailed description of our position here is set forth so specifically in order that the reader may appreciate the attack that occurred during the early part of November.

On the morning of November 11th, while some of the men were still eating their breakfasts and while the positions were only about half-manned, suddenly from the forests surrounding the upper village, the enemy emerged in attack formation. Lieutenant Dennis engaged them for a short time and withdrew to our main line of defense. All hands were immediately mustered to repel this advancing wave of infantry. In the meantime, the Bolo attacked with about five hundred men from our rear, having made a three-day march through what had been reported as impassable swamp. He occupied our rearmost village, which was undefended, and attacked our hospital. This forward attack was merely a ruse to divert the attention of our troops in that direction, while the enemy directed his main assault at our rear and undefended positions for the purpose of gaining our artillery. Hundreds of enemy appeared as by magic from the forests, swarmed in upon the hospital village, and immediately took possession. The Bolo then commenced a desperate advance upon our guns.

At the moment the advance began, there were some sixty Canadian artillerymen and one Company B sergeant with seven men and a Lewis (machine) gun. Due to the heroism and coolness of this handful of men – who at once opened fire with the Lewis gun – they forced the advancing infantry to pause momentarily. This brief halt gave the Canadians a chance to reverse their gun positions, swing them around and open up with muzzle bursts upon the first wave of the assault, scarcely fifty yards away. It was but a moment until the hurricane of shrapnel was bursting among solid masses of advancing infantry, and under such murderous fire, the best disciplined troops and most foolhardy could not long withstand. It was certain the advancing Bolo could not continue his advance. The Bolos were on our front, our right flank, and our rear, we were entirely cut off from communication and there were no reinforcements available. About 4 p.m. we launched a small counter attack under Lieutenant Dennis, which rolled up a line of snipers who had given us considerable annoyance.

We then shelled the rear villages occupied by the Bolos and they decamped. Meanwhile the Royal Scots, who had formed for the counter attack, went forward also under the cover of the artillery and the Bolo, or at least those few remaining, were driven back into the forests.

The enemy losses during this attack were enormous. His estimated dead and wounded were approximately four hundred but will never be known as to how many of them later died in the surrounding forests from wounds and exposure. This engagement was not only disastrous from the loss of men, but was even more disastrous from the fact that some of the leading Bolshevik leaders on the front were killed during this engagement. One of the leading commanders was an extremely powerful giant of a man, named Melochofski, who first led his troops into the village hospital in the rear of the gun positions.

He strode into the hospital, wearing a huge black fur hat, which accentuated his extraordinary height, and singled out all of the wounded American and English troops for immediate execution, and this undoubtedly would have been their fate, had it not been for the interference of a most remarkable woman, who was christened by the soldiers as 'Lady Olga.'

This woman, a striking and intelligent appearing person, had formerly been a member of the famous 'Battalion of Death,' and afterwards informed one of our interpreters that she had joined the Soviets out of pure love of adventure, wholly indifferent to the cause for which she exposed her life.

She had fallen in love with Melochofski and had accompanied him and his troops through the trackless woods, sharing the lot of the common solider and enduring hardships what would have shaken the most vigorous man. With all her hardiness, however, there was still a touch of the eternal feminine, and when Melochofski issued the order for the slaughter of the invalid soldiers, she rushed forward and in no uncertain tones threatened to shoot the first Bolo who entered the hospital.

She herself remained in the hospital while Melochofski, with the balance of his troops, went forward with the attack and where he himself was so mortally wounded that he lived only a few minutes after reaching her side. She eventually was sent to the hospital at the base and nursed there.

At daybreak the following day, five gun boats appeared around the bend of the river, just out of range of our three-inch artillery, and all day long their ten-inch guns pounded away at our positions, crashing great explosives upon our blockhouses, which guarded the bridge connecting the upper and middle village, while in the forests surrounding this position the Bolo infantry were lying in wait awaiting a direct hit upon the strong point in order that they could rush the bridge and overwhelm us. Time after time exploding shells threw huge mounds of earth and debris into the loopholes of this blockhouse and all but demolished it.

Here Sergeant Wallace performed a particularly brave act. The blockhouse of which he was in command was near a large straw pile. A shell hit near the straw and threw it in front of the loopholes. Wallace went out under machine gun fire from close range, about seventy-five yards, and under heavy shelling, and removed the straw. The same thing happened a little later, and this time he was severely wounded. He was awarded the Distinguished Conduct Medal by the British. Private Bell was in the blockhouse when it was hit and all the occupants were killed or severely wounded. Bell was badly gashed in the face, but stuck with his Lewis gun until dark when he could be relieved, being the only survivor in the shattered blockhouse that held the bridge across the small stream separating us from the Bolos.

For three days the (Bolo) gunboats pounded away and all night long there was the rattle and crack of the machine guns. No one slept. The little garrison was fast becoming exhausted. Men were hollow-eyed from weariness and so utterly tired that they were indifferent to the shrieking shells and all else. At this point of the siege, it was decided that our only salvation was a counter attack.

In the forest near the upper village were a number of log huts, which the natives had used as charcoal kilns, but which had been converted by the enemy into observation posts and storehouses for machine guns and ammunition. His troops were lying in and about the woods surrounding these buildings. We decided to surprise this detachment in the woods, capture it if possible and make a great demonstration of an attack so as to give the enemy in the upper village the impression that we were receiving reinforcements and were still fresh and ready to fight. This maneuver succeeded far beyond our wildest expectations.

Company B under the command of Lieutenant (later Captain) John Cudahy, and one platoon of Company D under Lieutenant Derham, made the attack on the Bolo trenches. Just before dawn that morning the Americans filed through the forest and crept upon the enemy's observation posts before they were aware of any movement on our part. We then proceeded without any warning upon their main position.

Taken as they were, completely by surprise, it was but a moment before they were in full rout, running panic stricken in all directions, thinking that a regiment or division had fallen upon them. We immediately set fire to the huts containing their ammunition, cartridges, etc. and the subsequent explosions that followed probably gave the enemy the impression that a terrific attack was pending. As we emerged from the wood and commenced the attack upon Upper Toulgas we were fully expecting stiff resistance, for we knew that many of these houses concealed enemy guns. Our plans had succeeded so well, however, that no supporting fire from the upper village came and the snipers in the forward part of the village, seeing themselves abandoned, threw their guns and came rushing forward shouting 'tovarish, tovarish,' meaning the same as the German 'kamerad.'

As a matter of fact, in this motley crew of prisoners were a number of Germans and Austrians, who could scarcely speak a word of Russian, and who were probably more than thankful to be taken prisoner and thus be relieved from active warfare.

During this maneuver one of their bravest and ablest commanders, by the name of Foukes, was killed, which was an irreparable loss to the enemy. Foukes was without question one of the most competent and aggressive Bolo leaders. He was a powerful man physically and had long years of service as a private in the old Russian Army, and without question a most able leader of men. During the four days of attacks, and counter attacks, he had led his men by a circuitous route through the forest, wading in swamps waist deep, carrying machines guns and mortars.

The nights were of course miserably cold and considerable snow had fallen, but Foukes would risk no fire of any kind for fear of discovery. It was not due any lack of ability or strategy on this part that his well-planned attack failed.

Out of our forces of about six hundred Scots and Americans we had about one hundred casualties, the Scots suffering worse than we. Our casualties were mostly sustained in the blockhouses, from the shelling.

It was reported that Trotsky, the idol of the Red crowd, was present at the battle of Toulgas, but if he was there, he had little influence in checking the riotous retreat of his followers when they thought themselves flanked from the woods. They fled in wild disorder from the upper village of Toulgas and for days thereafter in villages far to our rear, various members of this force straggled in, half-crazed from starvation and exposure and more than willing to abandon the Soviet cause. For weeks the enemy left the Americans severely alone.

Toulgas was held.

It was decided to burn Upper Toulgas, which was a constant menace to our security, as we had not enough men to occupy it with sufficient numbers to make a defense and the small outposts there were tempting morsels for the enemy to devour. Many were reluctant to stay there, and it was nervous work on the black nights when the wind, dismal and weird, moaned through the encompassing forest, every shadow a crouching Bolshevik. Often the order came through to the main village to 'stand to', because some fidgety sentinel in Upper Toulgas had seen battalions, conjured by the black night.

So it was determined to burn the upper village and a guard was thrown around it, for we feared word would be passed and the Bolos would try to prevent us from accomplishing our purpose. The inhabitants were given three hours to vacate.

It was a pitiful sight to see them turned out of the dwellings where most of them had spent their whole, simple, but not unhappy lives, their meager possessions scattered awry upon the ground.

The first snow floated down from a dark foreboding sky, dread announcer of a cruel Arctic winter. Soon the houses were roaring flames. The women sat upon hand fashioned crates wherein were all their most prized household goods, and abandoned themselves to a paroxysm of weeping despair, while the children shrieked stridently, victim of all the realistic horrors that only childhood can conjure. Most of the men looked on in silence, uncomprehending resignation on their faces, mute, pathetic figures. Poor *moujik*! They didn't understand but they took all uncomplainingly. Fate had decreed that they should suffer this burden, and they accepted it without question.

But when we thought of the brave chaps whose lives had been taken from those flaming homes, for our casualties had been very heavy, nearly one hundred men killed and wounded, we stifled our compassion and looked on the blazing scene as a jubilant bonfire. All night long the burning village was red against the black sky, and in the morning where had stood Upper Toulgas was now a smoking, dirty smudge upon the plain.

We took many prisoners in the second fight for Toulgas. It was a trick of the Bolos to sham death until a searching party, bent on examining the bodies for information, would approach them, when suddenly they would spring to life and deliver themselves up. They said that only by this method could they escape the tyranny of the Bolsheviki. They declared they never had any sympathy for the Soviet cause and were forced into the Red army at the point of a gun, and kept in the ranks using the same persuasion.

They were a hard boiled looking lot, those Bolo prisoners. They wore no regulation uniforms, but were clad in much the same attire as the ordinary *moujik* – knee high leather boots and high hats of gray and black curled fur. No one could distinguish them at a distance – every peasant could be a Bolshevik. Who knew?

In fact, we had reason to believe that many of them were Bolshevik in sympathy. The Bolos had uncanny knowledge of our strength and state of our defenses, and although no one except soldiers were allowed beyond the village we knew that despite the closest vigilance there was working unceasingly a system of espionage with which we could never hope to cope.

Some of the prisoners were mere boys seventeen and eighteen years old. Others were men of advanced age. Nearly all of them were hopelessly ignorant, likely material for a fiery-tongued orator and plausible propagandist. They thought the Americans were supporting the British in an invasion of Russia to suppress all democratic government and to return a Romanoff to the throne.

That was the story they had given to the *moujik*, and, of course, they firmly believed it, and after all why should they not judging from appearances? We quote here from an American officer who fought at Toulgas:

If we had not come to restore the Tsar, why had we come, invading Russia, and burning Russian homes?

We spoke conciliating of "friendly intervention," of bringing peace and order to this distracted country, to the poor moujik when what he saw were his villages a torn battle ground of two contending armies, while the one had forced itself upon him, requisitioned his shaggy pony, burned the roof over his head, and doing whatever was militarily necessary. It was small concern to Ivan whether the Allies or the Bolsheviks won this strange war.

He did not know what it was all about, and in that he was like the rest of us. But he asked only to be left alone, in peace to lead his simple life, gathering his scanty crops in the hot brief months of summer and dreaming away the long

dreary winter on top of his great oven-like stove, a worry free
fatalistic disciple of the philosophy of nitchevoo.

After the fierce battle to hold Toulgas, the only contact
with the enemy was by patrols. D Company relieved B Company
for a month. Work was constantly expended upon the winter
defenses. The detachment of the 310th Engineers was an
invaluable aid. When B Company went up to Toulgas again late in
January, they found the fortifications in fine shape. Meanwhile,
rumors were coming in persistently of an impending attack.

The Bolo made his long expected night attack January 29,
1919, in conjunction with his drive on the Vaga, and was easily
repulsed. Another similar attack was made a little later in
February, which met with a similar result. It was reported to us
that the Bolo soldiers held a meeting in which they declared that it
was impossible to take Toulgas, and that they would shoot any
officer who ordered another attack there.

On March first we met with a disaster. One of our patrols
was ambushed and a platoon sent out to recover the wounded
met a largely superior force backed with artillery. We lost eight
killed and more wounded.

From that time on the fighting in the Upper Dvina was
limited to patrol action. There, to be sure, was always a strain on
the men. Remembering their comrades who had been ambushed
before, it took the sturdiest brand of courage for small parties to go
out day and night on the hard-packed trails, to pass like deer along
a marked runway with hunters ready with cocked rifles. The odds
were hopelessly against them.

The vigilance of the patrols, however, may account for the
fact that even after his great success on Vaga, the commander of
the Bolshevik Northern Army did not send his forces against the
formidably guarded Toulgas.

And so the fighting in and around Toulgas sputtered out
with the two sides sparring but neither trying for a knockout punch.
The Polar Bear Memorial Association lists the four-day battle that
began the day the Armistice was signed as the most costly single
action fought by the Polar Bears. Though they lost 28 killed in
action and 70 were injured, the Polar Bears still bested the enemy,
whose loses were estimated at 500.

Other fatalities ranged from a single death at milepost 445
to 32 in a series of four engagements in and around the town of
Kodish over a four-month period.

For readers old enough to remember the war in Vietnam,
the action in Arctic Russia was, in many ways, strikingly similar.

In both conflicts the houses of the villagers, usually inno-cent bystanders, were destroyed if they were considered of value to the enemy. Villages were taken, then abandoned, only to be fought over again. In both instances it was virtually impossible to tell friend from potential enemy and "collateral damage" was extensive.

And in both cases, American forces left without being able to claim a victory.

Were There Mutinies?

"What we have here is a failure to communicate" is a fa-mous line from the movie *Cool Hand Luke*. A failure to communicate may have led to one or more acts of mutiny by members of the Polar Bears. Though the Army did its best to downplay the stories, they are worth considering.

The primary incident took place near the end of March 1919, four months after World War I had ended, and involved members of Company I of the 339th Infantry.

The incident allegedly involved members of the company failing to follow an order of the first sergeant to load their sleds and move down the railway to relieve another company. After the American commander talked to the soldiers, they changed their minds and loaded the sleds and moved out.

According to National Archives and Records Administra-tion records, more than a year later, in June 1920, Major H. N. Scales, former Adjutant and Inspector, American Forces in North Russia, filed a report with General W. F. Richardson, former commander of American Forces in Russia, Subject: Alleged Mutiny of Company I, 339th Infantry. In his report, the major wrote:

Pursuant to your request, the following are the facts, from memory, as to the investigation made by me relative to the alleged mutiny of Company I, 339th Infantry, at Archangel, Russia, in the spring of 1919.

Company I, 339th Infantry, was in a rest area at Smallney Barracks, on the outskirts of Archangel, Russia, when orders were received to go to the Railroad Front and relieve another company. The following morning the First Sergeant ordered the company to turn out and load the sleds. He reported to the Captain that the men did not respond as directed. The Captain then went out to the barracks and demanded of the men standing around the stove, "Who refuses to turn out and load the sleds?" No reply came from the men. The Captain then asked the trumpeter, who was standing nearby, if he refused to turn out and load the sleds and the trumpeter replied that he was ready if the balance were, but that he was not going out and load the packs of others on the sleds by himself, or words to that effect. The Captain then went to the 'phone and reported the trouble as "mutiny" to Colonel Stewart, the Commanding Officer, American Forces in North Russia. Colonel Stewart directed him to have the men assemble in the YMCA hut and he would go out at once and talk to them. The Colonel arrived and read the Articles of War as to mutiny and talked to the men a few minutes. He said he was ready to answer any questions the men cared to ask. Some one wanted to know "What are we here for and what are the intentions of the U.S. Government?" The Colonel answered this *as well as he could* (emphasis added) and asked if there was anyone of the company who would not obey the order to load the sleds, if so, to step up to the front. No one moved. The Colonel then directed the men to load the sleds without delay, which was done.

It seems that a day or two before orders were received to move to the front, mail had been received from the United States by various members of I Company in which were newspaper clippings from Detroit, Michigan, of an alleged speech by a Senator in the U.S. Senate demanding information from the government as to why the 339th Infantry was being kept in Russia, suffering hardships from freezing and hunger, and being murdered by the Bolshiviki, after the Armistice had been signed. In addition to this, comments alone the same line (were made) by the editor of a Detroit paper, which is the hometown or area of practically every man in the 339th Infantry.

The testimony showed that the Captain commanding Company I, 339th Infantry, did not order his company formed nor did he ever give a direct order for the sleds to be loaded. He did not report this trouble to the Commanding Officer (a field grade officer) of Smallney Barracks but hastened to 'phone his troubles to the Commanding Officer, American Forces in North Russia. The Captain is alleged to be a socialist and closely allied with Victor Berger (a Socialist Congressman from Milwaukee, see chapter five) before the declaration of war. He impressed me as being rather weak and totally unfit for duties as Company Commander, yet his tours of duty at the front were considered to be satisfactory by his commanding officer.

As I remember, the testimony of the First Sergeant was not available at the time.

The Company was at the front in May when the investigation was made and the service of all concerned was considered satisfactory by the Battalion Commander.

I might mention that there was an American newspaper correspondent in Archangel and news was rather scarce from the American standpoint and a 'thriller' would put Archangel on the map and that the press reports had to pass through a British censor where they should have been stopped.

Further, both the British and French each had some 3 or 4 similar troubles or "mutinies" of a worse type, but not one word of it got by the British censor of wires.

"My conclusions were that from such evidence as could be obtained, the alleged mutiny was nothing like as serious as had been reported, but was of such a nature as could have been handled by a Company Officer of force.

My recommendations to the Commanding General of American Forces in North Russia were that the matter be dropped and considered closed, in which the Commanding General concurred as you will doubtlessly remember.

H.N. SCALES
Major, A.G.D.

What does this document indicate about communications?

A year after the incident, the major was able to recall what the trumpeter said about loading the sleds. His recollection as to how the commander answered the question about what the Polar Bears were still doing in Russia was vague. He could only recall that the colonel answered "as well as he could."

What does this report say about the American military mindset in the World War I era?

First, as MSNBC pundit and author Craig Crawford writes in his book, "*Attack the Messenger*," the media is always a ready target, in this case the Detroit newspapers and the Detroit editor asking why the men from his home state were still in Russia. Second, attack the British censor for letting presumably factual stories get to the American public. Third, when all else fails, point out that the Allies, the British and French, had even bigger problems.

Neither the Army nor the men of Company I wanted the word "mutiny" hung around the necks of the Detroit Doughboys. A "clarification" was printed in the *New York Times* of July 1, 1919 under the headline:

339TH SAY MUTINY CHARGE IS FALSE, OFFICERS AND MEN RETURNING FROM ARCHANGEL ASSERT INCIDENT WAS EXAGGERATED.

The 339th Infantry, one company of which was reported to have mutinied in Archangel in April as a result of Red propaganda, returned yesterday on the transport *Von Steuben*, and its officers and enlisted men were unanimous in branding the charge as unfounded, although they admitted there had been much dissatisfaction in the ranks. They said it was true that the enlisted men had demanded from their officers the reason for being kept in northern Russia, but maintained they had a right to do so. One enlisted man summed it up thus: "If Senator Hiram Johnson and others can ask such questions in the Senate, why shouldn't we, the ones involved, ask them? And we did, and that was all there is to it." Major J. Brooks Nichols of Detroit, Mich., commander of the 46 officers and 1,495 members of the regiment who returned on the *Von Steuben*, said the incident that inspired the report that there had been a mutiny had been exaggerated. "I have heard more bunk about this alleged mutiny than could be written in a dozen books," he said. "The incident that gave rise to the rumors was a misunderstanding between a sergeant and one of the privates. The men of the 339th are the best disciplined and the most courageous of any outfit I know, and all any officer could desire."

Major Nichols declared that conditions in northern Russia were chaotic, and no one could prophesy the future. The better classes were hoping that the Bolsheviki would eventually hang themselves if given enough rope.

Captain H. G. Winslow of I Company said he was very anxious to clear up the stigma that his command received by the reports of the mutiny. He said, "There was positively no mutiny. Statements which my boys read in newspapers received from the United States caused them to question their officers as to the reason they were being held in Russia. The feeling that nobody knew just why we were there spread among the men. Then Colonel Stewart explained at length to them that the reason we came there originally could be summed up in four points. The four reasons, he said, were: First, to guard the huge stores of war material at Archangel which had been sold by the Allies to the old Russian government; second, to preclude the Germans from coming through Finland and establishing submarine based on the White Sea and at Murmansk; third, to assist the Russians in re-establishing the Eastern Front and reorganizing their own army, thus diverting some of the attention of the Germans from the Western Front; fourth, to assist the Czechosolvaks (sic)."

The argument between the sergeant and the private, which started the mutiny story, was a trivial incident. The noncommissioned officer ordered a Polish boy to load a truck.

Because of the lack of knowledge of the English language, the boy refused the orders that had been given to him. Later, after the order had been explained to him by officers of the company, the soldier readily loaded the truck. That was the nearest thing to a mutiny that we had.

Captain Winslow said that the men of the 339th were amused by the report that they had served in Siberia. Where they did serve, he said, was at Archangel, protecting the Vologda Railroad, in the northern Russia district. He said the weather was intensely cold, and no one could blame the soldiers for complaining, as they frequently experienced days when the thermometer registered 50 degrees below zero. Food conditions were not exactly satisfactory, he said.

The 339th went to Archangel in September from Newcastle, England. When they arrived at their destination they found that the Bolsheviki forces had fled, leaving the inhabitants virtually starving to death, according to officers of the contingent. They said they set up a provisional government along the lines of Kerensky's. The returning soldiers were loud in the praise of the YMCA and Red Cross. "We do not know what the Y has done on other front," one officer said, "but they certainly did treat us right. The YMCA also won a place in our hearts when they erected a Hostess House for us."

The Detroit *Free Press* of July 4, 1919, offered a somewhat different version the "incident" with Company I:

I Company was credited with a mutiny some time ago. I Company said we kicked like hell, but we didn't mutiny.

Here's the story they tell: The men complained for a long time because they did not understand why there was fighting in Russia when the war was over. Late last March, I Company was ordered to entrain at Archangel for the front. When the top sergeant transmitted the instructions to the men in the barracks, they refused to don their packs.

"Why the hell are we here?"' someone roared. The "'top kick", who was not any favored visitor at general headquarters, couldn't answer. The "buck" was eventually passed to Colonel Stewart.

The report in the Detroit paper, attributed to Colonel Stewart, that it was virtually "every man for himself" in North Russia, is probably more accurate. The reasons for which the mission had begun had been overcome by events.

As Germany had been out of the war for more than four months, the threat of it moving into northern Russia from Finland and establishing submarines bases in Murmansk was moot. The Czech Legion problem had been overcome by events and the military stores had been pretty well picked over with little of value remaining. With no real mission to perform, the Polar Bears were fighting just to stay alive.

Dennis Gordon tells of a more troubling incident in his book *Quartered in Hell: The Story of the American North Russian Expeditionary Force 1918-1919.* This incident took place in Toulgas.

Four members of Company B, 339th Infantry, drew up a petition that listed their gripes and then threatened a mutiny unless their officers addressed their complaints by March 15, 1919.

The plot was discovered and six officers were brought to the town to conduct a court martial. A private was brought before the court first. The articles of war covering mutiny, treason and desertion were read.

The soldier responded by tearing open his shirt and shouting, "Look at the lice, the dirt, the filth. We are half starved. But none of you have lice or go hungry."

The courtroom was deadly quiet for a long minute before the head officer rose and told the soldier that if he would use his influence to keep down further trouble, the soldiers would be out of Toulgas in ten days. The other soldiers were similarly excused. The subject was not discussed again.

What was the psychological warfare being used by the Bolsheviki that Major Scales referred to in his report on the I Company incident?

The Bolos must have picked up early on that the American soldiers hated the British officers. The feeling was mutual. The British general who first commanded the sector felt the American officers were unprofessional and that the American enlisted were not even regulars – but draftee scum. The general conveniently overlooked the fact that the British troops were no better than the junior varsity – soldiers not considered physically capable of being sent to France.

The Bolos tried to drive home to the Americans that they were simple pawns in the game, being manipulated by the British who had dreamed up the invasion of northern Russia to be able to exploit the rich stands of timber.

Likewise, they made the point that the Bolo army was made up of working class laborers and peasants. Did not the

American farmers, mill workers, and shopkeepers, have more in common with them than with the autocratic, garishly dressed White Russians, and their former tsar?

The charges of mutinies, or incidents, if they ever took place, and if so, how serious they were, were soon forgotten. The action in northern Russia was coming to an end and all the Polar Bears could think of was the long awaited "exit strategy."

The Czech Legion

If the Detroit Doughboys could have been called the pawns on the Russian chessboard, the Czech Legion would have been the queen, moving this way and that, forward and backward, and ultimately being partially responsible for the deaths of many of the young Americans who perished in Arctic Russia.

The World War I era Czechs, and to a lesser degree, the Slovaks, were ethnic peoples without a country. What are now the Czech Republic and Slovakia were parts of the Austro-Hungarian Empire when World War I burst into flame. Both the Czechs and Slovaks hated the Austrians and Hungarians and longed for independence.

When World War I broke out, there were thousands of Czechs and Slovaks living in Russia. A separate unit, called the *Druzina*, was formed in Kiev, now the capital of the Ukraine, made up of Czech soldiers serving under Russian officers. The unit fought on the Eastern front and was highly regarded as a well-disciplined group.

At the same time, the Austrian Army was filled with Czechs and Slovaks fighting *against* the Russians, and at times, their fellow ethnic members. Thousands were taken prisoner; others "reflagged" themselves and joined the tsar's army.

The Czechoslovak National Council pushed hard during the war to have the Czech forces fight with the Allies against Germany.

As mentioned earlier, 1917 was pivotal in World War I as Tsar Nicholas II was deposed and the Bolsheviks grasped power in Russia. The Bolsheviks did not object to the Czechs building a powerful force – later to be known as the Czech Legion – partly in the hope the legionnaires would side with the Communists and join their revolution.

France, and future Czech president Thomas Masaryk, wanted the Legion to exit Russia and reemerge as a fighting force under a French commander. The Czech Legion was even fancifully considered to be part of the French Army.

With Russia spiraling toward the Red-White Civil War, the Czech Legion was largely on its own. To preclude unnecessary problems, the Legion pledged neutrality in the Civil War.

France was still adamant that the Legion be moved to the Western Front. The British were formulating a different plan. The Americans stood on the sidelines.

In the chaos that was Russia in early 1918, the Bolsheviks gave permission for the Czech Legion to leave Russia via Vladivostok, an arduous journey east on the Trans-Siberian Railway, or through Archangel.

A trickle of Legionnaires headed east, supposedly to be picked up at Vladivostok by British vessels to route them back to France. The Czechs in the Ukraine moved north toward the railway.

In April 1918 the British offered an alternative plan: The Czechs going to Vladivostok would be used to bolster the Allied Intervention Force in the Far East, while another part of the Legion would make its way to the Arctic to bolster the Allied force there.

Facilitating the movement of the Legion to Arctic Russia was one of the reasons given for requesting thousands of American soldiers join the Allies in Northern Russia. For this change in plans the British, Canadian, American, and other allied soldiers in Arctic Russia would pay dearly.

The Czech Legion first headed east toward Vladivostok, then part of the Legion reversed course back to the west to attempt the linkup with the Allies in Arctic Russia, a linkup that was never made. The Legion never got closer to Archangel than 500 miles.

Then came the incident at Chelyabinsk on May 14, 1918.

As described by George F. Kennan in the January 1958 issue of *The Russian Review*, the incident was minor and could have been handled on the spot. But Moscow got involved and the incident spiraled out of control.

Trains carrying Czechs east and Hungarian POWs west for repatriation ended up parked side by side. A missile, a rock or piece of metal, was thrown at the train carrying the Czechs and a soldier was killed. The Czechs poured out of their train cars and lynched the offender.

The local Soviets jailed a number of Czechs and three days later the Czechs seized the arsenal and freed the prisoners.

Moscow was furious and ordered that the Czechs be disarmed. Commissar for War Leon Trotsky ordered local Soviets to detain the Czechs and organize them into labor groups or impress them into the Red Army.

So ended the plan for a peaceful exit from Russia for the Czech Legion.

The Legion now had the option of fighting its way north through hundreds of miles of tundra or the Allies could strike south to open a channel for the Czechs. The Legion also had the option of battling back to Vladivostok.

The Polar Bears and their Allies in the Arctic North could barely hold their footholds in the arc south of Archangel. To drive some 500 miles through territory held by an ever-increasingly aggressive Communist force to link up with the Czechs would have been impossible. The problem was compounded by the fact warmer weather was turning the tundra into a huge swamp.

With the Archangel route foreclosed, the only alternative was to head back east, but this time there would be opposition stemming from the Chelyabinsk incident.

The vanguard of the Legion rolled into Vladivostok on May 5, 1918. But the bulk of the Legion was stretched along almost 5,000 miles of the Trans-Siberian Railway.

Like wildfire, and no one can explain the communications, the whole Trans-Siberian flamed into open warfare between the Communists and Czechs. Orders came from Moscow that the Legion was to be stopped and interned. The Legion captured and controlled key stretches of the railway. Lost in the inevitable "fog of war" was any plan to move part of the Legion to France via Archangel.

As the Legion moved east, it continued to grow, with former POWs and ethnic Czechs living in Russia swelling the ranks. The Legion, which began as two companies, eventually numbered up to 70,000 men.

Evacuation was an arduous process. At any one time as many as 20 or more groups claimed to be the legitimate government of Russia. Different factions controlled different stretches of the railroad and clashes were frequent. According to *Land Forces of Britain, the Empire and the Commonwealth*, more than 13,000 Czechs died in Russia during the Allied Intervention; Japan suffered the second largest number of casualties, 1,500.

The Czechs did have two important bargaining chips with them as they rolled eastward.

They had control of Russia's gold cache and had also captured Admiral Alexander Kolchak, self-styled dictator of the White Russian force in Siberia. Turning over the gold and the admiral smoothed the way for the Czechs to roll on east. The gold was reported to have been sent to Moscow and the admiral was liquidated. One report said the Communists chopped a hole in the ice in a frozen pond and stuffed his body into the chill water, never to be found. This especially brutal way of eliminating an enemy, dated back to the reign of Ivan the Terrible. Its premise was that once submerged, the person went directly to hell.

A less colorful account, but perhaps more likely, is that he was merely shot.

The first Czechs, the sick and wounded, exited Russia on an Italian ship in January 1919. The last group arrived in Vladivostok in May 1920, almost a year and a half after the Armistice. According to Robert L. Willett in *The Russian Sideshow*, some 37,000 members of the Legion had exited through Siberia by September 1920.

Both the Polar Bears of Arctic Russia and the American Expeditionary Force in Siberia had left Russia before the last of the Czech Legion departed. Some of the Legionnaires returned to Italian ports via the Suez Canal; others sailed to the United States on American ships, hop scotched to the East Coast, and then crossed the Atlantic. Almost all were home by the end of 1920. None, of course, fought on the western front in World War I.

Meanwhile, in the Far East

At the same time the Polar Bears were battling frozen fingers and toes – and an ever more belligerent Bolshevik army – a separate American force was in the field some nine times zones to the east, on a equally fuzzy mission.

Some 6000 miles to the east, Vladivostok, in far-off Siberia, was sinking under loads of Allied equipment meant for the Russian Army fighting the Germans. The problem for the Allies was moving the gear across Russia using the creaky Trans-Siberian Railway.

The United States agreed to send an armed force into Siberia to help safeguard the war supplies. It was also to serve as a shield protecting the special force of civilian contractors helping to rebuild the Russian railway system and to play a role in the redeployment of the Czech Legion.

The American Siberian force was joined by a few thousand colonial French soldiers, a smattering of Italians, the ubiquitous English, who also had also landed forces in two parts of southern Russia, and the new bully on the block – Japan. Of all the forces, those of the "Rising Sun" presented the greatest problems.

When Commodore Matthew Perry pried open Japan in 1854, the island nation had been insulated for more than 250 years, since Toyotomi Hideyoshi's ill-fated plan to conquer Korea,

China, India, and beyond at the end of the 1500s (see chapter four). Commodore Perry's visit was a wake-up call for the ambitious Japanese.

Japan flexed its new military muscle for the first time in 1895 when it soundly defeated China in the Sino-Japanese War. It added Taiwan (renamed Formosa) to its empire and gained suzerainty over Korea, whose independence it guaranteed in perpetuity. A scant 15 years later it annexed the peninsula nation!

The island nation became a world power a decade later when it went to war with Russia in a dispute over Korea.

At the time China was the "sick man" of Asia with no less than a half-dozen Western nations having carved out spheres of influence and extra-territorial rights in various parts of the country. Russia's area of control was the Liaotung Peninsula and the city of Port Arthur.

In a move to be emulated some 35 years later at Pearl Harbor, the Japanese fleet attacked Russian ships in Port Arthur without warning and landed an army in Korea. A second Japanese army was landed in the Liaotung Peninsula.

Heavy fighting the next year resulted in some 150,000 casualties. In the end, the inept Russian commander surrendered Port Arthur. The Russian bear had been humbled in the eyes of the world.

The war ended in May 1905, when the Japanese Admiral Heihachiro Togo's fleet defeated the Russian Baltic Fleet that had sailed almost around the world to be battered into submission in the Tsushima Straits between Japan and Korea. With political unrest rising at home, the Russians had little interest in continuing the war and it was settled by the Treaty of Portsmouth in 1905.

The Treaty of Portsmouth, mediated by American President Theodore Roosevelt, codified the first time an Asian nation had defeated a Western power in combat. Japan gained the Russian concession in Liaotung and Port Arthur, half of Sakhalin Island, and recognition of its dominance in Korea. Russia and Japan jointly agreed to return Manchuria to China. The agreement was to prove temporary as Japan detached the province from China in 1932 and set up the puppet regime of Manchukuo.

Acting as the vanguard of an independent command, the first American combat troops to move into Siberia were the 27th and 31st Infantry Regiments that steamed up from the Philippines. They dropped anchor in mid-August 1918, three weeks prior to the Polar Bears arriving in Archangel.

The Japanese commander, General Kikajiro Ishii, informed the unit commanders that he was the supreme commander in Siberia and that they would take orders from him.

Two weeks later, reinforcements from the 8th Infantry Division brought the American units to full strength. With their arrival from California came Regular Army Major General William S. Graves, head of the American Expeditionary Force Siberia (AEFS).

General Graves informed General Ishii that the American forces would be under *American* command. General Ishii backed off and the Americans took their orders from General Graves.

The combat units were supported by a company of the 53rd Telegraph Battalion, Field Hospital #4, Ambulance Company #4, the 146th Ordnance Depot Company and Evacuation Hospital #17.

The force in Siberia differed from the Polar Bears in that the troops were Regular Army soldiers, not wartime draftees. While the Polar Bears were almost all from the Midwest, the members of the AEFS were from all parts of the country.

General Graves was a well-respected leader given an unclear mission. In his book, *The Unknown War With Russia*, Robert J. Maddox quotes the general as saying: "I was in command of the United States troops sent to Siberia, and I must admit, I do not know what the United States was trying to accomplish by military intervention." To borrow a page from the late columnist/humorist Molly Ivins, the general was as "confused as a billy goat on Astroturf."

General Graves was not alone in his confusion. American politicians also had a hard time grasping just what was happening in Russia.

Wisconsin was a major provider of the manpower that made up the 339th Infantry in Arctic Russia.

Its Progressive Senator, Robert La Follette, placed the following in the *Congressional Record* of January 7, 1919:

When my constituents appeal to me, and they do daily, to explain why their boys, having entered the service of their country, are retained in remote parts of the earth to wage a war, not against the common enemy, but against a people with whom we are at peace, *I have no answer* (italics added).

Although as befuddled as the senator, General Graves was determined to do his best in carrying out the directive of President Wilson that the American forces were NOT to take sides in the multi-faceted civil war raging in Russia.

His other missions, as he understood them, were to assist in rebuilding the Russian railway system, to safeguard supplies that had piled up in Vladivostok and to keep a channel open through which the Czech Legion could evacuate Russia.

In her book *America's Siberian Expedition 1918-1919*, Betty Unterberger points out that while these objectives were well understood by both the State and War Departments, the American public was allowed to believe that the Doughboys were in Siberia to oppose the Bolshiviki and help make the world "safe for democracy." Unspoken were the American goals of countering Japanese influence in the area and the desire to maintain an "Open-Door" policy to benefit American business. And running like a red thread through the entire venture into Russia were the twin fears of Germany moving east into Russia and that the Bolsheviks were somehow agents of the German Kaiser.

Unlike the Polar Bears in Arctic Russia who were sent out on offensive missions, the troops in Siberia fought only in self-defense, and fight that had to do, as Siberia was in chaos.

Scattered around Russia were up to 20 groups, each claiming to be the government of a slice of the country, or all of it. There were White Russians, Bolsheviks, Chinese bandits, Russian outlaws and probably the worst of the bunch, two Cossack warlords, Ivan Kalmykof and Geogorii Semenov.

Each of the groups murdered, raped, pillaged, and burned peasant villages as it suited them. Apparently the page "winning the hearts and minds of the people" was missing from the playbooks of all factions.

As if General Graves and his 7,000 or so soldiers didn't have enough to worry about, the Japanese were becoming a bigger and bigger problem.

In her study of the intervention in Siberia, *Between War and Peace*, Carol Melton wrote that President Wilson finally agreed to send U.S. troops into the theater to show the Western Allies that he was a "team player." Though unspoken, he undoubtedly believed such action would help sway the Europeans into supporting his pet project – the League of Nations.

The United States and Japan agreed that each would send some 7,000 men into Siberia. The Japanese *nodded* their agreement but had different plans.

Prior to the Communist revolution, the Kerensky government had requested that Japan send a quarter-million soldiers to fight with Russia on the Eastern Front against Germany. Not interested! Later the Japanese were asked to move forces into western Siberia to counter the Soviets. No! The Japanese were interested only in eastern Siberia, the Maritime Provinces, Manchuria and northern China.

The Japanese were similarly not interested in assisting the Russian people; their ambition was merely to add more land to their growing empire. The Japanese force grew to more than 70,000, by far the largest foreign army in Russia. And to make matters even worse, the Japanese allied themselves with the worst of the Cossack warlords, whom General Graves considered to be more blood thirsty than even the Bolsheviki. The theory was that a weak, divided Siberia would be more fertile ground for planting the Japanese flag. On a number of occasions, the erstwhile Allies – America and Japan – almost came to conflict.

Both the Japanese and American governments were divided as to policy in Siberia.

The American State Department was interested in staying in eastern Russia and supporting the anti-Soviet forces. The War Department could see little progress to be made and wanted an early exit.

The situation was even more fractured in Japan.

The military had rushed forces into Russia without asking the approval of the weak civil government. Ditto reinforcements. This same military clique would play a primary role in launching war in the Pacific a generation later.

While the battles were being waged in both Washington and Tokyo, American forces were spreading out along the Trans-Siberian Railway and into the coalfields of Siberia. Coal was needed to run the trains and General Graves had to medicate disputes between the Bolsheviki-leaning miners and the Imperialist-leaning mine owners. For this he was unfairly tagged as a Communist sympathizer though he was doing his best to comply with President Wilson's directive to stay out of disputes between the factions, while at the same time keeping the railroad running.

American Doughboys died in accidents and were killed in ones and twos by all sides. The most costly battle took place along the railroad at a place called Kanghaus. A group of some 75 members of the 31st Regiment were ambushed by a group labeled only as "partisans." By the time a rescue party arrived at the scene, some 20 Americans were dead and more than 20 were seriously wounded. And so it went. Russians who by day seemed friendly enough might be the same ones who were trying to kill the Doughboys at night. With no clearly defined mission, merely staying alive from day to day became the order of the day.

The intervention is Russia is sometimes called the "Shadow War." If this is true, the role of the Russian Railroad Service Corps (RRSC) was a shadow within the shadow. One of President Wilson's goals was to send a group of railway executives to offer ways to improve the creaky Trans-Siberian as it was the only way to move supplies from Vladivostok to the Eastern front for use of the Russian Army. This was months before the first U.S. combat soldiers arrived.

Five railroaders, led by John Stevens, an expert in the field who also played a prominent role in building the Panama Canal, traveled to Russia and made recommendations to the government of Alexander Kerensky (the Communists had not yet come to power). Among the recommendations were that American railroad men be sent to operate the line and that locomotives and rail cars be furnished.

Some 300 railroaders and 80 machinists were earmarked for Siberia to assemble the rolling stock and supervise the operation of the Trans-Siberian. Like most everything else, the plan ran into almost immediate trouble.

By the time the ship carrying the men was to have arrived at Vladivostok, the harbor was icing over. A quick decision was made to head back to Japan. By February 1919, part of the force was landed in somewhat warmer Manchuria, as one branch of the Trans-Siberian roadway ran through Chinese territory. Part of the railroaders stayed in Japan even longer.

Despite the best of intentions, the men of the RRSC accomplished little. Constant factional fighting, and endless bureaucracy forced the RRSC men to stay close to the railroad and out of danger, protected by the various Allied military forces.

By December 1919, World War I had been over for more than a year and the AEFS was still scattered about Siberia. The reasons for coming to Russia were no longer valid. The stockpiled supplies were no longer needed at the nonexistent Eastern Front and the railroad men could not do their work with constant fighting among the factions. The Czech Legion was more than capable of taking care of itself. The American public was becoming more curious as to why American boys were still in Russia while President Wilson was much more concerned with the League of Nations than a few thousand American soldiers so far from home.

American soldiers finally began boarding ships for Manila in January of 1920. General Graves and the last major contingent sailed out of the harbor on April 1, 1920. A Japanese band played, with some sarcasm, "Hard Times Come Again No More."

There was no flag waving as the American force moved back to the Philippines. Comrades had been left behind, casualties of a shadow war. The officers and men of the AEFS would be hard pressed to list their accomplishments, other than being able to leave Russia behind alive.

General Graves must be credited with doing a good job in Siberia, as all factions accused him of helping the others. A faction in the State Department kept demanding his removal for not being strongly pro-White. The British too felt he was not anti-Bolshevik enough.

But General Graves were strongly supported by Secretary of War Newton Baker, and Chief of Staff of the Army General Peyton March. It was a thankless job but one he performed with gallantry, especially in hewing to the line of President Wilson that his force not get involved in internal politics.

General Graves and his officers and men were commended by General March in the Report of the Chief of Staff, 1920:

The expedition affords one of the finest examples in history of honorable, unselfish dealings with an unfortunate people and a dignified and sincere attempt under very difficult circumstances to be helpful to a people struggling to achieve a new liberty and self-government. The situation that confronted the commanding general, his subordinate commanders, and troops, was a particularly difficult and hazardous one. The manner in which this difficult and arduous task was performed is worthy of the best traditions of the Army.

Marching Toward the Exit Strategy

With the French, Italian and American forces leaving the battle fronts, the task of keeping Arctic Russia out of the hands of the Bolsheviks was left to the British, their "legions," and the anti-Bolshevik Russian forces.

While General Ironside, in his book *Archangel 1918-1919*, admitted he knew little more about Arctic Russia than the mill hands from Detroit and the farmers from Wisconsin, he was determined to make "Russification" work but time was limited. According to Leonid I. Stakhovsky in his work *Intervention at Archangel*, the general received an order on March 19, 1919, stating that British forces would be withdrawn from Russia before Archangel was iced over in the fall/winter of that year. To give himself time to build up the indigenous Russian force, and to keep panic from seizing Archangel, the general put that knowledge in his kit bag.

Probably the primary problem faced by the general was the revolving door government policy in Arctic Russia. Much as would happen in Vietnam after the assassination of Ngo Dihn

Diem, governments were formed, names were changed, ministries were activated and dissolved, alliances with other anti-Bolshevik forces were forged and broken. As Robert McNamara pointed out in his book, *In Retrospect*, South Vietnam had six governments in the year following the coup that ousted Diem. And the situation got even worse. As Dana Lloyd writes in his work, *Ho Chi Minh*, the number of failed governments had grown to eight only six months later. Simply put, as in Vietnam, there was no strong leadership, no persons to whom the average Russian could rally. And it was all too transparent that no matter what the government was called, or who ran it, the British were still pulling the strings.

General Ironside's particular favorite to carry the anti-Bolshevik banner was the Slavo-British Legion activated in June of 1918 by General Poole. Also "stood up" were a Polish Legion, a Finnish Legion and the Russian Volunteer Army. All were officered by the British with London paying for the care, feeding, financing, and maintenance of the units. The French also organized a branch of its famous Foreign Legion; the Americans declined to set up a parallel force.

By the summer of 1919 the Russian landscape looked much like the tablecloth at a typical Italian restaurant – red squares and white squares.

The Russian leader on whom General Ironside pinned his hopes – a man with a very un-Russian sounding name – General Eugene Miller – was probably not the best choice.

The number of average Russians who were saddened by the death of the last Romanoff was probably small. And yet the leader of the White forces in Arctic Russia was a lieutenant general who had served tsarist Russia for more than 30 years. He had commanded both a corps and an army during the war with the Central Powers. He favored the pomp of the old army and loved epaulets, a symbol of tsarist rank universally despised by the Russian rank and file.

General Ironside, in the best traditions of the British imperialist, felt that any group of men could be whipped into an outstanding fighting force if led by a Sandhurst graduate or two and a few crusty sergeants major. This theory worked well in India where a small veneer of British soldiers commanded a huge native force. Why would not the same system work in Russia?

In India, the troops, the *sepoys*, were professional military men. The Russians swept into the Slavo-British Legion were impressed peasants, former deserters, common criminals, and the local riff-raff who would do anything for a few shillings.

Discipline began to unravel in February 1919 when a company of the British Yorkshire Infantry Regiment refused to go to the front.   They were faced down by General Ironside who, according to legend, once crushed an opponent with a bear hug. The British soldiers wisely reconsidered. This breach of command was followed quickly when a French battalion refused orders to go to the front. They were disarmed and sent back to France.

The "tablecloth" was becoming redder and redder. Part of the 3rd Russian Infantry Regiment at the front near Toulgas revolted, killed unit officers, and crossed over to the Bolos.   The story was the same with the 8th Russian Infantry Regiment at Pinega where officers were also killed.

The most crushing defeat for General Ironside came in July when two companies of his *Bolshies* revolted, killing four British and three Russian officers.   A large number of *Bolshies* defected.

At about the same time the anti-Bolshevik forces led by Admiral Kolchak in Siberia were being beaten; General Miller was given dictatorial powers to try to save the Arctic north, with disastrous results.

More defections quickly followed.

The 5th Russian Infantry Regiment surrendered to the Bolos on July 20. Revolts by the 6th and 7th Regiments that same day were broken up with great difficulty.   General Ironside had seen enough.   It was time to accept reality – the mission was failing.

The British moved back to Archangel by September 23, and were out of Arctic Russia four days later. On February 20, 1920, the Bolsheviks marched into Archangel, on the heels of General Miller and his staff as they fled for their lives. Russification, like the intervention, was a failure.   British forces had suffered 327 battle deaths. The cost to the exchequer was a hundred million pounds.

In his book, published a year after the withdrawal of all Allied Forces, entitled *Fighting Without a War*, Ralph Albertson listed half a dozen reasons why "Russification," as practiced by the British, didn't work.   Albertson, who worked with the Military YMCA, traveled widely in Arctic Russia and was among the last Americans to leave the war zone.

Among the reasons the British were unable to mold a fighting force among the Arctic Russians, he felt, was the British habit of referring to the Russians as "swine." These references were unfortunate as some of the Russians could understand English.

Other reasons he listed were that the British distrusted and disliked the Russians, made no effort to understand them and were utterly tactless in working with Russian soldiers. War-weariness among the British soldiers and populace also played a major role.

Sir Winston Churchill, Britain's Secretary of State for War, had always been the tip of the spear aimed at the heart of the Bolsheviks. He was not alone, having supporters on both sides of the Atlantic.

French Prime Minister Georges Clemensau and General Ferdinand Foch were anti-Communist to the point they refused to allow a peace conference to take place in Paris, not wanting their capital "contaminated" by the revolutionaries from Moscow.

Large segments of the American State Department were on the side of the Whites. American Ambassador to Russia David Francis kept up a steady barrage of letters to President Wilson urging a force of 150,000 British, French and Americans drive inland to capture Moscow and St. Petersburg. None of the major allies seemed interested.

Even President Wilson, working behind the scenes, would like to have seen an early end to Bolshevism, according to Robert J. Maddox in his work *The Unknown War With Russia*.

What else could explain the American government recognizing and working with an "embassy" of the defunct Kerensky government? That "embassy" was able to procure, often at very favorable rates, war material that found its way into the hands of the White Russians.

There is little doubt that Sir Winston was the leader of the anti-Bolshevik front. In his work *Churchill, A Life*, Martin Gilbert quotes the British leader thus:

Civilization is being completely extinguished over gigantic areas, when the Bolos hop and caper like troops of ferocious baboons amid the ruins of cities and the corpses of their victims.

After conquering all the Huns – tigers of the world – I would not submit to be beaten by the baboons.

Of all the tyrannies in history, the Bolos' tyranny is the worst, the most destructive, the most degrading ...incomparably more hideous, on a larger scale and more numerous than any for which the Kaiser is responsible.

As Sir Winston and his "strangle the baby in the crib" adherents were fighting a last ditch battle, American public opinion was souring against keeping forces in Russia as this excerpt from the *Congressional Record* of January 7, 1919, illustrates:

Senator Robert La Follette of Wisconsin: I should like to ask the Senator (William Kenyon of Iowa) a question which I was tempted to ask the Senator from Arkansas (William Kirby) when he was speaking, both of them taking the view that we should at once send a large army into Russia.

Senator Kenyon: Or withdraw the troops we have there.

Senator La Follette: Does it not occur to the Senator from Iowa that it would be a pretty wise thing for us to make a declaration of war before we go any further with this business?

Senator Kenyon: Yes; it is true; but the Senator does not get my viewpoint. I do not say send a large army. I say we should do one of two things – withdraw these men, or, if they are to be kept there for any purpose, put a sufficient Army there to keep them from slaughter. That is the point I make. *I say, however, withdraw them. We are not at war with Russia. Now that peace is in sight, are we to begin all over again with a new war? I say no.* (emphasis added).

The mothers of the boys who are in Russia are going to be heard. While the letter which I have is rather sarcastic in some places, it is from a woman in my State who has done wonderful work with the Red Cross ... who had one boy wounded on the battle fields of France and now in a hospital there and this other boy of hers, her only remaining boy, is fighting through the snows of Russia, *without any authority to put him there that anybody knows of.* (emphasis added). Her letter reads in part:

I trust you will pardon my troubling you again so soon, but I, at least, had the great pleasure of a response, which so far has been denied me by Secretary of War Baker. Perhaps he thinks he has something bigger than mothers' letters to think of, and, no doubt, he is a busy man; but if it were not for we mothers of men we might be under German rule today, and we resent silence when all is at stake for us... Why should ours be left there to be slaughtered? I'd like to send Mr. Baker and his boys (if he has any), perhaps then he would begin to think something to be done. And while he is waiting, what of our boys?

Senator Kenyon placed one more letter in the *Congressional Record*, from a mother, apparently from Detroit:

I read with much interest the demand of Senator Townsend on behalf of the Michigan people concerning the Three hundred and thirty-ninth Infantry. It is true most of these men are from Detroit...I notice that Secretary of War Baker says he never heard complaint(s). Well, perhaps they went where my letter went – to the wastebasket. At least I received no reply. Had he read it, he could not have truthfully said what he did.

Then he disclaimed knowing of influenza. If such be true, I think it is time he began to find out.

I think I sent you the letter received from my son, when he said 62 of their men – some of the best – died in four days after reaching Archangel.

He also told of the second lieutenant being taken from the barge as they were going up the river and dying three days later. I don't believe one of these deaths has been reported...and with all due respect to our President, I think no time should be lost to cable a demand that he pause in his receptions long enough to doing something for our boys at once there.

We visited Camp Custer a short time before they left for over(seas). And a more splendid body of men President Wilson will not meet in all his travel. The whole of Russia would not pay for one of their lives, as it is today or ever will be.

Senator La Follette spoke on the situation in Russia later in the month:

Mr. President, the armed forces of the United States (which) landed in Russia some months ago under the orders of the Commander-in-Chief are – if press dispatches can be relied upon at all – engaged at the present time in making war on Russia.

Some of the troops employed in military operations there are from my own State, and I ask to be officially informed as to the presence of our troops in Russia, and I think the Congress and the country ought to know why we are making war upon the Russian people.

On the 2d of this month there appeared in the *New York Times* a dispatch stating that soldiers from Wisconsin and from an adjoining State were at the time engaged in desperate military operations in Russia and against Russian troops.

I do not know how other Senators may feel, but I should be false to my State and her people if I did not exhaust every means at my power to find out by what right hundreds of young men from Wisconsin are engaged in conducting a war on Russia.

The Rest of the Story

As the late spring days lengthened in Arctic Russia, things began to look up for the Americans.

The haughty General Poole had been replaced by General Ironside, who was better liked by the Americans, and Brigadier General Wilds Richardson had replaced the ineffective Colonel Stewart, who had proven unwilling or unable to comply with President Wilson's directive not to involve American soldiers in combat. Colonel Stewart faded into obscurity soon after leaving Arctic Russia but must be recognized as one of less than 5,000 service personnel who have won the nation's highest military decoration – the Medal of Honor. He won the award while serving in the Philippines in 1899.

The Doughboys were on the move, but not south toward the front. They were moving north, toward Archangel. Had they only known, all would have circled February 16, 1919 on their "short-timers" calendar for it was on that day that President Wilson notified Secretary of War Baker to start making plans to withdraw the Polar Bears.

The last three soldiers to lose their lives in the Arctic were all from small towns in Michigan. Private Alva Crook, Company M, of Lakeview; Private Floyd Auslander, Company H, of Decker; and Corporal Rodney Sapp, also of Company M, hometown Rodney, were killed while defending fortifications near Bolshie Ozerki. The action took place on April 1, 1919, six weeks AFTER the decision had been made to withdraw from Russia. They were the last three American soldiers to die in combat for a dying cause.

By June 8, 1919, the Polar Bears had completely left the front and was ready for the trip home. The first units had left Arctic Russia on June 2. The last group, Companies A, B, and C of the 310th Engineers would pack up their tools and sail for home from Archangel on June 26, 1919.

A stop for logistical reasons in Murmansk allowed for the final bit of combat for the Polar Bears. As one of the ships carrying the Yanks docked in Murmansk near a British transport a mini-brawl broke out. Lumps of coal were tossed from ship to ship. As Robert L. Willett relates it in *The Russian Sideshow*, a Private Henkelman of the *Menominee* wrote:

On the Kola River near Murmansk, we tied up with our bow near an English ship just arriving in North Russia. I was below deck when I heard noises and sauntered up on deck and saw a pitched battle taking place between our gang and the English throng, each side hurling chunks of coal at each other and cursing loudly. Our men wanted to get off and attack the Limeys, but our officers doubled the guard at the gangplank.

What could have sparked this? Perhaps the British were upset thinking the Yanks arrived at the party late and were leaving early. For the Polar Bears, it could have been pay back for all the M & V rations they were forced to eat.

In late June 1919, the Polar Bears finally hit French soil, staying a few days in Brest before sailing home aboard an American ship. Undoubtedly, the food was better at that port of call.

Detroit welcomed the first of the returning Polar Bears on July 4, 1919. It proved a bittersweet homecoming as the Doughboys had lost 223 comrades to all causes with another dozen listed as prisoners of war. According to the Chicago *Tribune* of February 26, 1939, more than 2,400 total incidents of illness or injuries were recorded in the chief surgeon's log.

To show its appreciation, the state of Michigan awarded a bonus of $15 to each soldier for each month he had been in the service. Though not a great sum today, it did help smooth the transition back to civilian life as the average pay was for a laborer in 1920 was some $80 per month.

The saga of the Polar Bears did not end for another ten years when an additional 55 caskets were brought back from Russia for burial. Today a memorial to "Michigan's Own" stands in White Chapel Park outside Detroit – a marble Polar Bear with a cross and helmet under its front paws.

The Polar Bears were not awarded a special campaign ribbon for their service in Russia, but they did have one distinctive decoration they could wear.

Many Army units wear unit crests with mottos inscribed in English, Latin, or sometimes French. The Detroit Doughboys are probably the only ones to have Russian lettering on their crest. As translated from the "old" Russian, the motto reads – "Bayonet Decides."

And when it came to awards, the young men from the cities, villages and farms of the Midwest did themselves proud.

Awards

The Distinguished Service Cross is second only to the Medal of Honor in the hierarchy of U. S. Army awards for valor. Twenty-three of the awards were presented to the Polar Bears, more than double the Army's average. Fourteen were won by natives of Detroit while three others went to soldiers from other parts of Michigan. Six of the awards were made posthumously.

Eleven of the decorations were for heroism in action after the November 11, 1918 Armistice had been signed. Medals were won by lieutenants, sergeants, corporals, privates and even a bugler. The honor roll reads like this:

Private Charles J. Bell,
Company B, 339th Infantry, Louisville, KY

Sergeant William H. Bowman,
Company B, 339th Infantry, Detroit, MI

First Lieutenant Charles C. Chappel,
339th Infantry, Toledo, OH

First Sergeant George E. Comstock,
Company E, 339th Infantry, Detroit, MI

Sergeant Aulbert D. Cox,
Company D, 339th Infantry, Arthur, IL

Private Chester E. Everhart,
337th Ambulance Company, Detroit, MI

Sergeant Matthew G. Grahek,
Company M, 339th Infantry, Detroit, MI

Corporal Robert L. Green,
Company D, 339th Infantry, Lincoln, NE

Corporal Clement A. Grobbel,
Company I, 339th Infantry, Warren, MI

Private Lawrence B. Kilroy,
337th Ambulance Company, Detroit, MI

Sergeant Cornelius J. Mahoney,
Company K, 339th Infantry, Detroit MI

Private Hubert C. Paul,
337th Ambulance Company, Detroit, MI

Second Lieutenant Howard H. Pellegrom,
339th Infantry, Grand Haven, MI

First Lieutenant Clifford F. Phillips,
Company H, 339th Infantry, Falls City, NE

First Lieutenant Ralph E. Powers,
337th Ambulance Company, Amherst, OH

Corporal Robert M. Pratt,
Company M, 339th Infantry, Detroit, MI

Bugler James F. Revels,
Company I, 339th Infantry, Detroit, MI

Corporal William H. Russell,
Company M, 339th Infantry, Detroit, MI

Corporal Theodore H. Sieloff,
Company I, 339th Infantry, Detroit, MI

First Lieutenant Albert M. Smith,
339th Infantry, Kalamazoo, MI

Private Victor Stier,
Company A, 339th Infantry, Detroit, MI

Private First Class Homer A. Tuley,
337th Ambulance Company, Detroit, MI

Private Clarence H. Zech,
337th Ambulance Company, Detroit, MI

Epilog

The Polar Bears, as well as their counterparts who fought in Siberia, have all departed this earth. Undoubtedly the other members of the Allied Coalition and the Russians against whom they fought are also gone. The action, which took place some 85 years ago, is just a minor footnote in history.

In fact, it is so little known among Americans that the speech writers for President Ronald Reagan slipped this paragraph into his January 25, 1984 State of the Union address:

Tonight, I want to speak to the people of the Soviet Union to tell them it's true that our governments have had serious differences, but our sons and daughters have never fought each other in war. And, if we Americans have our way, we never will.

That statement would come as quite a surprise to the families and friends of the Polar Bears, 139 of whom were killed in action or died of wounds in combat in Arctic Russia with the Bolos, or were swallowed up by the endless tracts of forest and never heard from again. The same would be true for the 189 members of General Graves' command who lost their lives in struggles against the Communists, the Cossacks, the bandits and the cold in forbidding Siberia.

At this point one question must be considered: Were the Soviets really serious about pushing the Polar Bears back into the White Sea? Upon a close reading of the available records of the Shadow War, the answer appears to be "No."

There were a number of instances where the Bolos were on the verge of overrunning an Allied position and able to inflict heavy casualties only to pull back. Artillery barrages stopped suddenly for no apparent reason. Fire was withheld while the Allies went forward to collect their wounded.

Why would this have been done? To paraphrase feisty old Nikita Khrushchev, the Allied Forces in Arctic Russia may have been a bone in the Bolshevik's throat, but not a dagger pointed at the heart.

The Communist revolution would be won in Moscow, St. Petersburg, Kiev and Odessa, not in backwater Archangel, much as the American Civil War was settled in Virginia and not rustic Arkansas. As Evan Mawdsley writes in *The Russian Civil War*, the Bolsheviki had committed only three under-strength divisions to the Arctic front – one in the Murmansk area and two around Archangel.

An all-out Bolo offensive, by a larger force, causing a "Last Stand" for the men from Camp Custer, could possibly have brought "massive retaliation" from France, Great Britain, and the United States as Ambassador Francis urged so many times. An Allied force of several hundred thousand British, French and American troops aimed at Moscow and St. Petersburg, could doubtless have strangled the revolutionary baby in the cradle.

No doubt the Bolsheviki knew that demands of the American and British political leaders, like American Senators La Follette and Kenyon, and the public to "bring the boys home" were growing ever louder and more shrill. Time was on the side of the Bolos.

Even more outspoken than Senators La Follette and Kenyon was California's Senator Hiram Johnson, a bitter enemy of President Wilson. He kept up a steady drumbeat of "what are our soldiers doing killing and being killed by Russian peasants in the freezing cold in a country with which we are not at war?" Throughout Michigan, particularly Detroit, letters and petitions, first a trickle and then a torrent, flooded into Washington demanding that "our boys" return home from what most family members considered to be a fool's errand.

The Russians sparred with the Allies, bided their time, and were successful in watching from the sidelines as the last of the Allies sailed home.

The action in Arctic Russia has usually been considered an interesting, but minor sideshow. It may have been minor, but it was deadly.

Though the raw number seems small, the Doughboys, individually, faced an exponentially greater chance of being killed than the GIs who have fought in the Second Gulf War.

From the start of September 1918 to the end of March 1919, the Doughboys served in a combat zone for 212 days. Doughboys died at the rate of two every three days. During the first five years of the Second Gulf War there were roughly two fatalities each day. But the average troop strength in Iraq has been more than 30 times that of the young Americans who fought in Arctic Russia, reducing the odds of any one solider being killed by a factor of nine or more.

The final irony is that all of the fighting, almost a century ago, in this bizarre twilight contest took place in a country with which the United States was ostensibly at peace.

A conversation that could well have taken place in Detroit in 1920 sums up the adventure best:

Albert: Understand you were in Europe in the War.

Chester: Yup.

Albert: What was it like in France?

Chester: Don't know – didn't go to France.

Albert: Where did you go?

Chester: To Russia.

Albert: Why in the world did you go to Russia?

Chester: Danged if I know. Danged if anybody knows.

PRIMARY SOURCES

Ralph Albertson, *Fighting without a War, an Assessment of Military Intervention in North Russia*, Harcourt, Brace and Howe, 1920

Michael Beschloss, *The Conquerors*, Simon and Schuster, 2002

Hugh Borton, *Japan's Modern Century*, Ronald Press 1955

Neil G. Carey, editor, *Fighting the Bolsheviks, The Russian Memoir of PFC Donald E. Carey, U.S. Army, 1918-1919*, *Presidio Press*, 1997

Chronicler (John Cudahy), *Archangel, The American War with Russia*, A.C. McClung and Company, 1924

Foster Rhea Dulles, *The American Red Cross, A History*, Harper and Brothers, 1950

R. Ernest Dupuy, *Perish by the Sword*, Military Service Publishing Service, 1939.

Niall Ferguson, *The War of the World, Twentieth-Century Conflict and the Descent of the West*, The Penguin Press, 2006

Thomas L. Friedman, *From Beirut to Jerusalem*, Anchor Books, 1989

Martin Gilbert, *Churchill: A Life*, Henry Holt and Company, 1991

Ann Hagedorn, *Savage Peace, Hope and Fear in America 1919*, Simon and Schuster, 2007

E.M. Halliday, *When Hell Froze Over*, ibooks, 2000

Richard Holmes, *Battlefield, Decisive Conflicts in History*, Oxford University Press, 2006

Sir Edmund Ironside, *Archangel 1918-1919*, T & A Constable, LTD, 1953

George F. Kennan, *The Decision to Intervene*, Princeton University Press, 1958

Ian Kershaw, *Fateful Choices*, Penguin Press, 2007

Phyllis Lee Levin, *Edith and Woodrow*, Scribner 2001

Dana Lloyd, *Ho Chi Minh*, Chelsea House, 1986

Evan Mawdsley, *The Russian Civil War*, Allen and Unwin, 1987

Robert McNamara, *In Retrospect*, Time Books, 1995

Roy MacLaren, *Canadians in Russia, 1918-1919*, Macmillan of Canada, 1976

Robert J. Maddox, *The Unknown War in Russia, Wilson's Siberian Intervention*, Presidio Press, 1977

Gary Mead, *The Doughboys, America and the First World War*, The Overlook Press, 2000

Carol Willcox Melton, *Between War and Peace*, Mercer University Press, 2001

Joel Moore, Henry H. Mead, and Lewis E. Jahns, *The History of the American Expedition Fighting the Bolsheviki*, Battery Press (reprint), 2003

Louis G. Perez, *The History of Japan*, Greenwood Press, 1998

Richard Pipes, *A Concise History of the Russian Revolution*, Alfred A, Knopf, 1995

Jim Powers, *Wilson's War*, Crown Publishing Group, 2005

John B. Romeiser (editor), *Combat Reporter, Don Whitehead's World War II Diary and Memoirs*, Fordham University Press, 2006

James L. Stokesbury, *A Short History of World War I*, William Morrow and Company, 1981

Betty Miller Unterberger, *America's Siberian Expedition, 1918-1920*, Duke University Press, 1956

Robert L. Willett, *Russian Sideshow, America's Undeclared War*, Brassy's Inc., 2003

SECONDARY SOURCES

Bentley Historical Library
"Detroit's Own" Polar Bear Memorial Association
Onwar.com

MEDIA SOURCES

Chicago Sunday *Tribune*
Detroit *Free Press*
Detroit *News*
The *Russian Review*
Washington *Evening Star*

Walker Flag

The Original "Contra"

Had William Walker's artillerymen been better at fusing mortar shells, Oliver North, of Iran-Contra fame, may well have retired as an obscure Marine colonel and Managua might be playing baseball in the American League.

For had Walker's band of adventures – the original "Contras" – won the battle of Masaya, Nicaragua in November 1856, he could well have gained control of all Central America, opening it to massive colonization by North Americans, and possible statehood or commonwealth status.

From this near miss, Walker, one of the best known personalities on the 1850s, and onetime President of Nicaragua, slipped into obscurity, but not until three final desperate attempts to bring American-style democracy to the Central Americans, if they wanted it or not.

Walker, son of a successful Nashville, Tennessee businessman, packed many careers into his adventuresome life – doctor, lawyer, journalist, self-appointed army commander, and the nineteenth-century's most famous "filibuster", as soldiers of fortune were known in those days.

Young William Walker's family belonged to the fundamentalist Disciples of Christ sect, a group of Protestants who shunned all of life's pleasures. Small, shy, and bookish, applying today's standards, the teen-aged William Walker would have been considered a geek. Walker was devoted to his mother – Mary Norvell Walker – who was in ill health when he was young. His father was correct and distant, once telling a friend that he would not *object* to hearing news of his wayward son.

An accomplished scholar, Walker entered the University of Nashville at age 12 and graduated two years later *summa cum laude.* He was versed in Latin, Greek, French, German and Spanish, as well as English. In one of the many quirks of fate concerning Walker's life, his alma mater, after a number of mergers and name changes, has been incorporated into Vanderbilt University, named for one of his main antagonists, Commodore Cornelius Vanderbilt, who richly endowed the school he never visited.

From the University of Nashville, Walker traveled to Philadelphia where he enrolled in the medical school of the University of Pennsylvania. He earned his medical degree at age 19.

Walker then journey to Europe where he studied at the top medical colleges on the continent. He was an accomplished surgeon and was considered one of the best in the city when he returned to Nashville.

Medicine had little lure for the idealistic Walker. He was especially appalled by the public hospitals he found in Europe where the poor received inadequate or no treatment at all.

Life in New Orleans

He soon gave up medicine and moved to the vibrant city of New Orleans where he "read the law" and began to practice at 23.

New Orleans brought to him his two true loves – a girl named Ellen Martin and the doctrine of "Manifest Destiny".

Mark Twain once said that the ante-bellum south was afflicted with the Sir Walter Scott syndrome. Honor – and dueling if necessary – marked a true gentleman. Respect for women was an absolute must. Fighting for a "lost cause" only added to the romance.

Ellen Martin was part of a well-to-do family – intelligent, charming, and attractive. But what may have drawn William Walker to her even more was that scarlet fever in childhood had left her a deaf-mute. What could be more romantic, more dashing, than to love, cherish and protect one who had suffered a disabling illness early in life?

To further his romance with Ellen, Walker learned sign language. He also wrote long letters to her as writing came natural to him.

While William Walker was "courting" Ellen Martin, he began another career as an editor of the left-leaning, mildly anti-slavery New Orleans *Crescent*. Walker devoted himself to politics while another writer who would later make his mark in literature, Walt Whitman, wrote about life in the exiting city of New Orleans.

While no newspaper in the South could survive on an ardent anti-slavery platform, the *Crescent* was less vocal in its support of the "peculiar institution" than the others.

William Walker was making a name for himself in journalism and might have moved into politics when tragedy stuck – an epidemic of yellow fever hit the city and Ellen Martin was a victim. With Ellen gone, Walker's life turned around and his next destination would be California.

As young Walker was working with the newspaper in New Orleans in the late 1840s, a man who would become instrumental in Walker's eventual downfall was entering the scene is Nicaragua – Commodore Cornelius Vanderbilt.

Gold was drawing prospectors by the thousands to California. There were two ways to get to the goldfields, overland or by ship. Vanderbilt's idea was to transport travelers through Nicaragua, cutting the sea voyage by more than half. He set up Accessory Transit Company to facilitate this venture.

Miners and other travelers would take a Vanderbilt-owned ship to the east coast of Nicaragua, travel by river to Lake Nicaragua, steam across the lake, and trek the last 12 miles to the Pacific Coast overland and then grab a waiting Vanderbilt steamer for California. A canal would eliminate the hot, dusty, pestilence-ridden overland leg and make a non-stopped trip possible. In a few years the ambitions and millions of Vanderbilt would clash with "President" William Walker.

Onward to California

Following the death of Ellen, Walker trekked overland to California, arriving in San Francisco in 1852, unemployed and almost penniless.

Walker took up journalism once more in San Francisco getting a job with the *Herald*. It was one of the newer papers in town, also left-leaning. It supported such causes are the right to divorce, was for free trade, and opposed slavery being introduced into California.

The *Herald's* major crusade was calling for law and order in wide-open San Francisco. With Walker doing much of the writing, the paper attacked judges, city officials, and the law enforcement community. For his efforts Walker was fined $500 for contempt of court. He refused to pay. Public opinion was on his side and he was freed from jail.

Walker began his career as a filibuster in 1853 with the target being the mineral-rich Mexican state of Sonora. The state was being ravished by Apache Indians and American settles near the border had asked for help as the Mexican government was unable to protect them. This Scott-like venture appealed to Walker, a chance to help the downtrodden. Wealthy Californians looked at it as a way to pry the mines of Sonora from Mexico.

Sonora was the big prize but Walker had neither the man-power nor money to go after it. So he set his sights on sparsely populated Lower (Baja) California. In October Walker and his group of 45 adventurers headed south.

Filibusters were rough and ready men. Some were disap-pointed miners, others worked the docks, while others just drifted around. To control a group like this one would expect to find a man like First Sergeant Milton Warden, played by Burt Lancaster in *From Here to Eternity*. He could whip every man in his company and they all knew it.

William Walker – Adventurer

In his memories *With Walker in Nicaragua,* published in 1909, J.C. Jamison, a captain of infantry and a survivor of Nicaragua, described Walker thus:

He was a man of small stature, his height being about five-feet five-inches, and his weight close to 130 pounds. His body, however, was strong, and his vital energy surprisingly great. The expression of his countenance was frank and open, and heightened by the absence of a beard of any kind. His aggressive and determined character was plainly indicated by his aquiline nose, while his eyes, from which came his sobriquet, 'Grey-Eyed Man of Destiny' were keen in their scrutiny and almost hypnotic in the power. A woman's voice was scarcely softer that Walker's, and so imperturbable was he that his praise of a valorous deed or his announcement of a death sentence were equally calm in tone and deliberated in enunciation.

Though affable in intercourse, he suppressed his emo-tions, whether of joy or sadness, and did not permit himself to be startled by surprise. In common with other men, I cannot recall ever having seen him smile. But with all his placidity of voice and demeanor, men leaped eagerly into the very cannon's mouth to obey his commands.

The well-known poet Joaquin Miller wrote of him:

General Walker was the cleanest man in word and deed I ever knew. He never used tobacco in any form, never drank anything at all except water, and always ate most sparingly. He never jested and I cannot recall that I ever saw him smile. He was very thin of flesh and of most impressive presence, especially when on the firing line. At such times he was simply terrible, his grey eyes expanding and glittering like broken steel with the rage of battle. He was, in the eyes of his devoted Californians, truly "the bravest of the brave."

The manner of his death showed not only the true courage but the serene Christian peace and dignity of this 'Grey-Eyed Man of Destiny'...his dress, language and bearing were those of a clergyman, when not on the firing line, and his time was spent in reading. He never wasted a moment in idle talk, never took advice, but always gave commands, which had to be obeyed. On entering a town he, as a rule, issued a proclamation making death the penalty alike for insulting a woman, for theft, or for entering a church, save as a Christian should.

Not everyone had such a high opinion of the diminutive warrior.

Samuel Absalom, in the 40,000-word essay in the *Atlantic Monthly* of December 1859 and January 1860, charged that Walker was an unfeeling tyrant who took no pains in supporting the welfare of his soldiers. Absalom, who wore the letters "MR" – for Mounted Rangers – on his collar while serving in Nicaragua said Walker was distant, haughty and acted every bit that of the Eastern tyrant.

Absalom said he would have been much more comfort-able being led by Walker's second-in-command, Brigadier General Charles Frederick Henningsen.

Henningsen, a true soldier of fortune, had fought in Spain, Russia and Hungary before coming to the United States and marrying southern money. Hating to miss a good fight, the son of Swedish parents joined Walker's force in Nicaragua, and more importantly, brought along handguns, rifles and mortars.

Colonel/President Walker

Thus the leader of the expeditions to Lower California and Nicaragua was not the tough guy first sergeant in *From Here to Eternity*, but rather Mayberry's Barney Fife.

Dr. William O. Scroggs, in his work *Filibusters and Financiers,* commented that officials in California didn't try all that hard to prevent the self-styled "Colonel" Walker and his group, called the "First Independent Battalion" from slipping into the Pacific Ocean with Lower California as its destination. The action took place just a few years after the successful war with Mexico through which the United States gained the American Southwest. Americans distained the Mexicans and most probably cheered Walker on as he sailed off to rip another slice from the southern neighbor.

Walker's ship, the *Caroline,* touched land at San Lucas and then moved on to the capital La Paz, at the southern tip of the state. Walker men captured the governor, pulled down the Mexican flag, and ran up the colors of the independent "Republic of Lower California", William Walker, president. His first proclamation stated: "The Republic of Lower California is hereby declared free, sovereign, and independent, and all allegiance to the Republic of Mexico is forever renounced."

La Paz and San Lucas are both at the southern tip of Lower California, some 800 miles south of San Diego. As Walker needed to be closer to the United States border to replenish his stock of men and supplies, it was necessary to hoist anchor and head for Ensenada, about 100 miles south of San Diego, on the Pacific Coast. There the Independent Battalion could get supplies and reinforcements.

Californians, like most Americans, were swept up with Manifest Destiny. Walker's venture into Lower California was hailed as a great victory, "releasing Lower California from the tyrannous yolk of declining Mexico and establishing a new Republic," reported the *Alta California.*

In his essay *Young American Males and Filibustering in the Age of Manifest Destiny: The United States Army as a Cultural Mirror*, in the *Journal of American_History*, Robert E. May points out that thousands of young Americans were swept up in "Filibuster Fever."

Among those who gave at least some consideration to becoming filibusters were Mexican War general and governor of Mississippi John A. Quitman and four others who would go on to become generals in the American Civil War – P.G.T. Beauregard, James Longstreet, George B. McClellan and even Robert E. Lee.

Had not the Civil War intervened, any or all of them may have followed William Walker or any of the others who planned adventures in Latin America.

This was almost the case in 1850 when renegade Spanish General Narciso Lopez was making plans for an expedition into Cuba.

In his book *Last in their Class, Custer, Pickett and the Goats of West Point*, James S. Robbins relates that Lopez offered, in turn, command of his force to both Jefferson Davis and Robert E. Lee. Davis was offered $200,000 but declined. Lee was more than a little interested but also passed. Both men were fortunate for in 1851 Lopez, himself leading the expedition, landed in Cuba with William L. Crittenden, nephew of the attorney general of the United States J.J. Crittenden, by his side.

The peasant uprising Lopez was counting on to fill out his ranks failed to materialize, and his band of filibusters were captured and executed in August of 1851 in Havana.

A recruiting office was opened in San Francisco and soon more than 200 fortune seekers were ready to join Walker's troops. They arrived in December.

Walker, in the meantime, had been busy setting up a government with secretaries of state, war, and the navy in place.

In mid-December the Mexican forces started to take Walker's band seriously and attacked his troops. During the fighting, his "flagship" the *Caroline*, pulled up anchor and headed to sea with the bulk of his supplies. Though the exact reason is not known, it is speculated that the Mexican officials being held captive on the boat offered a few pesos to the right people.

The arrival of the second ship with the 200 plus new adventurers was not entirely good news. Men were aboard – but no supplies. Stealing food and cattle along the way, Walker made his move to his original objective, Sonora. On January 18, 1854, Walker proclaimed that the state of Sonora had been annexed to the Republic of Lower California and that the new country would be called the Republic of Sonora, divided into two states, Sonora and Lower California. Walker had his country, now he had to hold it.

That was not all that easy. Food was bad. Desertions began. A Mexican ship blockaded Walker's supply route by patrolling the harbor at Ensenada.

The Independent Battalion now had three problems: The pipeline of men and supplies had been chocked off with Ensenada being blocked, the Mexican government was beginning to swing into action and the *bandito* chief known only as Melendrez was sniping at its flanks.

The only choice was to try to get to Sonora, with its promise of mineral wealth, which was the ultimate goal of Walker and his band. Driving a herd of cattle and horses stolen from Melendrez and others, the battalion headed for the Colorado River to cross into Sonora.

The river was running swiftly and swept the animals away. Walker and his band arrived in Sonora without supplies, without reinforcements and without hope. Not surprisingly, the force melted away with deserters heading back for the United States.

Walker's only chance was to get to the American border and take his chances with the American army and courts.

Melendrez dogged his men to the border, hoping to nab the footsore, hungry, and dejected Americans. But the Americans made good their escape.

On May 8, 1854, the "President", wearing just one boot and a homemade sandal, and 33 survivors, surrendered to Major J. McKinstry, and Captain H.E. Burton. On their words of honor, they promised to go to San Francisco to stand trial for violation of the Neutrality Act of 1794.

Only a few pages in William Walker's book, *The War in Nicaragua*, are given to the adventure in Mexico. It was one aspect of his life that Walker was willing to forget.

Back in San Francisco, Walker, his second-in-command Henry Watkins, State Secretary Frederick Emory, Secretary of War John M. Jarnigan and Navy Secretary Howard Snow were all indicted by a grand jury. Watkins and Emory were found guilty of violating the Neutrality Act and fined $1,500 each. Walker pleaded not guilty on June 2 with trial set for October.

Walker's defense was that the acts he committed were done in Mexico and that if any country should try him, it should be the southern neighbor.

Notwithstanding that two of his underlings were found guilty, Walker was cleared with the jury taking only eight minutes to reach a verdict. The cases against the secretaries of war and the navy were dropped.

How could Walker have been found "not guilty?" Jury nullification was part of the answer but more correctly, most people admired what he had done. Twelve years earlier a group of American settlers moved to the Mexican province of Texas and took up residence. In 1835, led by Davy Crockett, Jim Bowie, and Sam Houston, the settlers began a revolution that wrenched Texas from Mexico and set up the Republic of Texas. The Republic was admitted as an American state in 1845.

The next year, after being turned down in an attempt to buy California and New Mexico from its southern neighbor, the

United States declared war on Mexico and pounded the Mexicans into defeat a year later. The peace treaty called for Mexico ceding to the United States more than a half million square miles, including all of California, Nevada, Utah and parts of Colorado, Arizona and New Mexico. The United States made a modest payment for the land.

How could the population at large object to William Walker trying to grab another piece of Mexico? The acquittal in eight minutes showed it could not.

William Walker had proven that he knew little about being a military commander. He had almost mystical powers to get men to flock to his cause, but he didn't know what to do with them. In today's parlance, he should be done a "lessons learned" analysis before planning his next military action.

Failings in Lower California/Sonora

He made four major errors in judgment in invading Lower California/Sonora:

He was acting on faulty intelligence, or none at all. He did not realize just how desolate were the areas he planned to rip away from Mexico.

He suffered unrealistic expectations. He had convinced himself that the Mexicans were just waiting for someone to "rescue" them from the Mexican government. At best the population was apathetic. They had no reason to believe that Walker's government would be any better than rule from Mexico City. They basically wanted to be left along.

No secure supply line was established. When the port of Ensenada was blocked, he had no way to get additional troops or supplies. He had to fall back on foraging to feed his men and stealing from the peasants – no way to win friends to his cause.

No exit strategy was considered. Walker was certain he would be successful so he had no "Plan B". When he was outgunned and his men were starving and deserting, he had to scramble back to the U.S. border as best he could.

Round one had been lost. No jail time but the "president/colonel" was back in California as a private citizen.

117

"Citizen" Walker returned to journalism writing for the Sacramento *Democratic-State Journal* and later the San Francisco *Commercial Advertiser,* both of which supported the Free Soil movement.

While with the *Advertiser,* Walker met a New Englander who would greatly influence his career, Byron Cole.

While living and working in San Francisco, Walker had long talks with Cole about Nicaragua. Would it not make more sense to set up shop in that lush country than to think of a return to hot, dry Sonora? Cole sold his interest in the paper and headed for Central America. Walker moved back to Sacramento.

While waiting in California, Walker became a minor power in Democratic politics. He became active in the wing of the party controlled by David Broderick, strongly anti-slavery.

When the Democratic state convention met at Sacramento in July of 1854, Walker played a prominent role as a speaker for the Broderick faction favoring "Free Soil." No doubt his notoriety earned in Mexico helped make Walker an attractive politician. His most powerful message was for all to avoid extremism.

While Walker was in California using his pen as a journalist, interest in Nicaragua was picking up.

The gold rush was bringing thousands to the West Coast. The trip around the horn of South America was long and tedious; the trek across the plains and Rocky Mountains was brutal. The obvious thing to do was cut sailing time in half by making the short trip from ocean to ocean by cutting a canal through either Panama (at the time still part of Colombia) or Nicaragua.

America was not the only country interested in Central America; England also had a stake in the area.

The east coast of Nicaragua was the home of the Miskito Indians over which England had long claimed a protectorate. The English had even renamed the only quality port on the East Coast, the former San Juan del Norte, Greytown. The United States and England had a treaty agreement that any canal though Central America would be jointly controlled by the two powers.

Commodore Vanderbilt

Vanderbilt and his group had set up a corporation known as the Accessory Transit Company which was transporting travelers through Nicaragua on to California and back.

The plan to dig a canal had to be abandoned. Lake Nicaragua, the key to the waterway, was some 1,300 feet above sea level. To get from the Atlantic to the lake would require a series of locks. Even the wealthy commodore's pockets were not that deep and financing from Great Britain was impossible to find.

So the Accessory Transit Company settled on sending boats up the San Juan River to Lake Nicaragua, traversing the lake by steamer, and then sending the travelers on their way overland to the Pacific.

The company had even macadamized the 12-mile stretch to the Pacific Coast to make that part of the trip more tolerable. By 1854 comfortable coaches, painted Nicaraguan blue and white, were traveling in convoys of 25, each pulled by four mules. The baggage train followed. Business was booming with as many as 2,000 people making the trip in a good month.

It was time for William Walker to get back into the "game".

Byron Cole noticed several things in Nicaragua that were sure to be of interest to William Walker. Revolutions, revenge killings and almost non-stopped fighting had left the country impoverished. The adobe houses were abandoned. Lands were fallow. Public buildings were pockmarked. And there was a severe shortage of men, the fighting having taken its toll. Could there be a better place to get back into the "game".

Nicaragua in 1854 was in one of its periodic political crises. There were two parties – the Legitimists represented the landed gentry from its capital in Granada while the Democrats, the party of the poorer classes, had their seat of government in Leon. The feuding was non-stopped. There had been 15 presidents in six years.

By early 1855, the Democrats, who wore red ribbons as their military badge, were on the defensive. Their ally Honduras had abandoned them and the white-ribboned Legitimists had the Democrats backed up to the northern city of Leon. Should that city fall, the game would be up for the party which a century later would give the world Arturo Sandino and later the Sandinistas.

Democratic leader Francisco Castellon was desperate. He contacted Walker's newspaper friend Cole and offered a contract through which Cole would bring 300 Contras to Nicaragua to help his cause. Cole hustled back to California to show the contract to Walker.

Looking at the contract with a lawyer's eye, Walker turned it down. To join the Democrats as mercenaries would certainly be a violation of neutrality. He could not hope to be so lucky if he were to be tried again. But "colonization" would be another story.

Cole made another trip to Nicaragua and sent back a second contract. Castellon offered a grant of land for "peaceful settlers" with the provision that they could carry arms. He also gave Walker the right to settle all disputes between the government of Nicaragua and the Accessory Transit Company.

According to Jamison, who served as a captain in Walker's army, pay was set at $100 per month per man with a grant of 500 acres of land to be given at the end of the campaign.

One hundred dollars was enough to lure men by the hundreds. Compensation for a top cowhand in that period was "beans, a bunk, and 30 bucks a month". An American Army private was paid $13 at best while a captain, with a dozen years or more seniority, drew $60 across the pay table.

A force of 300 would seem modest and hardly enough to tip the scales in favor of the Democrats. Not so.

Battles in Central America in that era usually were fought with armies in the hundreds, occasionally a thousand or two. Most of the troops were conscripts who had little interest in fighting, other than to stay alive. An American force of 300 quality soldiers would have been quite a prize for the hand-pressed Democrats.

Walker was ready to select his colonists and head for Central America. But things didn't go according to plan.

While preparing for the trip and lining up his forces, Walker took time off to fight a duel, one of at least four he took part in, and was shot in the foot. This slowed down preparations but finally a leaky old brig, the *Vesta*, was secured. After getting approval from both the district attorney and General John Wool, the new military commander in San Francisco, that his traveling to Nicaragua with a group of settlers was acceptable, his group of 58 followers, later known as the "Immortals", were ready to cast off – when in stepped the law.

Walker had obtained supplies by issuing stock in his venture. Just before the *Vesta* was to leave, the stockholders changed their minds and demanded cash. A lien was placed against the ship and its cargo and the venture nearly ended before it began.

Off to Nicaragua

A little slight of hand, a lie here, a lie there, a bit of whisky and the *Vesta* slipped out of the harbor on May 4, 1855. William Walker was on his way to Central America to fulfill his date with destiny.

Six weeks later Walker and his little band of Contras arrived near the Democratic stronghold of Leon, some 50 miles north of the Legitimists' capital of Granada. Walker's thinly veiled guise of colonization quickly evaporated in the tropic heat.

The Democrats were truly desperate. General Ponciano Corral was ready to march on Leon to claim the city for the Legitimists. If successful, the war would be over for capturing the enemy faction's capital in that era usually ended hostilities. The Democrats could expect wholesale revenge killings – slaughter of this kind being one of the main reasons the population of Nicaragua was 60 percent female.

Walker's force, to be augmented by 200 native soldiers, was organized as a separate corps, *La Falange Americana* (American Phalanx). Walker wanted to get as close as possible to the transit route. The 2,000 travelers crossing Nicaragua each month would prove to be a fertile recruiting ground.

Colonel Walker had one additional obstacle to overcome: The Democrats already had an army commander.

General Trinadad Munoz, tall and resplendent in his scarlet and blue gilded uniform, towered over Walker, dressed in his non-descript civilian clothing, looking like an undertaker or a ribbon clerk.

Munoz ordered Walker to break up his force and assign groups of ten to the units commanded by Munoz. He ordered Walker and his men to stay away from the transit route. Walker rebelled. Unless his unit stayed intact, and could proceed to the route, they would pack up and leave. Walker's bluff worked. He and his force would remain together and would move down to the route.

First Combat

Rivas was not much of a town but Walker had to control it to control the transit route. His force of 200 native soldiers, along with his Invincibles, headed for the Pacific Coast port of San Juan del Sur. Landing safely, the little band moved to Rivas.

On June 29, the Legitimist forces attacked Walker's force at noon. When the bullets started flying, so did Walker's Nicaraguan *pistolares* who were to supplement his force. All he had left were 55 *falanginos* to fight it out with an opponent numbering some 500. Walker's forces, outnumbered ten to one, fought for four hours before breaking out of the encirclement. Dazed, the Legitimists let them slip away. Walker lost five killed and 12 wounded. Five of the wounded had to be left behind and were butchered by the natives, their bodies burned.

The Legitimists, with odds of ten to one in their favor, suffered casualties of ten to one. The North Americans had proven they could fight; Walker also learned that the natives would only be of value to him if they were true volunteers.

Walker and his group, scraggly, bareheaded, some shoeless, all dirty and hungry, many limping, made it back to port at San Juan del Sur. Again proving his magnetism, two men, one from Ireland, one from Texas, wondering around the port city, joined his band. Two days later the *falanginos* were back near Leon.

Walker was enraged. Someone had tipped the enemy that his band would be in Rivas. It had to be his rival Munoz. Again Walker threatened to pack up and return to California. Again his bluff worked. Walker would stay and take his force into Leon where the inhabitants feared a raid by the Legitimists.

Fortune smiled on Walker as Munoz soon exited the scene, variously reported to have been killed in combat near Leon or a victim of the ever-present killer cholera.

Though the situation was still murky, Walker was now the military leader of the Democratic forces. He again set sail for San Juan del Sur and the transit route. But opposition was on the way.

The Honduran general who had bested Walker at Rivas, Santos (the Butcher) Guardiola, was on the march with 600 troops. Even with the reinforcements from California, Walker had only 200 guns.

The clash took place at Virgin Bay on Lake Nicaragua. With their backs to the lake, Walkers troops, westerners and native volunteers, routed Guardiola. Walker lost only two native soldiers; the enemy left 60 dead on the battlefield before fleeing, every man for himself.

Virgin Bay was the first victory for Walker and his forces. He was hailed as a military genius. His force was growing as more recruits were coming in from California. His next target would be the Legitimists' stronghold of Granada.

Walker knew that the enemy's forces were still concentrated at Rivas leaving Granada for the taking. He marched his men to Virgin Bay and commandeered the steamer *La Virgen*. On October 12, the *La Virgen* steamed quietly, lights out, past the city of Granada. The troops were landed some three miles north of the target city.

Starting their march about three in the morning, Walker and his troops arrived at Granada as the sun was rising. The few defenders scattered like sheep and Walker had captured the Legitimists capital. He made points with the Democrats by freeing political prisoners but lost them just as quickly by refusing to allow his followers to sack the hated city.

The next day, being Sunday, William Walker went to mass. Later that day the city fathers made an offer to Walker that he could not accept – as they had no right to offer it – the Presidency of Nicaragua. The job of chief executive would come his way a little later.

Walker's next move was to try to form a coalition government among his forces, the defeated Legitimists, and the Democrats. Everyone got something. The job of Provisional President went to elderly Patricio Rivas, a political moderate. Corral became Secretary of War. Walker saved the most important job for himself – Commander-in-Chief of the Nicaraguan Army.

The first thing he did was strip off the red and white ribbons of the warring factions and replace them with "Nicaraguan Blue". Then he dissolved both armies, leaving the Americans the only force to represent the nation. This made the little man from Nashville virtual dictator of the new republic. As a bone to the Democrats, Maximo Jerez was named Minister of Relations (Interior).

The coalition soon began to fall apart. Corral tried to smuggle letters to the rightwing factions throughout Central America saying that if they did not come to the aid of the old Legitimists, all would be lost to the *gringos*.

The letters were intercepted and fell in Walker's hands. Knowing that he would be creating a martyr, Walker nonetheless ordered the favorite of the Legitimist faction be to shot as a traitor. It was done.

Things were going pretty well for the *gringos*. Money was coming in drips and dabs; Granada's streets were being patrolled by the Americans; a weekly newspaper, in both English and Spanish, began publication.

An early edition of Walker's paper, *El Nicaraguense*, trumpeted that the "Grey-Eyed Man of Destiny" had arrived in Central America.

Local legend had long held that some day a"Grey-Eyed Man of Destiny" would come to relieve the suffering of the peons. Walker, whose grey eyes were his only distinguishing feature, certainly considered himself to be that man. The impoverished Nicaraguans tended to agree.

Like the legendary Joan of Arc who had appeared from nowhere to lead the French against the occupying English in the middle ages, Walker was the toast of the country.

Elections and more elections

An election was held on April 13, 1856 with votes being split among Rivas, Maximo Jerez and Mariano Salazar, all leaning toward the Democrats. None had enough support to claim the office and with the Costa Ricans having invaded the south, a strong government was needed.

Though Walker had come to Nicaragua as a champion of the Democrats from the northern part of the country, he was now a favorite of the citizenry of Granada who feared that any of the three contenders in the April election would move the capital back to Leon.

Rivas, who was still the provisional president, agreed to a new election with the voting set for June 29. Though he later withdrew his approval, the election went ahead as scheduled with Rivas, Salazar, and Fermin Ferrer, another one-time provisional president, joining William Walker on the ballot.

Provisions of the constitution of Nicaragua, much like that of the United States, provide that a person had to be a natural-born citizen to stand for the presidency. Though Walker had probably become a citizen of his adopted country, a mere declaration of wanting to become one was all that was required, he certainly didn't meet the natural-born criteria.

The election went on as planned. The totals were:

Walker	15,835
Ferrer	4,447
Salazar	2,087
Rivas	867

The "election" was neither fair nor legal. "Ghost" votes from villages destroyed in earlier battles were counted. A large vote from Leon was tallied, though no voting took place in that area of the country. Other irregularities dotted the countryside.

Walker was now in de facto and de jure control of Nicaragua. But that was just the first of the countries he planned to bring into his "confederation", the others being Guatemala, Honduras, San Salvador, Costa Rica and Cuba.

On July 12, William Walker took the oath as President of the Republic of Nicaragua. On bended knee, he swore to maintain the independence and territorial integrity of the country, to do justice in accordance with republican principles, to uphold the laws of God, the true profession of the Gospel, and the religion of the Crucified One.

William Walker had been playing a zero sum game for some time. Ordering the execution for treason of the Legitimists' favorite, Corral, made points with the Democrats in Leon. Squeezing out President Rivas, a favorite of the Democrats, caused hatred among the Democrats. With Walker getting the bulk of his votes in the election from the area of Granada only fanned the flames.

Allowing his soldiers to forage helped their food supply but earned the resentment of the peons. What good was a piece of paper when the *gringos* marched off with two bags of beans and the family cow?

While many of William Walker's recruits were greeted as saviors, at least for a time by the peons of Nicaragua, some betrayed the cause from the start.

In July 1856, a band of volunteers from Texas – styling themselves as the "Texas Rangers" – journeyed to Nicaragua and immediately disappeared into the countryside to pillage and steal. Walker vowed the have them hanged but there is no evidence they were ever found.

Was William Walker ever recognized by the United States as the legitimate president of his adopted country? In a manner of speaking, he was.

The administration of President Franklin Pierce had instructed American Minister to Nicaragua John Wheeler to recognize the de facto government as the legitimate rulers of the country. There is little doubt that the administration meant the government of President Rivas.

In the era before electronic communications, messages took weeks to be delivered. By the time President Pierce's instructions had reached the minister, the new election and inauguration had taken place and Walker was in charge. Wheeler, a good friend of the Nashville native, either felt he was carrying out the wishes of his government by giving the nod to Walker, or overstepped his authority, with his friendship for Walker being the key to the decision.

William Walker lost no time in governing his country. He issued bonds to be sold in the United States, he selected a cabinet of Nicaraguans with Americans as sub-cabinet ministers, he paved the way for the possibility of slavery being reinstated in the country, he confiscated the lands of his opponents and offered them for sale, with North Americans having first pick, and he exercised his right to control the Accessory Transit Company.

While Walker was putting his government into shape, the fortunes of the Transit Company became ever more tangled. Commodore Vanderbilt was challenged as its rightful owner by

C.W. Garrison and Charles Morgan. Money was made; money was lost. The price of the stock was manipulated. The contenders sued and counter sued. The Costa Ricans were involved. Garrison and Morgan had advanced Walker's government $20,000 and had provided free passage to Central America for some of Walker's recruits.

William Walker's Navy

While in Sonora/Lower California, Walker had a secretary of the navy but no fleet. In Nicaragua, he had a fleet – if one ship could be called a fleet – and no navy secretary.

As he had done so many times previously, Walker obtained what he wanted – this time a ship – by confiscation. A schooner owned by a Walker rival in Leon was making regular trips to Costa Rica flying, illegally, the American flag. When the schooner dropped anchor in San Juan del Sul, Walker's forces captured it. They reflagged it with the blue and white striped banner, with a red star in the middle – Walker's Nicaraguan flag.

Two small cannons were loaded on the ship, renamed the *Granada*, with Lieutenant Callender Fayssoux in command.

Fayssoux, a native of Missouri, was an excellent warrior who had fought in Cuba with the filibuster Narciso Lopez. He had faced down the crew of the British man-of-war, the *Esk*, which had demanded, in vain, that he allow the British to board his schooner.

Fayssoux and his crew of 28, sailed up and down the Pacific Coast of Nicaragua, ready to act as an escape hatch should Walker's men need to be evacuated from Central America.

The crew of the *Granada* fought a two-hour battle with a well-armed brig of British ancestry manned by Costa Rican sailors. When the smoke cleared, the Costa Rican ship was kindling and its sailors were bobbing around in the Pacific. Much to the surprise of the defeated ship's sailors, the crew of the *Granada* rescued half of the brig's 114. Even more astonishing to the Costa Ricans, they were treated humanely.

Walker's grip on power was tenuous, at best. His forces had abandoned Granada. The Democrats in Leon had turned against him. Most of the population of Nicaragua wanted the *gringos* to leave. Writing in *American History Illustrated*, Roger Burns and Bryan Kennedy tell of a Nicaraguan youth, Andres Castro, who killed a *gringo* with a rock. A monument was dedicated to him in San Jacinto.

Troops from San Salvador, Guatemala and Costa Rica were ready to march. British warships and Marines were in the harbor at Greytown on the Atlantic Coast, chocking off a possible reinforcement route from North America.

Against all odds, Walker's men fought their way back into Granada. But it would be a short reprieve.

Reenter Cornelius Vanderbilt

Now battling two other syndicates, the financier was ready to reestablish his claim to the hopelessly tangled Transit Company. Walker the filibuster had been an irritant. As commander of the army and as de facto president, he had cost Vanderbilt more than a million dollars in seized property and lost profits. When he became president, on the advice of Edmund Randolph and C.W. Garrison's son, William, Walker cancelled Vanderbilt's claim to the Transit Company. The commodore would have his revenge.

In his book, *Commodore Vanderbilt*, Arthur D. Howden Smith, wrote that the commodore referred to Walker as that "*cheap tin-sojer in Nicaraguey.*" Though some of Vanderbilt's associates felt an accommodation could be made with Walker, a fellow American, none was ever made.

The confrontation was blatantly unfair. Vanderbilt was a multi-millionaire. When he died in 1877, Vanderbilt left an estate of more than $100 million ($100 billion at the current rate). He had power and powerful friends. Walker had to scratch for a few thousand dollars to feed and equip his troops. Much of his income was from the sale of worthless bonds.

Years earlier Vanderbilt had been, or so he though, cheated in a business deal. He told his rivals he did not plan to sue, he would break them financially. And he did. This was the type man Walker had made a bitter enemy.

Walker's men were now battling anti-American Nicara-guans and the rest of the Central American powers.

Fishing in Troubled Waters

Vanderbilt encouraged and bankrolled Walker's growing list of enemies throughout Central America, partly to regain his company but mainly to settle scores with the little man from Nashville.

Smith also quoted the commodore as saying that giving money and guns was not enough – he would also have to teach the "greasers" how to fight.

To do this he hired as many soldiers of fortune as he could find in Central America to "stiffen the spine" of the native soldiers. Among his recruits were an Englishman named the Honorable W. R. C. Webster and an American Sylvanus Spencer. They played important roles in driving Walker and his forces from Nicaragua.

In his book *Patriots and Filibusters*, written in 1860, the English globetrotter Laurence Oliphant gives Spencer much of the credit for forcing the surrender of Walker in 1857. Oliphant's version was that he joined a boisterous crowd of about 250 in New Orleans in 1856 who were awaiting passage to Greytown to journey across Nicaragua to join Walker's forces. He described his shipmates as being Germans, Hungarians, Italians, Prussians, Frenchmen and Englishmen, as well as Americans. All were headed for adventure aboard the steamer *Texas*.

As the *Texas* was about to dock at Greytown, Oliphant observed an Anglo, later identified as Captain Spencer, leading a group of some 300 Costa Ricans. To the chagrin of the men on the ship, Captain Spencer and his Latin American charges had captured the riverboats which should have been waiting to take the new recruits up the San Juan River en route to joining Walker's forces on the west side of Nicaragua.

With the lifeline of men and supplies from the Eastern and Gulf states severed, Walker would get no men or materiel. Oliphant and his shipmates had little choice but get back to the United States any way they could. Vanderbilt's boast to "teach the 'greasers' how to fight" was far from idle

The critical battle for "President" Walker was at Masaya. Though outnumbered nine to one, Walker chose to attack the city. To win meant he would be master of Central America. The weapon that might make this possible was the mortar for the enemy lacked artillery.

But the fuses were too short. The shells that might have brought all Central America under American domination burst harmlessly in the air. After three days of fighting, Walker's band retreated to Granada. By April 11, 1857, Walker's force had evacuated and burned Granada and was effectively trapped at nearby Rivas.

In fighting in and around Rivas, the opposition peasant army of 2,000 suffered 700 casualties; Walker's losses were light. But conditions continued to grow more foul. Walker's men were covered with lice, living on mule meat, cut off from supplies and reinforcements, and weakened with fever.

Jamison, in his book, *With Walker in Nicaragua*, tells of taking refuge in a large building in a corner of the plaza in Rivas.

He related that the building was filled with large blocks of Spanish quese (cheese), impervious to bullets.

Temporary breastworks were quickly made of these mammoth cheeses, behind which were placed a body of sharpshooters, much to the discomfort of the Costa Ricans, who soon learned to avoid that particular locality. That these breastworks of cheese were far from Quixotic was further shown by the fact that while our sharpshooters were making targets of Costa Rican heads, they were satisfying their hunger by digging into the heart of the barricades with their jack-knives.

At this point, Juan Rafale Mora, the Costa Rican leading the allied army, applied a telling piece of psychological warfare.

Upon invading Nicaragua, Mora vowed to drive Walker and the filibusters into the sea, claiming that his quarrel was with the North Americans alone and not the Nicaraguans. Now he was offering safe passage to the United States to any of Walker's surrounded force who would defect. His enemy now was Walker alone.

While overwhelmingly winning the "body count" on the field, Walker could not replace his forces being thinned by desertion and fever. By five and tens his men left camp. The battle was being lost.

The filibusters never lost a battle in which they had parity of forces with the Central Americans. But the numbers game was just too much.

On May 1st, Walker surrounded to U.S. Navy Commander Charles Davis. Walker's "navy" was also deactivated as the *Grenada* was surrendered to Commander Davis's force. Losing round two of his quest to Americanize a slice of Latin America, Walker was again on his way to the United States, a prisoner, but not for long.

Newly elected American President James Buchanan, a Democrat from Pennsylvania, ordered that Walker not be tried for violation of the Neutrality Act.

In New Orleans Walker was not only free – but a hero!

To understand why Walker was not tried for an obvious violation of the Neutrality Act, it is necessary to review the 1856 Democratic Party platform. Reading between the lines, that party indicated that Manifest Destiny was part of its agenda and that should non-government agencies attempt to spread the doctrine, the government would not object.

The exploits of Walker and his Immortals were the subject of stage presentations from New York to California.

At Purdy's National Theater in New York, patrons were treated to *Nicaragua, or General Walker's Victories* while in California the bill of fare was *The Siege of Grenada, or Walker and his Men.*

Walker wasted little time in forming another "army" and obtaining another ship, the *Fashion*. He was ready to get back into the game.

On the 24th of May, Walker and his band splashed ashore near British-controlled Greytown on the Atlantic shore.

Walker's force was captured less than two weeks later by American Marines, backed by more than 200 cannons. Another round has been lost. (A third venture was intercepted on the high seas.)

Walker went on trial, this time in sympathetic New Orleans. By a count of ten to two, he was found "not guilty" and was again a free man.

With Civil War clouds gathering, the antics of the little man from Nashville and his band of misfits were crowded off the front pages. And landing in Nicaragua with both American and British warships patrolling the coasts would be impossible. Walker settled down to plan his next move and write his version of history in *The War in Nicaragua.*

Walker decided to give filibustering one more try. After all, in his mind, he was still the "president-in-exile."

Walker and his band of some 100 slipped out of Mobile in the late summer of 1860 with Honduras as the destination. There he would try to link up with Trinidad Cabanas, the local Democratic leader, who was in rebellion against the right-wing government.

Once Honduras was freed of the reactionaries, Walker and his troops would move to the southern border. From that sanctuary, he and his Contras would sweep back into Nicaragua and regain control.

The plan began well. Walker's men stormed the old stone fortress of Fort Truxillo. A chronic shortage of supplies, and a marching Honduran army, forced Walked out of his stronghold to seek the Honduran rebels.

Walker and company slipped out of the fort under the cover of darkness and plunged into the jungle. Help was not found. Instead, Walker's force ran into a Honduran patrol. The North Americans scrambled into some decaying bunkers and held out for a week.

Surrounded, with no supplies, his force shrinking daily, Walker was once again forced to turn over his sword, this time to the British.

Walker's force was returned to Fort Truxillo for repatriation to the United States.

Aboard the British warship *Icarus*, 25-year-old Captain Nowell Salmon, commanding, announced that Walker would not be going home with his men. Walker would be turned over the Hondurans. Walker protested that he had surrendered in good faith to the British Crown. Salmon would not be swayed.

On September 12, 1860, Walker, amid a crowd of laughing, jeering Hondurans, was led to the outskirts of Truxillo. A squad of soldiers stepped forward. A hail of bullets tore though his gaunt frame. A second squad fired a volley into his lifeless body. An officer put a pistol to Walker's head and pulled the trigger.

William Walker was 36.

Media Coverage

The percentage of Americans who can name, in order, the four men who served as president of the United States in the 1850s is probably minute. Asking for a list of their major accomplishments would probably elicit a blizzard of blank pages.

The four chief executives – Zachary Taylor, Millard Fillmore, Franklin Pierce and James Buchanan – consistently rank in the bottom third of presidents as to achievements, the only four consecutive men to hold the office to fall into that category.

Abraham Lincoln, U.S. Grant, and Robert E. Lee would become household names in the next decade. Babe Ruth, Joe McCarthy, Elvis Pressley – and Oliver North – would have to wait until the next century for their notoriety.

In the 1850s, William Walker, the diminutive man from Nashville, probably rated more printer's "ink" than any other American, some of it laudatory, some of it not.

Stories about Walker were carried in publications from California to New Orleans, to Mobile, to Nashville, to New York.

A typical example of the coverage given the freebooter was that of the New Orleans *Sunday Delta* of July 27, 1856.

Walker's exploits were splashed across more than five of the seven columns on the front page, wrapped around a two-column photo of the man dressed in a white shirt, black coat, and black tie. The cut line read:

MAJOR GENERAL WILLIAM WALKER
President of the Republic of Nicaragua

In the flowery writing typical of the period, the tiered head-lines on the top of the left column read:

THE SUNDAY DELTA
THE MAN OF DESTINY
A LESSON FOR OLD AND YOUNG FOGIES
"The History of the World is the Biography of
Great Men" – Thomas Carlyle on Heroes.
THE CHARACTER AND IDEAS OF WM. WALKER

In its story of some 7,000 words, the *Delta* did consider Walker, through not an overpowering physical specimen by any means, to truly be a man of destiny. He was compared favorably with his fellow Tennessee native General/President Andrew Jackson.

He has driven the Costa Ricans from the field and had consolidated his power in Nicaragua. He had confounded the moneyed men of Wall Street and had bested, at least temporarily, Commodore Vanderbilt. He was bringing Anglo-Saxon "know-how" to a Central America stuck centuries behind life in the United States. What was not to admire?

In that pre-radio, television, and cinema era, the *media* consisted of newspapers and magazines, *Harper's Weekly*, the *New York Times* and its predecessor, the *New York Daily Times*, being among the publications of record. All splashed the exploits of Walker and his filibusters lavishly throughout their pages.

In a more than 2,000 word article in its January 31, 1857 issue, *Harper's* detailed Walker's adventures in Nicaragua, comparing his landing at Realejo in June of 1855 with William the Conqueror's arrival in England more than 800 years earlier. *Harper's* made known its admiration of the little man from Nashville by saying: *"We have again and again called Walker a hero. We will not take it back"* (emphasis added).

On March 4, 1857, James Buchanan was sworn in as President of the United States. The *New York Daily Times* of the next day devoted little more than *five* columns to the inauguration, including the inaugural address.

Little more than two weeks later, March 21, the same pa-per devoted its entire front page and half of page eight, more than *eight* columns, to the exploits of Walker and his band of filibusters in Nicaragua.

Notwithstanding the publicity given Walker and his band, The *New York Daily Times* wrote the general off as an adventurer in its May 28, 1857 issue:

After two years of unprofitable filibustering in Central America, our notorious countryman, General WILLIAM WALKER, has returned home, safe and sound with a small remnant of his army, and a reputation considerably worse for wear. He has ingloriously abandoned the field of his operations, after sacrificing a large amount of property and hundreds of lives; he has done a vast deal of mischief, without any compensating benefits to the country he has ravaged, or to those who trusted in his courage and sagacity. Considering the opportunities he enjoyed, the readiness of the people among who he intruded himself to be governed by any one who had the facility to govern them, the aid that was lavishly extended to him, and the good fortune that followed his career, his utter failure as a filibuster is altogether disgraceful to him.

The telegraphic dispatch announcing his arrival in New-Orleans, gives so meager an account of the 'Capitulation' of General WALKER, that we can know nothing of the condition on which he surrendered himself, nor why he should have capitulated to the Commander of a United States man-of-war? *But the important fact is that with this fizzle of Gen. WALKER ends the last filibustering expedition in which our countrymen have been engaged. We doubt if there be another until General WALKER shall be forgotten, which will not be very long.* (emphasis added)

Fast Forward Three Years

The *Times* would have no way of knowing that General Walker would make three more attempts to regain his presidency, the last, in 1860, resulting in his death.

On September 19, 1860, the *Times* gave a brief sketch of the capture of the General and his remaining troops in Honduras:

PARTICULARS OF WALKER, CAPTURE
FROM OUR OWN CORRESPONDENT

HAVANA,
Thursday, Sept. 13, 1860

The Spanish man-of-war steamer *Francisco de Asis*, which arrived here on the 12th inst. from Truxillo, brought intelligence of the capture of the "Gray-Eyed Man of Destiny," WALKER and his second in command RUDLER, and seventy of his followers by the English screw war steamer *Icarus*, who handed them over to Gen. ALVAREZ, under condition that

WALKER and RUDLER should be dealt with according to law, and that the seventy followers, who were represented to be in a most deplorable condition, should be permitted to return to the United States, their passages to be paid by the United States Commercial Agent, which was done, and it was believed WALKER and RUDLER would be forthwith shot...

...The captain of the English screw-steamer *Icarus*, having directed WALKER to leave Truxillo, as the customs of that port were hypothecated to the English debt, the filibuster left in the direction of the Ionon River, some ten leagues distant. On the 2d, the *Icarus* and a packet left with native troops under Gen ALVEREZ, and reached the River Negro, the boats of the *Icarus* went up and captured WALKER, RUDLER, and 70 others. Many of them were sick and almost all were in a deplorable state. They were all afterwards taken to Truxillo with arms and baggage, and the whole were then put, by the British commander, at the disposition of Gen. ALVAREZ, under the condition that WALKER and RUDLER should be dealt with according to the law and that his followers should be allowed to return to the United States on giving their oaths never again to serve in any expedition against Central America.

Gen. ALVAREZ took possession of the captives, who were lodged in the castle. It is supposed that the two chiefs will be immediately shot.

The Times was correct in its supposition.

With the execution of William Walker on September 12, 1860 in Honduras, the era of filibustering basically ended. Both the *New York Times* and *Harper's Weekly* would summarize his life in obituaries later in the year.

The *Times* ran its final tribute to the late general on September 22nd:

The Late General Walker

Without waiting for the particulars of the closing catastrophe to Gen. WALKER'S eventful career, we may assume that he died like a soldier in the truest sense of the term. His friends in this City attribute his fate to an unyielding moral courage and proud contempt of the consequences before him, which forbid the slightest approach to a petition, on his personal account, for leniency or mercy.

Whatever hard things have been said of Gen. WALKER – and much, we doubt not, would have been left unsaid had his fortune been more propitious – he was, at least, no vulgar adventurer, either by birth, habits or education, or the honorable purpose with which he set out in life. His parentage was unsullied; his private walk and temperance unquestioned; his learning profound, and his original aims, however subsequently misdirected by an unchastened ambition, such as commended to success, while enlisting the warm esteem of numerous friends.

Even those who deny him all claims to military skill or political sagacity as a leader, pay the highest compliment to his moral force and personal integrity, since without these his first failure as an adventurer must inevitably have been his last.

Harper's slammed the lid down on William Walker's coffin in its October 1860 issue, but not before a few choice words for the British skipper of the *Icarus*, Commander Nowell Salmon, who accepted Walker's surrender and then turned the adventurer over to the Hondurans for execution.

Under the headline "THE END OF WALKER", the staff of *Harper's* unloaded on Salmon thus:

We record, in another column, the end of filibuster WALKER. No one regrets that he has received the merited penalty of his repeated infractions of law and sacrifices of life and property. He lived by the sword, and by the sword he has perished – as was fit. One may pity him, as one may pity any wrong doer who is justly chastised; but no one can say that, in his case, the chastisement was undeserved on inappropriate, or that the world would have been a gainer had he escaped his doom. Mankind and civilization acquiesce in his death.

At the same time public opinion will not justify the conduct of Commander (Nowell) Salmon, of the British Navy, who betrayed WALKER into the hands of the Hondurans. We have now the details of the filibuster's capture. He surrendered to Commander Salmon of her Britannic Majesty's Navy. He became a prisoner to the English, not to the Hondurans. Commander Salmon claimed his sword, not as an agent of Honduras, but as a British officer, and on those terms he received it.

ALVAREZ and the other Honduran officials, WALKER would have resisted to the last, and would have died, had he been overpowered, as become a soldier. It was on the faith of Commander Salmon's demand for surrender to him as a British officer that WALKER gave himself up. And Commander Salmon no sooner had him in the power than he surrendered him to the Honduran authorities.

Commander Salmon had better resign the commission he holds, and seek employment in the pawn broking or lottery policy, or some other business which requires no exercise of honor or conscience. He is evidently out of place in the British Navy. British naval officers are generally believed to be men of honor and spirit; Commander Salmon cannot feel at home among them. By resigning his commission and developing his energies to some disreputable pursuit – such as nature intended him for – he will probably forestall the action of the British Admiralty, which will doubtless remove him without delay.

He has had the glory of betraying to his death one of the most wrong headed but bravest men of the age. It is time now that he retire on his laurels. A meaner act that his can not be found in history.

There is no indication that Salmon became either a pawn-broker or a seller of lottery tickets, notwithstanding *Harper's* advice to the Royal Navy.

Rather, Salmon, who entered the service of his sovereign at age 12, retired in 1905 as Admiral of the Fleet after serving as First and Principal Naval Aide-de-Camp to Queen Victoria. Salmon commanded in waters off Asia, Africa, the Americas, as well as Europe.

At age 22, Salmon won the Victoria Cross, the highest decoration given by the British military for valor. He also was a Knight Commander of the Bath and Knight Grand Cross of the Bath.

In the same issue of *Harper's,* the magazine ran a large portrait of General Walker, together with a final story summing up his life and deeds in Baja California and Nicaragua and other countries in Central America.

Under the headline "THE LATE GENERAL WALKER", the magazine had this to say about the man who was probably the best known American in the 1850s:

We publish herewith, as a matter of history, the portrait of the famous filibuster Walker, who was executed in Honduras on 12th ult. His life had been eventful and romantic.

Walker was undoubtedly a mischievous man, better out of this world than in it. He never displayed any constructive ability; his energies were wholly destructive. He was brave, persevering and energetic; but he had not a spark of human pity in his breast.

His works, from first to last, have been injurious rather than beneficial to the world.

A strange tribute to a man just three years earlier the publication called a "hero"!

The Rest of the Story

Abraham Lincoln would be elected president two months after Walker's death. The United States raced toward civil war with casualties to run into the millions. William Walker and his little band of "Freedom Fighters" would soon be forgotten.

With John Bell of greater Nashville being one of four candidates for president in the 1860 election, the capture and execution of William Walker received little more than passing mention in his hometown.

He had commanded no more than 3,000 North American and Western European filibusters. About 1,000 had died. Another 700 hundred had deserted. Some 250 of the wounded had been discharged. The rest were captured and presumed murdered. Walker's largest single force numbered less than a thousand.

Walked faced combined forces of some 20,000, half of whom were killed or died of disease. Through repeatedly indicted, he spent just ten days in jail, for contempt of court while a journalist in California.

Vanderbilt lost interest in Nicaragua, turning his restless energies to railroading in the U.S. and Trans-Atlantic shipping. A canal was never dug in Nicaragua.

William Walker and Slavery

One aspect of William Walker's ventures has never been settled – his views of slavery.

Some historians and biographers insist that Walker's interest in Central America was solely to promote slavery and add slave territory to be exploited by the American South. Others say the evidence is not that clear.

There is no evidence that Walker or his family ever owned slaves.

It should be remembered that Walker wrote for two newspapers which were not pro-slavery – the *Crescent* in New Orleans and the *Herald* in San Francisco.

As a politician in California, between filibuster missions, Walker was a member of the David Broderick faction of the Democratic Party that opposed slavery.

On the other hand, Walker, as president of Nicaragua, repealed a provision in the Nicaraguan constitution that outlawed slavery. He also was gaining support in the American South at the expense of backing in the North.

Nicaragua would remain a battleground between the conservative and liberal factions and become a regular port of call of the U.S. Marines in the first half of the twentieth-century. Later that country was contested by the Sandinistas (liberals) and the conservatives who were funded, after the fall of the last Samoza dictator, by the United States, with the help of Colonel North.

There is no evidence that Walker ever married and left no heirs. There is no evidence of a will. His only worldly possession, his sword, was taken for display to a museum in Nicaragua. Walker was buried in a simple grave in Honduras under a small marker on which his name was misspelled. Requests to have his remains moved to Nashville have been denied.

William was not the only Walker to fight in Nicaragua. Brother Novell served him as an officer but was later reduced to the ranks for being drunk on duty. Younger brother Jack died of cholera. Walker's good friend from his days in California, Byron Cole, was captured by Nicaraguans and hanged. The Texas Rangers dropped out of sight.

So ends the saga of William Walker. Unanswered is the question how close did Walker come to being successful in colonizing Central America?

From what evidence can be obtained, he could have been successful had he had a few thousand more filibusters available in key battles. And he probably could have had them had he worked with – and not against – Commodore Vanderbilt.

Had he sided with Vanderbilt, and had he given the commodore the right to operate the Accessory Transit Company, Vanderbilt could have kept the supply line of men and material open for Walker. The Central American armies were poorly led. The soldiers were mainly conscripts who had no desire to fight for the landowners. Walker's forces were, man for man, considerable better. Vanderbilt could have opened the door and Walker could have come through.

In his biography of Vanderbilt, *Commodore, the Life of Cornelius Vanderbilt*, Edward J. Renehen, Jr. writes that the door was once opened a crack. He related that the commodore was once willing to forget differences and work with Walker. Walker's emissary to England, the Cuban ex-patriot Domingo de Gricouria, met secretly with Vanderbilt's people in New York. The financier offered credits of $100,000 should Walker agree to return the franchise of the Accessory Transit Company.

When de Gricouria reported this to Walker, the self-styled president/general adamantly refused the offer and stripped the ambassador of his diplomatic post.

In his book, *Freebooters Must Die*, Frederick Rosengarten, Jr., quotes the perennial fighter Henningsen, who later rode with the 59th Virginia in the American Civil War, as saying this about the men who fought with William Walker:

I have often seen them marching with a broken or compound-fractured arm in splits; and using the other to fire a revolver or rifle. Those with a fractured thigh, or wounds which rendered them incapable of removal, often (or rather in early times, always) shot themselves sooner than fall into the hands of the enemy. Such men do not turn up in the average of every day life, nor do I ever expect to see their likes again. I was on the Confederate side in many of the bloodiest battles of the late war, but I aver, that if, at the end of the war, I had been allowed to pick five thousand of the bravest Confederate or Federal soldiers I ever saw, and could resurrect and pit against them one thousand of such men as lie beneath the orange trees of Nicaragua, I feel certain that the thousand would have scattered and utterly routed the five thousand within an hour.

All military science failed, on a suddenly given field, before assailants who came on at a run to close with their revolvers and who thought little of charging a battery, pistol in hand.

Why, then, did Walker not join with Vanderbilt? The commodore could easily have provided transportation for a few thousand more men to fight with Walker. They could have reshaped Central America. Why not join forces with one of the most influential men in America?

Loyalty.

His friend from California, Edmund Randolph, worked with the syndicates that *opposed* Commodore Vanderbilt. Walker would not betray a friend.

Honor and loyalty must be put into nineteenth-century context to fully understand Walker's decision.

Just a few years later Robert E. Lee would be faced with a similar decision: Would he be loyal to the nation, and army he had served, with distinction, for 32 years or would he stand with his state – Virginia? As a point of loyalty, he chose Virginia though the decision cost him his wealth and his plantation, now part of Arlington National Cemetery.

Honor and loyalty were two traits required of all Sir Walter Scott's heroes. Honor and loyalty were just as dear to William Walker, and in the end, may have cut short his adventuresome life.

Postscript

Ironically, neither "General" Walker nor "Commodore" Vanderbilt earned their titles in the service of their country as neither served in the military. Vanderbilt was given the honorary title "Commodore" for his nautical skills. Walker became a "General" because he said so.

PRIMARY SOURCES

Merritt Allen, *William Walker, Filibuster*, Harper and Brothers, 1932

Charles H. Brown, *Agents of Manifest Destiny*, University of North Carolina Press, 1958

Albert Z. Carr, *The World and William Walker*, Harper and Row, 1963

O. Edward Cunningham, *Shiloh and the Western Campaign of 1862*, Savas Beatie, 2007

C. W. Doubleday, *Reminiscences of the "Filibuster War"*, G. P. Putnam and Sons 1886

William W. Freehling, *The Road to Disunion, Volume II*, Oxford University Press, 2007

Amy Greenberg, *Manifest Destiny and the Antebellum American Empire*, Cambridge University Press, 2005

Laurence Greene, *The Filibuster*, Bobbs-Merrill, 1937

Stephen Kinzer, *Overthrow, America's Century of Regime Change from Hawaii to Iraq*, Henry Holt and Company, 2006

J. C. Jamison, *With Walker in Nicaragua*, Stephens College Press, 1909

Judge Daniel B. Lucas, *Nicaragua: War of the Filibusters*, B. F. Johnson, 1896

James M. McPherson, *Battle Cry of Freedom* – the Civil War Era, Oxford University, 1998

Laurence Oliphant, *Patriots and Filibusters*, William Blackwood and Sons, 1860

Edward J. Renehan, Jr., *Commodore, the Life of Cornelius Vanderbilt*, Basic Books, 2007

Frederick Rosengarten, Jr., *Freebooters Must Die!*, Haverford House, 1976

Arthur D. H. Smith, *Commodore Vanderbilt, An Epic of American Achievement,* Robert M. McBride and Company, 1927

W.O. Scoggs, *Filibusters and Financiers*, Macmillan, 1916

Glendon G. Van Deusen, *Horace Greeley, Nineteenth Century Crusader*, University of Pennsylvania Press, 1958

William Walker, *The War in Nicaragua*, S. H. Goetzel and Company, 1860

MEDIA SOURCES

Alta California
Harper's Weekly
Journal of American History
New Orleans *Sunday Delta*
New York *Times*

Turtle Boat

The Turtle and the Samurai

Conventional wisdom says the first time ironclad ships were used in combat was in March 1862 when the *Monitor* and *Merrimac* fought to a draw in the waters off Hampton Roads, Virginia during the American Civil War.

Conventional wisdom gets a "C".

While it is true that the battle between the *Monitor* and *Merrimac* marked the first time ironclad ships fought each other, iron-coated warships were used more than 250 years earlier in the Korean Straits in the seven year, on-again-off-again, conflict between Japan and Korea, often called the Imjin War (War of the Water Dragons).

The story unfolds like this: In the 1590s, Toyotomi Hideyoshi had united the warring factions in Japan, and seeking to make his name known for all time, set out to conquer China and perhaps India. Hideyoshi planned to use Korea as a "ladder" to reach China. Korea, which always considered itself China's "little brother," refused an alliance with Japan. This set the stage of

Asia's Seven Years War, or as Barry Strauss terms it in his article, *Korea's Legendary Admiral*, "The Japanese-Started Invasion of the Year of the Dragon."

Toyotomi Hideyoshi and Yi Sun-sin

Toyotomi Hideyoshi and Yi Sun-sin were both born into modest families. Hideyoshi's father was a farmer and part-time soldier not prominent enough to rate a surname. Hideyoshi's father died when the future leader of Japan was seven. His stepfather was also a common man with no pedigree or claim to landholdings.

Admiral Yi was born in Seoul in 1545. While little is known about his early life, by age 31 he had passed the military civil service examination and was posted to the northern part of Korea where he served for the next ten years.

Though his repute was as the supreme commander of the Korean fleet, he was, in truth, a soldier who had no naval training. In 1591 he was assigned as a military commander in the southwestern province of Cholla.

Unlike Hideyoshi who ruled Japan for more than a decade, the future admiral served as but a loyal subject of the Korean royal family. As a military man, he did as he was instructed and played only a minor role in Korean history until the advent of the Seven Years War.

A much better known historical figure, Hideyoshi began his climb through the ranks of the Japanese military as a teenager as a page serving a local warlord. During this period of Japanese history, serving with a warlord was typical as the country was fractured among more than a hundred local leaders, each with his own army. This factionalism was a direct cause of the Seven Years War between Japan and Korea that brought fame to Admiral Yi and infamy to Hideyoshi.

Hideyoshi grew to manhood during the period known in Japan as *Sengoku* which translates roughly into the *Time of the Warring States*. Boundaries were unsettled. Fighting was endemic, the emperor was a shadow power and the shoguns were often ignored. Fighting raged in all corners of the country with the leaders of the strongest armies ruling the land.

Knowingly or not, young Hideyoshi made a brilliant career move when he joined the camp of Oda Nobunaga. A powerful leader and able strategist, Nobunaga began to consolidate power in his hands. One by one the local leaders (daimyo) either were beaten in the field by Nobunaga's forces or joined his faction as it was best able to provide security and spoils. Hideyoshi remained loyal to Nobunaga until his leader died in 1582.

Hideyoshi was anything but an imposing figure. Even his mentor Nobunaga referred to the younger man as a "bald rat". He was also known as the "monkey regent". In physical appearance, he was short, slim, and quite homely. Being without money or pedigree, and also lacking in height, beauty or a powerful body, he was clearly not to achieve fame based on family ties or physical attributes.

None of these shortcomings prevented Hideyoshi from moving up the ranks of Nobunaga's forces. By 1565, at the age of 29, Hideyoshi commanded a force of some 3,000 men. Seventeen years later, Nobunaga was dead and Hideyoshi was the senior warlord. He soon completed the consolidation of Japan into a centrally controlled country.

By 1590 the job of consolidation was complete and Hideyoshi ruled as the *generalissimo*. His modest birth did not qualify him to claim the title *shogun* (supreme commander). This was not a serious handicap as previous shoguns had little power and the title was of little practical value.

Hideyoshi was a brilliant warrior but an even better negotiator and administrator. He unified Japan more through a series of alliances than by the sword. He was meticulous and what would be called today a micromanager.

Although he was headquartered in Kyoto and not Tokyo, Hideyoshi shared many traits with Japan's twentieth-century viscount General of the Army Douglas MacArthur. Both felt they were supreme commanders whose word was law. Each man proved to be an able administrator modernizing the country in the era in which he ruled. And both demilitarized large portions of the country.

As author Mary E. Berry points out in the book *Hideyoshi*, the generalissimo issued one of his most sweeping "red seal" proclamations in 1588. Such proclamations were an edict from the leader and not subject to discussion. This document has three provisions worth noting in their entirety:

Item 1: "The farmers of the various provinces are strictly forbidden to possess long swords, short swords, bows, spears, muskets, or any other form of weapon. If there are persons who maintain unnecessary implements, cause hardship in the collection of annual taxes, and foment uprisings, or commit wrong acts toward their retainers, they shall, needless to say, be brought to judgment.

"Since the paddies and dry fields of the places concerned will not be cultivated, and the fiefs will be wasted, the lords of the provinces, the retainers, and representatives shall therefore strictly collect all these weapons mentioned and deliver them to us.

Item 2: "So that long and short swords collected shall not be wasted, they shall be melted down and used as rivets and clamps in the forthcoming construction of the Great Buddha. This will be the act by which the farmers will be saved in this life, needless to say, and in the life to come.

Item 3: "If farmers possess agricultural tools alone and engage completely in cultivation, they shall prosper unto eternity, even to generations of their children and grandchildren. It is with compassion for farmers that we rule in this manner. Truly these orders will be the foundation of the safety of the country and the happiness of the people. In another country the rules of Yao of China have pacified the realm and used precious swords and sharpened blades as farming tools. There has been no such attempt in our country. Observing the meaning of our orders and understanding their various purposes, the farmers shall invest their energies in agriculture and the cultivation of mulberry trees for silkworms.
"Collect the above-mentioned implements without fail and deliver them to us."

This red seal edict had far-reaching implications both for the Seven Years War and even into modern times.
Disarmed, the farmers became virtual serfs bound to the land. They had no right to present grievances, to revolt, and even to demonstrate.
On the other hand, the warrior class, the samurai, was vested with almost limitless power. A scene in the film version of the novel *Shogun* by James Clavell well illustrates this authority.
The samurai march into a fishing village. One of the fishermen is decapitated for bowing too slowly and not deeply enough. The other villagers are silent. The entire village is given the task of teaching the shipwrecked English ship captain James Blackthorn to speak Japanese. If this could not be done in one year, everyone in the village would be killed. Again, the samurai order was met with silence.
With the exception of the "Self-Defense Force" and the police, post-World War II Japan is almost completely disarmed. As recently as a quarter-century ago, a sports hero had to appear on national television and apologize, not because he USED a firearm, but because he MERELY owned one. Needless to say, he disposed of it.

146

Hideyoshi's ban on weapons is probably the main reason why Japan's crime rate, more than 400 years after his death, remains so low.

Recent statistics place the murder rate in the United States at 6.32 per 100,000. In Japan the rate is 0.58, less than a tenth of the occurrences in the U.S.! Robbery and violent theft in the U.S. is more than 169 per 100,000 persons; in Japan the rate is less than three.

As important as was the red seal proclamation of 1588, one even more important was issued three years later.

Again quoting from Mary Berry's book, the new regulations were both unprecedented and far-reaching:

Item 1: "Should there be any (upper- or lower-ranking) military men, including hokonin, samurai, chuge, komono and arashiko, who have newly become townsmen or farmers since the campaign of Oshu of the previous seventh month (1590), the villagers and townspeople shall conduct an examination and shall absolutely not harbor them. If there is any concealment, all in the neighborhood and that place shall be brought to judgment.

Item 2: "Should any farmer, abandoning his fields, go into trade or wage labor, that person, needless to say and all his village, shall be brought to judgment. Moreover, the officials shall strictly examine and shall not harbor anyone who neither performs military service nor engages in the fields. If there is no compliance with these orders, the retainers shall be found negligent and their investitures confiscated. If there is any concealment by the townsmen or farmers, the whole village, or likewise the whole neighborhood, shall be in offense.

Item 3: "You shall absolutely not employ any military man – whether samurai or komono – who has left his master without asking leave. Conduct a thorough examination of a military man who seeks employ(ment) and establish a guarantor for him. If the military man in question has a lord and this is reported, you shall accordingly arrest him and hand him over to his previous master. If you violate these laws and permit such a person to go free, three heads shall be cut off and dispatched to the previous master in place of that one man.

"Should you fail to order restitution with those three men's heads, the new master shall be brought to judgment without inquiries into the merits of the case."

What Hideyoshi had done was establish three strata of society – farmer, laborer, and military – with no movement between the three.

This was particularly important for the military who were not able to establish a land base and were required to live apart from civilian society. The warrior was to be just that – a fighting man.

Hideyoshi didn't confine himself to setting only primary instruction for living. He even established rules regulating how many concubines a man could have, based on his status in the community. Sake could be consumed according to one's ability, but heavy drinking was prohibited. It was strictly prohibited for anyone to wear a kerchief that concealed the face.

Of all the red seals and other rules, the one establishing a separate warrior class was the most crucial in laying the groundwork for the Seven Years War.

While Hideyoshi was busily working his way through the ranks of the Japanese samurai culture, Admiral Yi was a loyal subject of the reigning king.

Admiral Yi Sun-sin

Yi Sun-sin was born into a middle-class family in Seoul in 1545. In that era military skills were not valued; poetry and philosophy were.

Choosing his own path, the admiral passed the military civil service examination at 31 and was assigned to the Yalu River area adjacent to China for the following ten years.

The admiral lived by a philosophy that could be described as three, four, five, and ten:

The three roads are knowledge of the world; understanding of things as they are; and wisdom toward humanity.

The four obligations are to provide national security at minimal cost; to lead others unselfishly; to suffer adversity without fear; to offer solutions without laying blame.

The five traits of the warrior are to be flexible without weakness; to be strong without arrogance; to be kind without vulnerability; to be trusting without naiveté; to have invincible courage.

The ten keys to security are purity of purpose; sound strategy; integrity; clarity; lack of covetousness; lack of addiction; a reserved tongue; assertiveness without aggression; being firm and fair; and having patience.

Had it not been for the Seven Years War, Yi Sun-sin would have remained an obscure figure, a simple soldier among many. Hideyoshi would always be remembered, together with Garibaldi in Italy and Bismarck in Germany, as leaders who brought unity to their countries.

Prelude to War

Master strategist though he was, Hideyoshi had *red sealed* himself into a corner. The warrior class, the samurai and the foot soldiers, were forbidden to farm the land or live in towns. They were restricted to barracks-like structures on the land of the lords they were sworn to protect, and to fight for when called.

Hideyoshi had painstakingly knitted Japan into one country under his rule. Too many samurai with too little to do could spell rebellion.

Thus the invasion of Korea on the road to China was a shrewd move for three reasons: The major lords of Japan would have to use vast parts of their wealth to finance the forces they would send across the straits. Vast numbers of samurai and foot soldiers would be out of the country where they could not cause trouble for the generalissimo. Conquest of China would be the first step in making Hideyoshi's name immortal. Another aim would be to fulfill his pledge that even though a country be thousands of miles distant, his rule would "deeply achieve amity and so build with foreign lands the spirit of the four seas as one family." This boast would next be seen in the twentieth-century when Japan promised Asians a "Co-Prosperity Sphere."

Though he was probably not aware, Hideyoshi's plan of keeping the soldiers occupied in a foreign war had been tried very successfully some 400 years earlier.

Western Europe of a millennium ago was fractured among dozens of entities, controlled by kings, princes, dukes, barons and lessers. Castles dotted the landscape. Rivalries and bloodshed were endemic. Add in this mix the facts that the Holy City of Jerusalem had been controlled by Islam for almost 400 years and that the Eastern Christian Church was under pressure from the Islamic Ottomans.

The only possible unifying force was the Catholic Church led by its succession of popes.

In 1095 Pope Urban II hit upon a brilliant plan. He would unite the Western European nobility and send it off to the Middle East to fight the Arabs. With the nobility out of Europe, peace would prevail. This was the start of the period known as the Great Crusades.

There was only one problem: Asking the knights of the period to invest their fortunes, travel hundreds of miles, and devote years of their lives to this venture, at the very risk of life and limb, was not very appealing.

So Urban II packaged the deal by imploring the knights that it was their Christian duty to aid the Eastern Christian Church and to free Jerusalem from Islam. Those who would die "Carrying the Cross" would receive absolution. Thus – "Freeing Jerusalem" – became Urban II's "weapons of mass destruction" and Christian Europe launched its *jihad*.

The Crusaders met with some success. The Christian Army did free Jerusalem from Islam and imposed its will for about 100 years. Islam won Jerusalem back in 1187. By 1300 Crusading fever had about run its course. And in 1337 England and France began on-again, off-again warfare for the next 116 years – the so-called "Hundred Years War". This was followed by a series of wars of succession and various religious and civil wars. Urban II's idea of sending the European warrior class off to a foreign adventure had been vindicated.

Planning for War

Hideyoshi was fortunate that his hobby was the tea cere-mony and not boxing. For few fighters who telegraph their punches as he did prior to the Seven Years War ever wear a championship belt.

As early as 1585, seven years before the first landing craft sailed for Pusan, Korea, he had told the Jesuit Priest Gasper Coelho of his plans to conquer China en route to India. He even asked the priest to try to arrange to have Portugal offer two ships for the venture. The plan fell through.

So it should have come as no surprise to the Koreans that they would have to deal with an aggressive Japan in the near future. That they were not better prepared would cost thousands of lives and almost destroy the country.

Korea had three options in dealing with the Japanese "issue":

Korea could have joined with Japan in attacking China, as Hideyoshi had proposed. But, as a country in which Confucianism was a primary belief system at the time, this would have been unthinkable. China was the "big brother," Korea was in its shadow. To join in on an attack was out of the question. Korea could have remained neutral and allowed the Japanese Army to march, unmolested, into China. Again how could the smaller member of the family not do all in its power to protect the dominate force? Staying neutral was almost as unthinkable as joining in the attack. Korea could have geared up for the conflict it knew was coming.

As war approached, Hideyoshi was the unchallenged leader of unified Japan. Admiral Yi was commander of half of Cholla – one of Korea's eight provinces. Hideyoshi had a huge force at his command; the admiral had a small sliver of the Korean Navy.

In his book *Surviving the Sword, Prisoners of the Japanese in the Far East 1942-45*, Brian MacArthur states that the Japanese Army which invaded Malaya at the outbreak of World War II was the largest invasion force ever launched by the island nation. He credits the Japanese landing with three divisions and enough armor and artillery to bring the front-line strength to some 60,000. An interesting statistic, but not quite true.

In his book *Samurai Invasion, Japan's Korean War 1592-98*, Stephen Turnbull credits Hideyoshi's Army of invasion with some 160,000 troops, divided into ten divisions. *Nanjung Ilgi, the War Diary of Admiral Yi Sun-sin*, credits the invasion force with 158,000 soldiers and 10,000 sailors.

Korea had an army of some 100,000 scattered throughout the country. The force was little more than a "home guard."

Overconfidence

Both sides entered the Seven Years War overconfident. The Japanese were closer to being right.

Japan invaded with its army split into two wings – one led by Buddhist commanders, the other by Christians. The Japanese soldiers were battle-hardened from years of internal wars. They were bolstered by thousands of samurai warriors, dedicated fighters as depicted in the Tom Cruise movie *The Last Samurai*. The Japanese were known for their *bushido*, or *fighting spirit*.

The Japanese had even made what would be known today as "civil affairs" plans, allocating each division an area of Korea to govern under a form of martial law. The collection of swords actually began in one province, reminiscent of Hideyoshi disarming Japan's peasants.

The Japanese troops were armed with swords, spears and bows and arrows. They also used *arquebusiers*, a European-designed firearm.

The invaders were reliable and highly disciplined. Drums and flags controlled movement on the battlefield. A well-defined chain of command ran back to Hideyoshi, who remained in Japan during the fighting.

The Korean forces, meanwhile, were weak, poorly armed, and even more poorly trained. Factionalism at the Korean court denied the country a strong central command. Though all its leaders must have known war was only a matter of time, they dismissed the Japanese as mere "robbers," a reference to the years of piracy that had been a staple of Korean-Japanese relations.

In *Nanjung Ilgi*, The Korean king and his court are quoted as having dismissed Hideyoshi's plan to conquer China by saying "The Jap's attempt to attack the Celestial Empire (China) is like that of a snail which strikes a rock."

Korean General Sin Rip, filling the slot comparable to the American chairman of the joint chiefs of staff, sneered that even if the Japanese had muskets, they could not hit anything with them. He paid for this blunder with his life in the battle of Chungju.

Two of Korea's provinces, Cholla to the southwest and Kyongsang to the southeast, border the Straits of Tsushima, the waterway the Japanese would have to cross to begin their invasion. The maritime safety of each province was split east and west. Thus the task of keeping the "robbers" from landing in Korea fell to Admirals Yi Ok-ki, Yi Sun-sin, Won Kyun and Pak Hong.

Admiral Yi worked well with Admiral Yi Ok-ki, and often their forces fought together. But he had a life-long blood feud with Admiral Won Kyun, referring to him in *Nanjung Ilgi* as a braggart and a drunkard. Admiral Pak Hong was a non-entity once the invasion began.

And begin it did as the first Japanese troops were ferried into the port of Pusan in May 1592. Hard as it might be to believe, with Korea having the superior navy, there was no opposition to the landing.

Upon hearing of the Japanese assault on Pusan, Admiral Won Kyun fled west by sea while Admiral Pak Hong escaped overland to the north and into infamy as a coward. Both scuttled the majority of their ships.

With no opposition, the army of Konishi Yukinaga sacked Pusan, stealing, burning, and killing civilians at random. Five days later the army of Kato Kiyomasa was landed, with units to follow in rapid succession. The only question seemed to be which of the rivals would be *ichban Seoul* and *ichban Yalu* – the first unit to march into Seoul and the first to reach the Yalu River separating Korea and China.

As happened in 1950 when the Communists exploded into South Korea on June 25th, a few Korean army units fought well; most did not. The Japanese moved up the peninsula, treating the Korean Army as little more than speed bumps along the way.

Less than a month after landing in Pusan, the Japanese were at the gates of Seoul. Konishi Yukinaga won the race to the Korean capital but to the surprise of all, the city was empty. The king and the court had flew north in a very unroyal manner, literally begging for food along the way. The only obstacles between Seoul and the Yalu were a series of swollen rivers as summer is the monsoon season in Korea.

As the area of action moved from river to river the exact scene would be repeated. The Korean forces would form up on the north side of the river; the Japanese on the south. And then they would negotiate!

The Japanese kept asking for safe passage to the Celestial Kingdom. After some talking the Koreans would say "No!" The Japanese would cross the river, either by boat or at fords if any could be found. Then the story would be repeated – retreat and march forward until the next river was reached.

The royal family managed to stay one step ahead of the "robbers" and finally reached the banks of the Yalu.

The last real obstacle to mopping up Korea and moving into China was to take the city of Pyongyang, now the capital of North Korea. Less than three months after having landed at Pusan, the Japanese army marched into an empty Pyongyang.

Like the United Nations Command that was on the banks of the Yalu River in September of 1950, Kato Kiyomasa's army reached China and even advanced a few miles across the border and fought a pitched battle with the Orangais, a fierce Manchurian tribe. This was the high water mark for the invasion forces of Hideyoshi.

For just when everything was going so well on land, disturbing news began to circulate among the Japanese forces – the Korean Navy was making its move.

As well organized and drilled as was the "robber" army, the Japanese Navy was almost completely neglected. The ships crossing the narrow Tsushima Straits were little more than troop transports and supply ships. Often the only armaments were the personal weapons of the soldiers being taken to the front.

The Korean maritime, on the other hand, had been battling pirates for centuries. The Japanese pirate ships were built for stealth and speed. Their strategy was simple – duck into a harbor, pillage and rape, and move on.

The Korean vessels, dating back hundreds of years, were solid and built to close with, and ram, the enemy. The ships were backed with rather sophisticated artillery.

Called *panokson*, the Korean ships were up to 100 feet or more in length and could carry a crew of up to 125. By adding a second deck, the oarsmen were separated from the fighters on the topside.

Heartsick that his fellow admirals from Kyongsang Province had run at the sight of the Japanese invaders, Admiral Yi was determined to fight.

Admiral Yi Swings into Action

The first battle took place at Okpo (modern Chinhae).

Admiral Yi was a master strategist. His ships could rain cannon balls, wooden arrows, fire arrows, and rounded rocks (like large marbles) down on the lightly hulled Japanese boats. The best the Japanese could offer were arquebusiers and arrows. The Korean sailors stayed safely out of range of the Japanese missiles and far enough away to prevent the Japanese from trying to board their vessels.

And just when it looked as if things couldn't get any worse for the Japanese sailors, they did. For into the battle at Sachon sailed the "Turtle Boats."

As strange looking as were the *Monitor* (a tuna can on a shingle) and the *Merrimac* (a floating barn roof), the Turtle Boats were even more so.

Properly called *kobukson*, or sea turtle, the ship was basically the size of a large *panokson*. But it had several distinctive features.

Above the ram was a dragon's head from which a cannon could be fired and sulfuric smoke poured. The smoke could screen the movements of the ship and also could terrify the superstitious Japanese who thought they were fighting a dreaded dragon.

It was equipped with both sails and oars and was heavily armed with artillery that could spit out cannon balls or fire arrows.

Its deck was covered with iron plating and upturned spikes that ensured that the sandal-clad Japanese seamen could not board.

The Turtles could dart among the vulnerable Japanese ships and cover the waves with splinters and dying sailors.

Word soon filtered to the front lines – where the Japanese were marching north like Sherman through Georgia – eating what they could, carrying off as much as possible, and burning the rest – and to Hideyoshi, back in Japan, that the Pusan supply line was being shredded. Serious as this was, it was only one of numerous problems now facing the "robbers."

With every "li" forward, the Japanese were taxing their tenuous supply line. And as they moved north the terrain became more hostile and the weather more forbidding. Most of the "robbers" were from southern Japan and could not handle the frigid winds that blew from Manchuria from September through late spring.

Though the Korean Army was not much of an obstacle, irregulars were. Guerrilla bands formed and sniped at the Japanese. Korea is well know for its mountains, increasing in height as one moves north. These proved very well suited for ambushes.

As the Japanese forces were stretched ever more thinly, the greater was the vulnerability.

Enter the Ming Chinese

As the Japanese moved further into what is now North Korea, the Ming had to make a decision: Would it be better to fight in Korea – and help ravish that country – or wait until the war brought death and destruction to their homeland?

Not surprisingly, the Ming soldiers poured across the Yalu to help their "little brothers" drive away the intruders. If this seems reminiscent of the fall of 1950 it should be. Chinese policy for centuries has been not to tolerate a hostile force on its borders. The Koreans were passive and a semi-satellite. The Japanese, and four centuries later, the United Nations Command force, were definitely "hostiles".

Naval Combat

Admiral Yi is credited with fighting four major campaigns in 1592 and 1593 during the first phase of the Seven Years War. He won each time, though always being outnumbered at least five to one.

True, he had the better ships, both the Turtles and the *panoksons*, but he outwitted the Japanese as well.

His most successful maneuver was the "crane" formation.

Admiral Yi and his ships would form into an arc, and pretend to move to open water with the center of the arc pulling away faster. The Japanese ships would follow as rapidly as possible. Just when they were about to catch up, the wings of the crane would swing around, the Koreans would reverse field, and the Japanese would be boxed in and picked off. The climatic battle was at Hansondo.

With moves like this, the Koreans were credited with destroying more than 400 enemy ships and scattering the rest. It was not unusual for the Japanese to beach their boats and run for cover in the hills. Among the "kills" was the *Nihon-maru*, the Japanese equivalent of *Old Ironsides*.

Once the Japanese at the front, and back in the homeland, heard of the disaster at Hansondo, they knew their plans to conquer China were futile. The only thing left to do was to pull back toward Pusan and dig in along the coast. The plan was to set up "fortified enclaves", which were later contemplated by American forces in Vietnam.

Korea's Army did little to drive the Japanese out of the country. Irregular forces, with leaders such as Kwak Chae-u, were more successful. And from the hills came another group of guerrillas, the "Warrior Monks".

Today it would seem odd to have members of the clergy fighting to protect their homeland. It was not in the sixteenth- and seventeenth-centuries. A few years after the conflict in Korea ended, Pope Julius II led the Papal Armies trying to regain land lost to the Italian city-states. The pope even went into the field to personally lead his forces.

Even entertainers played a role. A dancing girl named Non'gae is credited with waltzing off a cliff with the Japanese General Keyamua Mutsuke in her embrace, resulting in the death of both. Non'gae is honored each year in Chinju as a national heroine.

With the remnants of the Korean Army, the irregulars and the monks dogging their every step, the proud Japanese who had entered the country with so much promise a year earlier, were in full retreat. Of the landing force of some 150,000, less than 60,000 were able to make it back to the southern coast.

Admiral Yi, meanwhile, moved his headquarters to Hansondo as the Supreme Naval Commander of the Three Provinces (the southern third of Korea). Peace talks broke out. The next three years would be relatively quiet.

A Peace That Was Not

Relatively, but not completely quiet. Through the bulk of the Japanese forces had returned home, about a dozen enclaves in the greater Pusan area remained in Japanese hands. Admiral Yi and his mariners spent part of the respite sailing in and out of the many channels that separated the mainland and the many islands that dot the southern coast, chasing Japanese ships and fighting them when possible.

At this point the question must be posed: Why did the Koreans and Chinese leave the Japanese "off the hook?"

Peace feelers were advanced by the Ming. The Koreans were not involved and almost certainly would have objected. Hideyoshi felt he needed the time to refit and regroup his forces.

Fast forward to 1951 when the United Nations Command, primarily the United States, sat down to try to fashion a cease-fire with the Chinese Communists and the North Koreans. The government of South Korea, headed by crusty old Syngman Rhee was not invited. Only over Rhee's protests, and repeated threats to "go it alone", was an armistice signed after three years of fighting.

Peace talks in 1593 made perfect sense to the Ming. The "robbers" had been driven back from the Yalu River and were penned up in their little fortresses some 600 miles to the south. The Japanese had learned a hard lesson and the possibility of invading China was becoming more and more remote. Why not talk?

Both Japan and China felt the other was about to concede. The Chinese were certain Japan would accept vassal state status. Hideyoshi was certain that his new demands would be met by a surrendering China. He had toned down his demands, the major points being:

A daughter of the Ming Emperor would be married to the Emperor of Japan;

Japan would take only the southern half of Korea for itself, allowing China to have its "buffer" state in what is now North Korea;

Korea would send members of the royal household to Japan as hostages;

Trade between Japan and China would resume.

While the talks dragged on and on, Admiral Yi spent his days perfecting his archery skills and taking part in endless meetings with military and government officials. He also devoted much of his energy into blackening the reputation of Admiral Won Kyun, his blood-feud enemy. He also oversaw the building of new boats to add to his fleet.

Peace negotiations dragged on until in October of 1596 when Hideyoshi hosted a splendid banquet for the visiting Chinese delegation. He was in an expansive mood feeling that the Chinese were there to recognize him as the supreme ruler of Asia. It finally dawned on the Japanese leader that the Chinese were there to accept *his* pledge of loyalty as a subordinate to China. Hideyoshi exploded. The peace talks were ended; the war was to resume!

With Friends Like That ...

Rivalries were a way of life among the opposing sides the Seven Years War. Konishi Yukinaga and Kato Kiyomasa, who led the first invasion, were bitter rivals. Each wanted o be *ichban* in everything. That was not unusual for the Japanese fighting man.

There are tales of samurai warriors yanking each other off scaling ladders for the honor of being the first to reach the top of an enemy castle – *ichban nori* – and usually the first to be killed. But the rush of being first – and the "face" gained – was said to be something only a true samurai can understand.

Meanwhile, Admirals Yi Sun-sin and Won Kyun still hated each other. This rivalry almost opened Korea up to a crushing defeat.

A Japanese spy known only as Yosira told the Korean military command in the Pusan area that the Japanese were ready to sail. The commander urged Admiral Yi to venture out and rout the "robbers."

Admiral Yi declined. To meet the Japanese in open water would have been risky. Fighting among the many islands off the coast of Korea was much more advantageous. A major operation based only on the word of one spy seemed foolhardy.

The trap snapped shut. Admiral Yi's enemies and rivals, with Admiral Won Kyun in the mix, charged the man who had never lost a battle with being a coward! And the charge stuck.

Admiral Yi was returned to Seoul to stand trail. His reputation and very life hung in the balance.

The admiral's spotless record and military victories saved his life but he was commanded to return south and, for the second time in his career, to serve as a common solider. The first time was when he was serving in the army along the Manchurian border and had his reputation sullied by rivals. He was also cleared that time.

And who might take the job as Supreme Commander of the Three Provinces? Admiral Won Kyun.

With the disreputable rival commanding, the Korean Navy lost its only sea battle to the Japanese. Doing almost everything wrong, he sailed into a Japanese fleet of between 500 and 1,000 ships. Disregarding Admiral Yi's tenet of staying out of range and winning with artillery, Admiral Won Kyun allowed the Japanese to move close enough to board his ships.

When the carnage was totaled, the Korean Navy had lost more than 200 ships. Many of the sailors were hunted down and killed as they tried to take refuge on land. Among the dead were Admiral Yi Ok-ki, Admiral Yi's colleague from Cholla and, luckily for Korea, Admiral Won Kyun.

At the end of the battle, Korea's southern fleet had been reduced to just 12 ships.

From Cruise Control to Overdrive

With the Korean southern fleet well off to the west, and leaderless, the Japanese shifted, from the twilight war being fought in the southern fringes of the country while peace was being discussed, to a second invasion.

This time the goals were more modest. There was no more talk of conquering China and then India. The second phase of fighting would be in Korea, partly for revenge, partly for plunder, and partly for conquest.

Including the Japanese still in the enclaves around Pusan, the second army, comprised of about 150,000 men, was about the same size of the 1592 force.

Japanese forces in 1592 had moved up central and eastern Korea on their march to Seoul and China. Admiral Yi's home province of Cholla was hardly touched. This time the route would be different. The two wings of the Japanese Army would move on Chonju, the capital of Cholla, and then to Seoul.

Once again the Japanese made good early progress. The high water mark this time brought the intruders to within about 70 miles of Seoul. But with the Ming back in the war to guard their frontier, the pesky Japanese moved into Chiksan to await reinforcements for the move on Seoul.

In a move that anticipated General MacArthur's pincer of the North Korean Communists by some 350 years, the Japanese marched to the west coast port city of Sochon. There they would wait for the Japanese Navy to ferry them up to the Han River and into the capital. The Koreans would be trapped. But the navy never arrived.

Reenter Admiral Yi Sun-sin

Following the disastrous performance of his long-time rival, Admiral Yi was once again the Supreme Commander of the Three Provinces. But he had just a dozen ships; the number of Turtles is unrecorded. Japan's fleet outnumbered the admiral's ten to one.

As the Japanese made their way slowly toward the Yellow Sea and the rendezvous with the waiting Army at Sochon, the admiral stuck. As the robbers were making their way carefully through a treacherous channel called Myongyang, the tiny Korean fleet moved in with cannons blazing.

Admiral Yi was able to defeat the much larger Japanese fleet because he knew the waters off the southern coast and he employed what would become known to American football fans as "fresh legs".

The admiral knew the tides, the shoals, the narrows, and the sand bars. He was the master of the waterways. The Japanese could send only a few ships at a time through the narrow channel at Myongyang.

Using his signature move of staying just far enough away from the Japanese to prevent being boarded, the same tactic used by the British when they defeated the larger Spanish Armada in the summer of 1588, his fleet showered the Japanese with cannon balls and fire arrows.

Another brilliant maneuver was the use of "fresh legs."

The admiral stocked his ships with extra oarsman. Team "yin," pulling at the oars like distance runners, would set their sights on a Japanese ship and give chance. When the query was within range, the rowers would sidle aside and let team "yang" take over.

Like the well-rested football player – who had been sitting on the sidelines while both teams became more and more winded – and who would come into the game with "fresh legs" to break off several long runs – the yang team would stir up the waters in an all out sprint, at sixteenth-century warp speed. The iron ram would be driven into the thinly hulled Japanese boat and the waters would be filled with rice, dried fish, sailors, and soldiers who would never make it to the front lines.

Team yang would surrender the oars to team yin and the process would be repeated.

The Japanese lost 31 ships before breaking off contact. With no hope of flanking Seoul, the Japanese Army once again began the long road back to the southern coast. Admiral Yi's victory is known in Korea as the "Miracle of Myongyang" and is one of the least known significant naval battles in history.

With the Ming, the remnants of the Korean Army, the ir-regulars, and the monks keeping up the pressure, the Japanese were again penned up along the southeastern coast of Korea.

Then, suddenly, it all began to unravel. On September 18, 1598, Toyotomi Hideyoshi died peacefully at Fushimi castle. With him died the Japanese dreams of conquest. It now fell to five senior officers to ensure that the dead commander's infant son would succeed the father.

The dream of empire was basically that of Hideyoshi alone. When he exited the scene, the Japanese were ready to pull out of Korea. The Chinese, too, were tired of the war. Their southern flank was now safe. Chinese commanders were even willing to allow some of the invaders to sail away without pursuit.

Not Admiral Yi. Once again the invaders were on the run. He would make them pay.

The beaten army would have to evacuate by sea. The admiral would destroy as many of the hated foe as possible.

The last great battle was fought near Namhae Island. Admiral Yi and his forces destroyed half of the Japanese fleet in a night battle. The next morning, perhaps sensing that this would be his last chance to pay back the "little robbers," his fleet pitched into the retreating visitors making kindling of more enemy craft. The waters were filled with dead sailors.

At the peak of his admiralship, Korea's foremost hero, on the deck of his flagship directing the battle, was hit in the side by a ball from an arquebusier and slumped to the deck. Like the man he is often compared with – Admiral Horatio Nelson – Admiral Yi did not live to enjoy his greatest triumph. He was dead at the age of 53.

Epilog

Notwithstanding the romanticization of the samurai and the cult of the warrior, and the heroism of Admiral Yi and his mariners, and the patriotism of the fighting monks, by today's standards, combat in sixteenth-century Asia was brutal. Success on the battlefield hinged on the number of heads each unit could display. If there was no time to decapitate the dead, noses and ears were acceptable as trophies.

In one engagement, Admiral Yi's men fished from the water an ornately dressed Japanese. When it was determined that he was a man of prominence, his body was cut into pieces and displayed for the Japanese sailors to see. As could be expected, morale sank.

Near the Korean city of Sachon a large burial mound is said to contain the remains of some 30,000 Chinese soldiers, all nose-less! In Kyoto, Japan is a mound under which are buried the ears and noses of untold thousands of Chinese and Korean dead. It is *not* considered to be a major tourist attraction.

In addition to being a brilliant fighter, Admiral Yi was a strict disciplinarian, much like the American Civil War's Stonewall Jackson.

The penalty for desertion or treason meted out by the admiral was death by decapitation. To ensure that the rest of his men understood that he was serious, the heads of the victims were displayed in prominent places around the camps. Slackers and thieves lucky enough to avoid the supreme penalty could expect to be flogged almost to death.

Hideyoshi's dreams of a family dynasty were short lived. While his chosen heir was still a minor, Hideyoshi's foremost vassal seized power in 1600. By 1615, he had disposed of the Hideyoshi clan and began his own dynasty – the reign of the shoguns – which lasted until the restoration of Emperor Mejii in the late1800s. For the first time in almost 500 years Japan was generally at peace.

Hideyoshi is given his due as the man who unified Japan but his reputation has lost much of its luster as a man who overreached in a foreign adventure.

Admiral Yi, on the other hand, is still revered as Korea's greatest military genius. His statues dot the countryside, including the main intersection in the capital of Seoul. Replicas of his Turtle

Boats can be found from Seoul to the southern port city of Yosu. Fiberglass paddleboats are common in lakes and lagoons, fashioned to look like Turtles.

Numerous movies and a long-running television series relive his adventures. Especially popular are the scenes in which the Japanese fleets are battered by the admiral and his forces.

The Turtles were about 100 feet long and weighed about 150 tons. A full crew of what in Admiral Yi's days were known as "water soldiers" was some 150 men. To compare, the *Mayflower*, which brought the Pilgrims to Massachusetts, was a little shorter and weighed about as much. The *Mayflower* had a taller superstructure and more sails but had a manifest of about 100 souls.

The Turtle Boats were heavily armed, carrying up to forty cannons. Gun ports for archers dotted the ships. Being completed enclosed, the crew was impervious to Japanese assaults unless the "little robbers" were lucky enough to hit a gun port.

The number of Turtle Boats in Admiral Yi's fleet remains unclear as does the claim that they were, in fact, the world's first ironclad fighting vessels.

Some scholars claim that the admiral had between five and 60 Turtles under his command. One famous painting of the Imjin War-era shows eight such craft carving up a Japanese fleet. The Turtle fleet probably ranged from between three and 12.

Dr. Horace Underwood, one of the first Christian missionaries to settle in Korea, wrote that he doubted the ships were metal coated. Samuel Hawley, in his exhaustive work *The Imjin War*, writes in two places that the Turtles were armored and later than the whole story might just be national pride and mythology.

There is no reason to believe that the Turtle Boats could not have been plated with iron as Korean artisans were well acquainted with the arts of metallurgy.

In the war usually referred to as Shinmiyangyo (see chapter one) the American Asiatic Fleet claimed as booty not only the huge generalissimo flag of Lieutenant General Oh Chae-yun, but also five cannons, two of which had been cast in 1313!

In addition, the Koreans had fabricated an early version of the mortar capable of arching iron balls into the rear ranks of enemy troops. Filled with gunpowder and a wick held in place by a wooded peg, the balls were lit, and if all went well, would explode among enemy forces taking a toll by concussion and shards of metal.

One more innovation was a gunpowder-propelled device able to shoot a quiver of arrows in one burst, an early forerunner of the rocket launcher.

The iron plates on a Turtle's back would not have to have been more than two or three millimeters thick. The plating would have been useful in neutralizing the effect of fire arrows and musket balls. The curvature of the plating would have deflected cannon balls up and over the ship, the same as a flat rock can be skipped over a pond.

In his work *A Short Note on the Iron-clad Turtle-boats of Admiral Yi Sun-sin*, Bak Hae-ill estimates that the sheeting was indeed two to three millimeters thick and the iron spikes were some thirty centimeters high. The author also opined that the gates enclosing Seoul were iron-coated decades before the Japanese invasion, again attesting to the metallurgic skill of the Koreans.

In addition to being a "killing machine", the Turtle Boats had a great psychological affect on the Japanese. Plowing through the waves, they must have looked like fierce dragons breathing fire as they bore down on the enemy.

In a *History Channel* documentary, Admiral Yi's invention was ranked as one of the great naval innovations of the ancient world. The ships were not only cited for their armor, but the smoke of sulfur and saltpeter spewing from the dragon's head was probably the first use of chemical warfare. As a master of the winds and tides in the area, the admiral could ensure that the smoke would drift toward the enemy, and not back to his ships.

The real legacy of Admiral Yi Sun-sin is that by defeating the Japanese invaders in Asia's Seven Years War, he won for his country almost 300 years of peace. This respite was badly needed in order to rebuild the country that was horribly pillaged by the Japanese. Not until the early 1900s would Japan again become dominate in Korea – the "Hermit Kingdom" being "first prize" in the Russo-Japanese War. Japan defeated Russia in 1905; five years later Japan annexed Korea. This time there was no Admiral Yi to drive back the "little robbers."

Postscript

In his very entertaining book *The Military 100*, author Michael Lee Lanning ranks the 100 most influential military leaders of all time – George Washington as number one to Marshal Edmund H.H. Allenby, a British World War I leader, at number 100.

In his listing, Lanning included nine admirals. Four are American – Alfred Thayer Mahan, Chester Nimitz, David Farragut and George Dewey; two are British – Lord Horatio Nelson and

Thomas Cochran; two are Japanese – Heihachiro Togo and Isoroku Yamamoto; and one is German – Karl Doenitz. Admiral Yi Sun-sin does not make the cut!

Lanning admits that it is a little difficult to rank military leaders during a period spanning more than 2,000 years. But it does seem a little odd that Admiral Yi is not on the list. His achievement in driving the Japanese from Korea is probably as important to world history as Lord Nelson routing the French-Spanish armada.

Korea does, however, have one representative in the top 100 – Kim Il Sung!

Kim was installed as the dictator of Communist North Korea in 1945 by the Russians who accepted the Japanese surrender north of the 38th Parallel at the end of World War II.

Kim was a guerrilla fighter in Russia and China but there is no evidence of great military leadership. The North Korean Army he built was on the cusp of defeat in 1950 in the Korean War and was saved from complete rout only by the intervention of the Chinese Communists. In his work The *Coldest Winter*, David Halberstam writes that Kim Il Sung never commanded more than 300 fighters at any one time. Halberstam credits the rise of Kim not to military prowess but to his ideological purity.

In his book *In the Ruins of Empire*, Ronald Spector agrees that Kim was a small-time guerrilla leader who only reluctantly accepted his role as leader of North Korea. He writes that Kim's real ambition in was to be a division commander.

Kim Il Sung is, of course, revered in North Korea and loathed in the South. On the other hand, Admiral Yi is considered a national treasure in both halves of the divided peninsula. The admiral and his Turtle Boats appear regularly on postage stamps in the South. He also was featured on a colorful commemorative in the North in 1983. The admiral has also been honored by the philatelic societies of both Australia and the Republic of the Marshall Islands.

Still in all, Kim Il Sung is ranked higher than the Muslim hero Saladin and World War II's General George Patton. As the author points out, it is hard to give a fair assessment of achievement. Perhaps a second edition of *The Military 100* will remedy the oversight of omitting from the list Admiral Yi Sun-sin, one of the great warriors of antiquity.

Probably the greatest compliment to the Korean admiral came from Japanese Admiral Togo who defeated two Russian fleets in the Russo-Japanese War of 1904-05, marking the first time in which an Asian fleet had defeated one from Europe.

Admiral Togo is reported to have said that while it might be fair to compare himself to England's great Admiral Nelson, in no way could his name be linked to that of Admiral Yi Sun-sin who the Japanese admiral considered to be the greatest nautical warrior of all time.

PRIMANY SOURCES

Bak Hae-ill, *A Short Note on the Iron-clad Turtle-boats of Admiral Yi Sun-sin,* Korea Journal, *1977*

Mary E. Berry, *Hideyoshi*, Harvard University Press, 1982

Max Boot, *War Made New, Technology, Warfare and the Course of History 1500 to Today*, Gotham Books, 2006

Bruce Cumings, *Korea's Place in the Sun*, W.W. Norton, 1997

R. Ernest Dupuy and Trevor Dupuy, *The Encyclopedia of Military History from 3500 B.C. to the Present*, Harper and Row, 1970

Major Karl W. Eikenberry, *The Imjin War*, Military Review, 1988

David Halberstam, *The Coldest Winter, America and the Korean War*, Hyperion, 2007

Samuel Hawley, *The Imjin War*, University of California, 2005

Michael Lee Lanning, Lieutenant Colonel, U.S. Army, Retired, *The Military 100*, Barnes and Noble Books, 1996

Hanjung Ilgi: *War Diary of Admiral Yi Sun Sin*, Yonsei University Press, 1980

Han Woo-Kewn, *History of Korea*, Eul-Yoo Publishing Company, 1970

Brian MacArthur, *Surviving the Sword; Prisoners of the Japanese in the Far East 1942-1945*, Random House, 2005

James B. Palais, *Politics and Policies in Traditional Korea*, Harvard University Press, 1975

Ronald H. Spector, *In the Ruins of Empire*, Random House, 2007

Barry Strauss, *Korea's Legendary Admiral, MHQ: The Quarterly Journal of Military History*, 2005

Stephen Turnbull, *Samurai Invasion – Japan's Korean War 1592-1598*, Cassell and Company, 2002

--------------------, *Samurai – the World of the Warrior*, Osprey Publishing, 2000

H.H. Underwood, Korean Boats and Ships, Yonsei University Press, 1934

Grave of Mother Jones

Revolt of the "Rednecks"

Gunfire echoing through the hills and hollows; soldiers crouching behind rocks with rifles trained on their fellow citizens; airplanes being rigged to carry chemical weapons as well as being fitted with machine guns; hired thugs acting as paramilitary enforcers; the militia smashing the presses of "subversive" newspapers; elected officials being denied their right to hold office.

Which country fits this scenario – the Soviet Union under Stalin? Nazi Germany? Chairman Mao's China? Iraq under the iron fist of Sadam Hussein?

Probably all four. But the scenario laid out above actually took place in the southwest corner of West Virginia, less than a century ago. Known as the "Great Coal Mine Wars," the action would have been perfect for CNN coverage had the television giant existed at the time. Though little remembered, the Coal Mine Wars constitute one of the most controversial, and darkest, chapters in American history.

Background

To understand the Coal Mine Wars it is necessary to gain some background of the "Wild And Wonderful" state.

West Virginia is now, and was at the time of the "wars," one of the least wealthy states in the nation. And it lives with the legacy of being not quite legitimate.

Data compiled in 2000 ranked West Virginia next to last in per capita income, with only Mississippi being lower on the list. Income in West Virginia was some 20 percent below the national norm and is slightly more than half that of the most prosperous state (Connecticut). These facts help explain why West Virginians were willing to dig coal by hand, one of the world's most back-breaking and dangerous professions.

Coal was first commercially mined in Wheeling in 1810. With reasonably good access to transportation, coal from what is now northern West Virginia was fed into the industries of the East with railroads playing a vital role in moving the commodity.

Geologists knew that rich veins of coal were to be found in southwestern West Virginia but the lack of roads and rails kept it locked underground until late in the nineteenth-century.

That all changed in 1893 when the Norfolk and Western Railroad laid tracks through Matewan to Williamson. About the same time the Chesapeake and Ohio Railroad ran spurs along Paint and Cabin Creeks.

The scramble was then on by coal producers to buy land, or at least obtain mineral rights, in southwestern West Virginia. The region was to change from basic subsistence agricultural endeavors to mineral extraction.

Few of the residents of coal country profited from mining. Title to land was generally in dispute with the farmers in possession of recent titles while the rapidly expanding coal companies staked their claims through older titles. Coal companies could usually find a friendly state or federal judge to rule in their favor.

When title could not be "proven," the mountaineers were forced to sell their land and/or mineral rights for next to nothing or were summarily pushed off the land.

This issue of legitimacy is a bit more complicated.

Until the American Civil War, West Virginia was merely "western" Virginia, the northwest outpost of the Commonwealth.

The United States government fought a four-year Civil War to deny South Carolina and 12 other southern states the right to succeed from the Union and establish the Confederacy.

When the vote was taken in Virginia, the *Cavaliers* of eastern Virginia, where slavery was an important economic factor, voted to leave the Union and join the Confederacy. The *Mountaineers* of northwestern Virginia, where slavery was not important, voted to stay within the Union, with only a quarter of the regional delegates voting for succession.

The "flatlanders" had the votes and Virginia left the Union. In May of 1861 delegates from 25 western counties met in Wheeling and called for a convention to meet in June.

Representatives from 40 counties voted to void the act of succession and declared independence from Virginia. The people of western Virginia also elected two senators and voted to establish a separate state.

In May 1862 the "Restored Government of Virginia" petitioned the U.S. Congress for admission to the Union.

With a wink and a nod President Abraham Lincoln, and the Republican-controlled Congress, approved and on June 20, 1863 West Virginia was added to the roster of states, notwithstanding that it had come into being through an act of secession that had been declared illegal just two years earlier.

The Company Store

"Sixteen Tons", a melancholy ballet written by Randy Travis and recorded in 1955 by Tennessee Ernie Ford, sold more than two million copies and graphically tells the story of the coal miner of the early decades of the twentieth-century.

The Paul Bunyan-type miner of whom Tennessee Ernie sang was able to bring an extraordinarily large amount of coal out of the pits each day. But no matter how hard he worked, he could never clear his debts. He was hardly able to live but more afraid to die as he owed his very soul to "the Company Store."

The company store was more than merely a "store." The coal miner lived in company-owned houses, or shacks, went to a company-owned school, received care at a company-owned clinic, if there was one, and had to shop at the company store. The coal operators paid the miners not in cash but in "script," a type of promissory note that could be spent only at the company store, at prices arbitrarily set by the owners. If for some reason the miners wrangled a pay increase, the company recouped by raising prices.

The closest the government ever came to issuing "script" was after World War II when military personnel in Asia and Europe were paid in Military Payment Certificates (MPC), multi-colored bills of various sizes and denominations. The MPCs could be used in post exchanges, at clubs and cafes, bowling alleys and theaters but had no value outside the military establishment.

Stacking the deck

If the feckless miner in the tune by Randy Travis – who was suspected of being a security risk during the red hysteria whipped up by Senator Joseph McCarthy in the 1950s – owed his soul to the company store, the state of West Virginia had sold its to the coal companies.

The poor miners had many strikes against them – the company store/village system, corrupt and brutal county sheriffs, weak state government and governors, a business-controlled judiciary and unfair labor agreements.

In labor relations they shared disadvantages much like those of the poor southern sharecropper, and incongruently, professional baseball players.

The sharecropper usually had no capital and had to borrow from the landowner to buy seed and fertilizer. When the crop was harvested, the landowner and the worker each took a share. Somehow the share left for the farmer was never enough to clear his debts and he had to borrow more and more. This system was ideal for the keeping the often illiterate farmer bound to the land like the serf in medieval Russia.

The professional baseball player was bound just as tightly through a system known as the *reserve clause*.

This devise was the invention of William Ambrose Hulbert who had, interestingly enough, earned his fortune in mining coal. He was an early owner of the team now known as the Chicago Cubs and was the first president of the National League, which was organized in 1876.

The "clause" simply stated that once a player signed with a certain team he was that team's "property" as long as the team wanted his services. The player *could not* bargain with other potential employers while the owner *could* trade or sell his contact to another team to which he would then be bound.

The system Hulbert devised worked well, at least for the owners, for almost 100 years. It ultimately earned him a plaque in the Baseball Hall of Fame at Cooperstown, New York.

The coal miner was often bound to his "owner" using the "yellow dog" contract and the blacklist.

In the rural South, the yellow dog was considered to be on the lowest rung of the canine hierarchy, much as the coal miner was at the bottom of the heap in the hills and hollows of southwestern West Virginia.

When the miner signed a yellow dog contract, he agreed not to join a union, and if he did, the mine owner had the right to fire him and evict him from the company-owned house in which he lived. Those who broke a yellow dog contract were then placed on the blacklist that was circulated to the mine owners. He then would not be hired by any of the mining companies and had little choice but to leave the area.

In most Southern states, in the early decades of the twentieth-century, one elected official was the real power in the county. In some states it was the county judge, in others the county commissioner. In West Virginia the power center was the county sheriff.

Joseph Kennedy is said to have worked through the sheriffs in West Virginia in the 1960 primary when his son Senator John F. Kennedy was running for the Democratic nomination for president. Seymour Hersh, in *The Dark Side of Camelot*, estimated that the Kennedy people spread some two million dollars around the state.

In his history of corrupt politics in the state, *Don't Buy Another Vote, I Won't Pay for a Landslide,* Dr. Allen H. Loughry II relates an interesting anecdote. A local official was asked what it would take in the way of "campaign literature" to "get out the vote" in his area? He answered, "35." He was floored when he open two satchels and found the "literature" was not the $3,500 he meant, but $35,000!

In his book *West Virginia Tough Boys,* F. Keith Davis identifies the recipient of the Kennedy family largess as Raymond "Cathead" Chafin, long-time Democratic power broker in Logan County, and cousin once removed of Don Chafin, one-time sheriff and long-time Democratic political czar in Logan County, who played a key role in the Battle of Blair Mountain during the great coal mine wars.

However much the Kennedy campaign spent in West Virginia, it got more than its money's worth with the future president winning more than 60 percent of the primary vote in heavily Protestant West Virginia, in effect ending the challenge of Hubert Humphrey. Raymond Chafin did his part as Logan County cast the majority of its vote for the senator from Massachusetts.

As part of his reward, Raymond Chafin was invited to the White House more than once to talk "West Virginia politics" with the new president. He originally supported Humphrey but switched to Kennedy when it became apparent that the money spread around the state was taking hold.

As the state and local governments were always short of revenue, the number of deputy sheriffs had to be limited. In southwestern West Virginia, this problem was solved by allowing outside interests to fund additional peace officers.

Not surprisingly, in the counties involved in the coal wars that outside interest was the mine owners. Not only did the companies usually have the sheriffs in their pockets, they financed the majority of the deputies. Little wonder that the concerns of the owners far outweighed those of the miners, many of whom were African-American, foreign-born, poor, illiterate, or a combination.

And when there was particularly dirty work to be done, the mine owners could always call upon the muscle of the Baldwin-Felts Detective Agency of Bluefield, West Virginia. Many "detectives" were former peace officers skilled in firearms and strong-arm tactics and were known by the miners simply as "the thugs."

Life underground was a daily challenge for the miner. He often went into the mine before the sun was up and didn't return until after sunset. The result was a vitamin D deficit.

The miner worked in total darkness except for his helmet light. He often had to work on his hands and knees with water dripping into the cavern in which he was laboring. The miner had to know how to use explosives to shake the coal loose so it could be scooped into the waiting coal cars. Too much dynamite and the roof of the mineshaft could cave in.

He constantly faced the dual threat of methane gas and fires. If he were not killed or maimed in an accident, coal dust could leave him crippled with tuberculosis, emphysema or "black lung," an ailment doctors hired by the mine owners insisted didn't exist. One doctor even said that breathing a certain amount of coal dust could be beneficial – not that farfetched considering that physicians could be found as late as the 1950s saying that while cigarette smoking may not contribute to better health, it was, at worst, benign.

Often the miner and his sub-teen aged sons would work together in the pits, the boys earning a dollar or two a week separating worthless rock from the coal.

The one "advantage" was that supervision was loose, pleasing to the West Virginians who were proud of the motto that "Mountaineers Are Always Free." Being paid by the amount of coal brought to the surface, the miner could work at his own speed or not work at all. Some miners dug coal part-time and worked their farms in season.

This independence was little enough consolation consider-ing that the macabre joke, "it was safer to be in France fighting the

Kaiser than working in the coal fields" was all too true. During all of World War I, less than 2,000 West Virginians were killed in action, an average of a less than five per day from all corners of the state.

By way of comparison, a mine disaster at Monongah, West Virginia on December 6, 1907 claimed the lives of 362 miners. One hundred eighty-one died at Eccles in April 1914 while 112 perished at Layland in March 1915.

Small pay and big risks made fertile grounds of union organizers in West Virginia.

Strikes at the Creeks

With the coming of the railways into southern West Virginia, coal mining boomed. When enough workers could not be found locally, the coal companies brought in African-Americans from the South. Additionally, immigrants from East Coast cities were recruited through ads in the foreign language press that thrived in that era.

As the need for heavy equipment was much less than in industries like iron and steel making, mine owners could make a handsome profit if they could control wages. And that meant controlling union activity.

Growing parallel to the coal industry in West Virginia was the United Mine Workers of America (UMWA) union, founded in Ohio in 1890. Its charter was to get better working conditions and higher pay for its members. Its weapon was the labor dispute, better known as the strike.

To the mine owners, the unions and strikes were radical, revolutionary, un-American and the tools of their bitter enemies – the Socialists.

To the miners the union was their vehicle to a better working conditions, more pay, and a better life for their families.

UMWA activities oozed across the border of northern West Virginia from Ohio and Pennsylvania, where a number of strikes had been at least somewhat successful.

The union movement had its first success in West Virginia early in the twentieth-century in the Kanawha-New River Coalfield near Charleston, the state capital. The coal producers fought back and hired "detectives" of Baldwin-Felts to act as mine guards, to harass the union and to put a stop to unionization.

According to his book *Bloodletting in Appalachia*, Howard B. Lee wrote that union miners along Paint Creek were being paid two-and-a-half cents less per ton of coal mined than diggers in nearby areas. To gain parity, the miners asked that their wages be brought up to the standard. The owners refused.

Two-and-a-half cents per ton may not seem like much, but for the mythical miner in the Randy Travis song, it would mean 40 cents more per day, enough to buy up to six loaves of bread for his wife and family, depending on how badly he was being gouged at the company store.

On April 18, 1912 the coal diggers along Paint Creek, a ribbon of camps running south from the Kanawha River, went on the strike. They were joined by the miners along Cabin Creek, a parallel waterway a few miles east of Paint Creek. The Cabin Creek miners were demanding union representation.

The miners listed seven demands, some economic, others dealing with their rights as citizens:

- Cribbing be prohibited

- Scales be installed at all mines to ensure accurate weighing of coal

- Unions be allowed to hire their own checkweight men to prevent cheating

- Miners be allowed to shop at alternative stores

- An end of blacklisting

- An end to private "contractors" providing mine guards

- The right of free speech, assembly and the right to organize

"Cribbing" was the most insidious of the devices used to cheat the miners. The diggers would be paid on the basis of how many coal cars they filled in a day. A car could contain, perhaps, a thousand pounds of coal.

By adding a wooden frame to the top of the car – the "crib" – another amount, maybe two hundred pounds, could be loaded. As the miner was paid by the carload, the "extra" two hundred pounds was clear profit for the owners. The miner who loaded "Sixteen Tons" actually brought to the mouth of the mine more than seventeen-and-a-half.

Scales and union check weightmen were additional demands to ensure that the workers were paid fairly.

The right to shop at stores other than those controlled by the mine owners would offer a little more variety and competitive prices.

Those alternative stores, which served the local populace other than the coal diggers and their families, were not the Super K-Mart variety, but rather along the line of the "Jot 'Em Down Store" of Pine Ridge, Arkansas, made famous in the long-running radio classic *Lum & Abner.* Crackers were sold out of a barrel, spirits from a fruit jar, and homespun philosophy was free. Far from luxurious, the stores would at least give the miners a sense of power in spending their money.

The owners were opposed on two grounds: They would lose their monopoly and the right to set prices arbitrarily and they would have to pay the miners in currency rather than script.

The fact that the rights to free speech, assembly, and to unionize needed to be negotiated in the twentieth-century attests to just how far the coal country in West Virginia had fallen behind the rest of the nation.

The yellow dog contract, found to be *legal* by the courts of West Virginia and the U.S. Supreme Court in 1917, established the "master-servant" relationship for housing. The master (mine owner) had the right to enter the house, uninvited and unannounced, at any time, and to force the servant (miner) to leave when his services were no longer needed. On strike, the miners offered no services.

The first measure taken by the owners when the strike began was to evict the miners and their families, breaking up, or tossing into the street, any furniture or belongs the workers might posses.

The union supported the miners by providing tents and funds for the striking miners. The operators tried to bring in "transportations" – scabs and strikebreakers --to keep the mines operating.

Tension mounted on both sides. On the night of February 7, 1913 an outburst of killing erupted.

On that night an armored train – the "Bull Moose Special" – similar to but more powerful than the armored car called the "Death Special" used in Ludlow, Colorado some years earlier – rolled past the tent colony at Holly Grove with mine owner Quinn Morton and Kanawha County Sheriff Bonner Hill in control.

The Bull Moose Special was ordinarily used to "transport" scabs and strikebreakers – hence the term transportation workers – to the mines where they could work without being harassed or attacked by the strikers.

On this night a special mission was planned.

Mine guards opened fire with rifles and a machine gun as the train rolled down the tracks, scattering the residents. Striker Cesco Estep was killed in the attack.

177

The miners fought back. In a later pitched battle near Mucklow, some 16 people died, most of them mine guards.

Enter Governor William E. Glasscock and "Mother" Jones.

Governor Glasscock, who was completing his term as governor, had called in the state militia on three occasions to try to keep the coalfields from exploding.

Mary Harris "Mother" Jones had been in West Virginia at least twice previously stirring up the miners with her fiery, and often obscene, speeches.

This time the 82-year-old sometime member of the Knights of Labor, sometime Socialist, was caught in the military dragnet and sentenced to an unspecified term for being part of a conspiracy to murder by a military court martial – a procedure many law scholars – then and now – insist was not legal.

Mother Jones refused to enter a plea at her "trial" saying she didn't recognize the court set up by Governor Glasscock, whom she referred to rather snidely as Governor "Crystal-*appendage*," as being legal.

Very few acts of the "courts" in West Virginia at the time were legal.

Strikers were arrested one day, tried and convicted the next, and sent off to prisons on the third, all with no access to counsel or even an explanation of the charges. Strikers were tried in batches and given long prison sentences for minor "crimes" which in normal times would have resulted in only a small fine.

The strikers were treated like a twenty-first-century "unlawful combatants." One was sentenced to five years in the penitentiary for cursing at a militia officer!

The strike was hurting three parties: The strikers and their families who were living under canvas in the most primitive conditions, the mine owners who were losing money, and the union, the treasury of which was being drained to support the strikers.

Help came just in time as Dr. Henry Drury Hatfield was sworn in as governor on March 4, 1913.

Hatfield, a progressive Republican, and a nephew of "Devil" Anse Hatfield, leader of the clan which fought the McCoys in the cross-border feud, was born in Mingo County where the Matewan Massacre would take place.

At age 37, he was West Virginia's youngest governor, well versed in the lives of the miners and the coal operators. He knew that West Virginia was bleeding and set to work to settle the strike.

By May 1, 1913 the governor had hammered out an agreement to end the strike which both labor and management were reluctant to accept. In the end, both sides complained loudly but did acquiesce to the "Hatfield Contract."

Several of the strikers' demands were met. A nine-hour day was agreed upon and the workers were given the right to organize and shop at non-company stores. Workers would be paid twice monthly and a token increase was made to the price to be paid for coal mined.

Peace had returned to the "Creeks" as World War I approached and coal would become an even more important commodity.

The militia was sent home but not before it took time off from patrolling the coal fields to vandalize two Socialist newspapers, the Huntington *Socialist and Labor Star* and the *Labor Argus* of Charleston, wrecking presses, scattering type, and jailing the editors.

Even the clergy was not "off limits."

When the Free Will Baptists met in convention in Logan, Sheriff Don Chafin and his men broke into the meeting hall and forced delegates from towns that hosted union locals to flee the county.

The Reverend Sam Betts, a 65-year-old traveling preacher, set up tents for a meeting near the Winding Gulf Coal Company, but several hundred yards off the company's property. He declared that the workers deserved more pay and went on to denounce the mine superintendent. He was beaten by company employees and suffered broken ribs. Miners who supported him were fired.

Journalism in the early part of the twentieth-century took on a personal tone not seen today, except in some of the tabloids and on talk radio shows. The Socialist *Labor Argus* was one of the most outspoken.

This example of its fiery invective in the issue of February 13, 1913 explains why the militia chose to effectively "shut it down." Much of what was printed would turn out to be false or exaggerated but it resonated well with its readers.

CIVIL WAR AGAIN IN WEST VIRGINIA
SCORES OF MINE GUARDS KILLED
IN BLOODY BATTLES WITH MINERS

The brutal and cold-blooded attempt of Sheriff (Bonner) Hill and his hirelings and thugs to murder the sleeping miners in their tents at Holly Grove last Friday night precipitated a condition that culminated in a civil war in which scores of men lost their lives.

Since Friday evening a reign of terror has existed on Paint and Cabin Creeks. No pen can paint the horrors of the situation. Never before in the history of the nation has a public official so prostituted himself to the interest of the coal barons or resorted to such cold-blooded and brutal tactics as the high sheriff of Kanawha County (Bonner Hill) attempted last Friday night.

The miners who had been evicted from the homes on Paint Creek last summer pitched their tents at Holly Grove where they have lived ever since, with nothing but thin canvass walls to protect them from the rain and winter wind.

This tent village was detrimental to the coal barons' interest, as the strikers who made them (the tents) their homes were active in keeping the transportation of strike breakers from going up the creek and assisting them in making their escape from these slave pens.

This did not suit the coal barons, so they decided to wipe out the camp at Holly Grove, even though they would have to kill every man, woman and child in the camp. It was for this purpose that Bonner Hill, in company with some of the coal barons and their cutthroat thugs, made this dastardly and cowardly attack on the camp.

There was no trouble on Paint Creek and everything was quiet until Hill and his murderous hirelings slipped up the creek in the dark of night with lights out on the train (the Bull Moose Special), and when just opposite Holly Grove at a given signal this band of bloodthirsty brutes, without provocation, opened up a murderous fire on the tents of the sleeping miners with a machine gun and high powered rifles, killing Sesco Estep as he was putting his children into a dugout to protect them from the hail of bullets.

Several other people were wounded, among them a Mrs. Hall, who was shot through both legs while asleep and will probably lose a foot as a result. The miners, taken by surprise, returned fire the best they could.

We learned from a reliable source that Bonner Hill gave the order to the machine gun operator to open fire on the tents. There are a score or more witnesses who will testify that the first shots came from the train and that the train was running with all lights out. Not satisfied with this attempt to murder the miners and their families the thugs came back to Holly Grove early Saturday morning and took a position in the hills and again opened fire on the camp with a machine gun and rifles.

But only the miners were the sufferers. So Governor Glasscock did not see fit to call out the militia to protect them.

At last, driven to desperation by the sight of the mangled corpse of their comrade, the suffering of their wounded women, and the frantic fear of their wives and children, the miners at last took up arms to protect themselves, and the man who would not fight under these circumstances is indeed a craven coward, not deserving the name man.

Is it any wonder the miners resorted to arms to rid themselves of the brutal guards and hirelings of the coal barons after the object murderous attack by the authorities of the county and not receiving protection by the state?

These are the causes that led up to the bloody battle that raged throughout the strike zone all day Monday and Monday night and resulted in the killing and wounding of scores of the mine guards and thugs. Driven to revolt by the inhumanities of the county officials and thugs, the miners waged a relentless war of extermination on their persecutors, with the result that scores of mine guards are know to be killed and wounded in the fight Monday while the miners never lost a man.

All day Tuesday the dead and wounded were being brought out of the creek. As a greater part of the fighting was done in the hills it will be impossible to know just how many were really killed, and it is more than likely it will never be known as the authorities are only too anxious to hide from the world the horrors of these damnable slave pens.

It is a deplorable state of affairs when the sovereign citizens are forced to resort to arms to protect their lives and the lives of their families in a state that claims to be civilized.

As long it was only the miners being shot and murdered – as long as was only the miners' homes destroyed and lives endangered – Governor Glasscock refused to send his tinhorns to protect them, but just as soon as the miners were driven to revolt and the guards and thugs were getting the worst of the battle, the governor again declared martial law and rushed his militia into the strike zone to protect the coal barons and their hirelings.

The guards acting under instructions from the coal barons have gradually grown more brutal and unbearable. They thought because the miners were quiet that their spirits were broken and that they would crush them with their brutalities, but their calculations were bad, they had underestimated the miners. Instead of weakening from their long struggle and suffering, they have grown stronger and more determined. The miners are not asking for any special favors. They are only asking for their constitutional rights and they are going to have those or die fighting for them.

It can only be settled in one way and that is by giving these men fair treatment. Justice is all the miners are asking for and this fighting and bloodshed will never stop until they get it.

The 'watchmen' thugs, Baldwins, and hirelings of the coal barons must go and if the authorities refuse to do their duty, then but one recourse is left open the miners.

Mother Jones

Mother Jones is reported to have heard Populist orator Mrs. Mary Ellen Lease tell Midwest farmers if they wanted to raise their living standards, they should "raise less corn and more hell." She followed Mrs. Lease's advice and raised more than her share of the latter.

Mary Harris was born in County Cork in 1830. Her most lasting memory of life in Ireland was watching British soldiers march through the streets with the heads of rebellious Irish on the tips of their bayonets. Mary Harris's paternal grandfather may have been hanged as a rebel. Mary and her family left for North America in 1835.

She eventually found her way to Chicago, where she worked as a seamstress, and then to Memphis, Tennessee where met and married George Jones, an iron molder and staunch union man. Thus Mary Harris became Mary Harris Jones.

By 1867, the Jones family had grown to six. That year yellow fever swept through Memphis and she lost her husband and her four children, all under the age of six. Ironically, it was a yellow fever epidemic in New Orleans a decade earlier that had robbed William Walker of his true love and started him on his path of filibustering (see chapter three).

Mary Harris Jones moved back to Chicago and took up her needle again. She sewed for the wealthy along Chicago's "Gold Coast" but could not help noticing the legions of poor who were barely able to eke out a living. Another tragedy stuck in 1871 when the Great Chicago Fire claimed her few possessions.

She joined the Knights of Labor near the end of the nineteenth-century and slowly worked her way up in the labor movement. With her family gone, she became the "Mother" of the working class and began to sign her letters either as Mother Jones or just "Mother" about 1900. She also adopted May 1 – the international workers' day – as her new "birthday."

Mother Jones was in Charleston, West Virginia on February 13, 1913, leading a group who wanted to present a petition to Governor Glasscock protesting working and living conditions in the Paint and Cabin Creek areas.

She was arrested by local police and taken to the "bull-pen" in Pratt, West Virginia where she was turned over to West

Virginia military authorities enforcing martial law as declared by the governor.

Along with 47 others, she would be tried by court-martial under provisions of the 1882 so-called "Red Men's Act."

That act, an elastic law designed to curb the excesses of "Vigilantes" and "Regulators", as well as "Red Men", could exact penalties as minor as a $25 fine for illegally carrying a gun, "mechanical knuckles" or a dirk (dagger) to capital punishment for being part of a conspiracy in which deaths occurred. Under the act, a person could be found guilty of conspiracy even if the person did not take part in the acts of violence, or was anywhere near the scene.

The Red Men, at the time of the trial of Mother Jones, were a secret supra-patriotic organization that liked to trace its linage to the Sons of Liberty who, disguised as Mohawk Indians, staged the Boston Tea Party in Boston harbor on December 16, 1773.

Though using terms such as keeper of the wampum, wigwams and palefaces, not a single Native American could be found in the ranks of the Red Men which, at the time of Mother Jones's trial, restricted membership to white males 21 and older who used English as their primary language and believed in some type of "Supreme Being." White women 18 and older could join the auxiliary known as the Order of Pocahontas.

As described by William J. Whalen in his book, *Handbook of Secret Organizations*, the rituals of the Red Men were built around fire, tomahawks, and bows and arrows

Mother Jones was moved from the bullpen and placed under house arrest where she remained in custody until March when the trial began in a converted fraternal meeting hall in Pratt, a few miles southeast of Charleston. The charge was conspiracy to commit murder. Thus in theory, Mother Jones could have ended her long and colorful life dangling from the end of a rope

The 83-year-old labor agitator stood mute when asked for a plea. This was her way of protesting that the trial by court-martial was not legal.

Legal scholars today tend to agree that the trial was not legitimate on several grounds: Mother Jones was arrested in Charleston, which was not under martial law at the time, and the civil courts in West Virginia were operating normally, thus negating the need for military courts. In addition, the Constitution of West Virginia, under Article Three – Bill of Rights – contained the following wording:

> **Section 4:** ... *The privilege of the writ of habeas corpus shall not be suspended. No person shall be held to answer for treason, felony, or other crime not cognizable by a justice, unless on a presentment or indictment of a grand jury...*

> **Section 12:** ... *The military shall be subordinate to the civil power, and no citizen, unless in military service of the state, shall be tried and punished by any military court, for any offense that is cognizable by the civil courts of the State...*

No grand juries were convened. The state courts were certainly cognizable and Mother Jones was not a member of the military.

If more evidence was needed to invalidate the court-martial, the United States Supreme Court had set a precedent in 1866 by ruling in *Ex Parte Milligan* that a citizen of Indiana was wrongfully tried by a military court in that state while the civil courts were functioning normally. Lambden P. Milligan had been sentenced to be hanged for alleged "disloyal activities." He was freed on grounds that a military court could not assume jurisdiction over a civilian while the civil courts were functioning, as was the case in West Virginia in 1913.

These arguments made by the defense attorneys were dismissed as "frills" and the trial began March 7, 1913. The military court marched along in lockstep. After a week of deliberation, the verdicts were delivered to Governor Glasscock.

In his book *The Court-Martial of Mother Jones*, Edward M. Steel, Jr. related the workings of the court but indicates that no accurate records could be found as to the sentencing of the defendants. Most were released soon after the trial ended. Some were put on a form of probation, with the threat of going back to the stockade if their behavior warranted. Mother Jones was held until May 7, thought she was in her 80s and ill.

Governor Hatfield, upon finding her with a fever of more than 100 degrees, had her rushed to Charleston by train for treatment, not certain that she would recover. She did and was put back under house arrest. Governor Hatfield eventually overturned the verdicts of the military court and all, including Mother Jones, were freed.

Mother Jones, wearing her signature floor-length black dress and white dickey, with her hair pulled back into a bun, was a powerful speaker who could bring tears to the eyes of the rough-hewn miners one minute and have them on their feet shouting

Mountaineer words of encouragement like "You'll Go Gal!" the next.

She could also paint exacting word pictures using the pen. One such example appeared in the *International Socialist Review* in 1902:

One of the saddest pictures I have among the many sad ones in my memory is that of a little band of unorganized miners who had struck against unbearable conditions. It was in a little town of the Tianawha where I spent an Easter.

When the workers had laid down their tools the company closed their 'pluck me' store and started to starve them out. While they were working the poor wretches had to trade at the company store and when the payday came their account at the store was deducted from their check. The result was that many a payday there was only a corporation bill-head in the pay envelope to take home to the wife and babies.

Enslaved and helpless, if they dared to make a protest or a move to help themselves, they were at once discharged and their names placed on a black list.

Ten tons of coal must go to the company each year for house rent; two tons to a company doctor who prescribes a 'pill every five hours' for all diseases alike. You must go the corporation doctor when sick whether you want him or not. Two tons must go the blacksmith for sharpening tools, two tons more for water half way up the mountainside, and ten tons more for powder and oil.

All this must be paid before a penny comes with which to get things to eat and wear. When one hears their sad tales, looks upon the faces of their disheartened wives and children, and learns of their blasted hopes, and lives with no ray of sunshine, one is not surprised that they all have a disheartened appearance, as if there was nothing on earth to live for.

Every rainstorm pours through the roof of the corporation shakes and wet the miner and his family. They must enter the mine early every morning and work from ten to twelve hours a day amid the poisonous gases.

Then a crowd of temperance parasites will come along and warn the miners against wasting their money for drink. I have seen those miners drop down exhausted and unconscious from the effects of the poisonous gases amid which they are forced to work.

In all of her speaking and writing, Mother Jones constantly hammered home one theme: The workers were being exploited and being forced to live under sub-human conditions by the rich and powerful and that the only way they would ever change the situation was by being willing to fight for their rights.

Mother Jones was one of three women among the first 33 persons inducted into the U.S. Department of Labor "Labor Hall of Fame."

The others were Mary Anderson, a women's rights advocate who worked in the Department of Labor for more than 25 years, and Frances Perkins, President Franklin Roosevelt's Secretary of Labor, the first woman to fill a cabinet chair.

Among the other labor giants in the "Hall" are John L. Lewis, Samuel Gompers, George Meany, A. Philip Randolph and Robert Wagner, for whom the Wagner Act is named.

Massacre at Matewan

Matewan, West Virginia today is a hamlet of some 500 people of moderate incomes living in modest homes on the northern side of the Tug Fork of the Big Sandy River that separates the "Wild And Wonderful" state from the Commonwealth of Kentucky.

Matewan was organized in 1895, the same year Mingo Country was carved out of Logan County and set up its own government. The organization of Matewan was insignificant in the mine wars – the separation of Logan and Mingo Counties was not, as later events would prove.

Until May 19, 1920, the town was best known as one of the venues of the long-running feud between the Hatfield clan of West Virginia and the McCoys of Kentucky. The feud, legend has it, was started over the theft of a hog. Part fact, and part fiction, the fighting, off and on, lasted some 12 years and cost a dozen lives.

By nightfall of May 19, Matewan would become known as the site of one of the bloodiest shootouts of the first half of the twentieth-century. When the shooting stopped and the counting began, ten fatalities were recorded.

To put it in perspective, the massacre claimed as many lives as the St. Valentine's Day killings in Prohibition-era Chicago and the carnage of the Gunfight at the OK Corral combined.

The Matewan shootout is told in its most graphic detail by the late Lon Savage in *Thunder in the Mountains*. His account is excerpted with permission of the University of Pittsburgh Press.

Thirteen Baldwin-Felts detectives, tall, heavy men in dark suits, arrived in Matewan on the noon train. The group was headed by two of the three Felts brothers who ran the company, Albert, the field manager, and his younger brother Lee. Miners watched sullenly as the men – "thugs" as the miners called them – stepped down from the train car. The detectives made their way on foot to the Urias Hotel on Mate Street, a block away.

It was Wednesday, May 19, 1920. Gray clouds blotted out the sun, and a light rain fell intermittently. Idle miners, men who had lost their jobs because they had joined the union, knew that the detectives' arrival meant some of them also would lose their homes.

The Baldwin-Felts men assembled at the Urias Hotel, where Anse Hatfield, the proprietor, fed them lunch. They came out on the main street again, carrying rifles, and climbed into three waiting cars. The vehicles chugged out of town along the road up Mate Creek toward the Stone Mountain Coal Company, a quarter mile away, where several striking miners still lived in company owned homes.

Word spread quickly. The hated thugs were back to throw more miners out of their homes. Soon, word came back to the miners waiting in Matewan that the so-called detectives, by force of arms, were evicting the first family from a home, throwing their furniture out onto the country road. Men hurried into town, fearful and angry, talked briefly, then headed back home for their guns.

Sid (Hatfield) was furious. He had warned Felts not to do this. He talked to Mayor (C.C.) Testerman, and they decided to talk to Felts. They walked up the railroad tracks as it forked up Mate creek to where the evictions were taking place. Angry miners fell in behind them. When they arrived at the Stone Mountain Camp, a small crowd was with them.

The Baldwin-Felts men were in the process of evicting the family of Charley Kelly when Sid and the mayor arrived. Kelly and his wife stood outside their weather beaten home. Mrs. Kelly had been washing clothes on the back porch when the detectives had arrived, guns in hand. She asked them to wait until her husband came home. "We haven't got time," a detective answered. Four of them went inside and reappeared moments later carrying furniture.

They dumped it unceremoniously in the unpaved road. Kelly arrived home in the midst of the process, and Sid, the mayor, and the miners arrived shortly afterward.

Sid approached Al Felts. Al wore a revolver in his holster but had given his rifle to another detective. Sid asked if the detectives had proper authority to make the evictions. Yes, Al responded, he had checked with the court and had gotten the authority to make the evictions. Sid asked to see the authority. Al told Sid if he didn't believe it, he could go back to Matewan to find out if they had proper authority. There was a minor argument. Finally, Sid and the mayor returned to town, the crowd of miners still behind them.

Sid called the sheriff's office in Williamson ten miles away. There, a deputy told him the detectives had no authority to evict families from their homes. Then, Sid said with some pleasure, he could arrest the detectives. He asked the deputy to send county warrants on the next train for the arrest of the detectives. Somewhere in the conversation, he said, "We'll kill the God dammed sons of bitches before they get out of Matewan."

A block away, two teenaged telephone operators looked at each other wide eyed. They had listened to the conversation.

To make certain that he could arrest the Baldwin-Felts men, Sid asked Mayor Testerman to prepare town warrants charging the detectives with illegally carrying weapons. One way or another, he would get them.

By then, everyone talked of violence. Union miners hurried from their homes with guns. The report circulated that a family with several children had been forced at gunpoint from their home, their furniture set out in the rain, the children left to stand in the drizzle. The stories got worse: The detectives had thrown out a pregnant woman, a sick child, a tiny baby in its crib, all with nowhere to go. The miners' fury rose.

Sid, waiting for the warrants on the five o'clock train, was livid. If the warrants didn't work to stop the detectives, he commented, they would "kill every God dammed one of them without any God dammed warrants." Testerman, alarmed at the mood, asked a miner who called himself a gospel minister to find some "sober-sided men" to act as policemen; the self-proclaimed minister later commented he planned to kill a few detectives himself.

Finally, shortly before four o'clock, the detectives returned. They had forced six families from their homes. The drizzle continued. The detectives ate an early dinner at the Urias Hotel under Anse Hatfield's care, put their rifles in cases, and left to walk toward the depot. At least four of them still carried their pistols in pockets or holsters. They planned to catch the five o'clock train to Bluefield, the same train bringing in the warrants.

Sid, his guns holstered, approached them as they passed Chambers Hardware on the square between the block of buildings and the railroad track. Armed miners looked on intently from the square, from the hardware store, and from the doors and windows of nearby buildings. Ed Chambers and several others crowded around as Sid spoke.

He had warrants, he told Al, to arrest all of the Baldwin-Felts detectives.

Felts was not bothered. "I'll return the compliment," he said. "I've got a warrant for you too." With that, he produced a paper and told Sid he was under arrest and would have to go with the detectives as they returned to Bluefield.

This was a new one. Miners looked surprised. One ran off shouting, "They've got Sid under arrest!"

Someone ran into Testerman's Jewelry Store and said sharply, "Sid needs you!" Mayor Testerman dropped everything and hurried out, leaving his five-year-old son behind.

Testerman arrived at the altercation as miners grumbled and began shifting weapons. Someone commented that the warrant for Sid's arrest might as well have been "written on gingerbread."

Testerman asked to see the warrant, and Felts produced a piece of paper. Testerman inspected it and announced, "This is a bogus warrant."

They stood by the door of Chambers Hardware. Inside the store, a half dozen armed miners watched, guns at the ready; scores of others stood around outside. As Testerman, Al Felts, and Sid glared at each other, the first shot was fired.

Mingo County folks still argue who fired it. Sid said Al Felts shot Mayor Testerman and he, Sid, then pulled a gun and shot Felts. Others say miners in the hardware store shot first, killing Testerman. The Felts family always claimed Sid shot first. Whoever fired it, Al Felts and Testerman fell to the ground, Felts with a bullet in his head, Testerman shot through the stomach. Sid pulled both of his guns and began firing. They all joined in, miners and detectives, shooting from the street, from the hardware store, from windows upstairs.

The detectives, realizing they were ambushed, tried to flee. John McDowell, a former policeman, jumped behind a telephone pole as shots zipped past him. He pulled his pistol and fired three times at a miner without hitting him, then ran toward the river.

Diving into the water, he waded and swam across, climbed the opposite bank and disappeared into the Kentucky woods.

Other detectives were less fortunate. One – Troy Higgins, a former Virginia police chief – broke out running when the firing started; the movement attracted the attention of William Bowman, a miner, who took aim with his rifle and shot, and the detective fell into the dirt.

Two detectives were brothers, Walter and Tim Anderson, and they jumped a fence and scurried into a house; inside, they ran into armed miners and a bullet slammed into Walter's shoulder. Still on his feet, he and his brother ran into the house next door. Outside, the battle raged so fiercely they were not missed. When the train pulled in minutes later, the brothers sneaked to it and boarded the last car as the train pulled out.

Lee Felts, Al's younger brother, drew two pistols when his brother fell. Art Williams, a miner, emptied his .32 pistol in a futile attempt to bring down the youngest of the Felts brothers. Unharmed, Lee emptied his pistol at Art without hitting him. Reece Chambers, Ed Chamber's father, then took aim at Lee with his rifle and fired. Lee dropped to the ground and died.

Art Williams was not through. He kicked one of Lee's pistols from the dying man's hand and ran with it to the nearby bank in time to see a detective lurching, apparently from a blow or bullet wound. Williams shot the detective from such close range that blood spurted back on the pistol. The detective was A.J. Booher, former Bristol, Virginia, police chief.

Another former policeman among the Baldwin-Felts men, E.O. Powell of Marion, Virginia, was shot to death. Powell's body was found among the others after the battle, but no one seemed to know who had shot him.

Booher, himself, had drawn blood before he died, and the victim was one of the day's most unfortunate. Bob Mullins, 53, a miner, had been fired that morning for joining the union, and he arrived in Matewan in time to witness the beginning of the battle. When the shooting started, Mullins ran toward the bank building. Booher shot Mullins as he ran. "Oh Lord, I'm shot," Mullins screamed as he fell, and those were his last words.

Lee Felts, too, may have killed a bystander before he went down. A witness said Lee shot in the direction of Tot Tinsley, an unarmed miner whose body was found afterward, a bullet hole in his head.

Oscar Bennett, another of the detectives, escaped because of a lucky choice. Just before the first shot was fired, he went in search of a pack of cigarettes. When the shooting began, he quickly grasped its meaning and calmly walked to the railroad station. There, in the waiting room, he quietly stood at a window and watched the battle, while silently tearing up his identification papers. When the train pulled in, he walked to the Pullman loading area and waited, still silent. When the train pulled away, Bennett was safely inside.

C.B. Cunningham, detective next in command behind the Felts brothers, stood beside Al Felts when the battle began. As Al went down, Cunningham drew a gun and fired into the hardware store. Sid and several miners all claimed to have brought Cunningham down, and perhaps all did. His body was found riddled, half of his head blown off.

Isaac Brewer, a friend of Sid's, was inside the hardware store and saw Cunningham draw his gun. A shot, probably Cunningham's, smashed into Brewer's right chest. Still on his feet, Brewer pulled his own gun, only to have it shot from his hand. Gravely wounded he retreated to the back of the hardware store to stop the blood.

Detective J.W. Ferguson, a former police chief, was wounded in the initial firing and he lurched down the street crying "I'm shot to pieces." A town employee helped him into a nearby home, and the lady who lived there eased him into a wicker chair. Suddenly, several armed men crashed through the house from the front, and the town employee ran in fright. Moments later, Ferguson lay dead in the alley behind the house, nine bullet wounds in his body. He was shot as he tried to climb a fence beside the alley, witnesses said.

C.B. Hildebrand had come with the detectives to carry furniture from the homes. Unarmed, he ran down the street when the first shot was fired. A bullet neatly lifted his hat from his head. He ran behind a home, ducked into a shed, and climbed inside an empty barrel. Several hours later, a woman and child entered the shed, noticed the barrel moving, and fled in terror. About 11:30 p.m., six hours after he had climbed inside, Hildebrand left the shed. Out on the now quiet street, he lit a cigarette and walked briskly through town, whistling, to safety.

When the battle ended, the streets were littered with dead and dying. Men hid beneath railroad boxcars, behind walls and trees and in ditches. Both Felts brothers, five other detectives, and two miners had been killed, and Mayor Testerman lay dying on a cot, ministered to by his wife. Five others had been wounded.

Moments later, the five o'clock train, No. 16, pulled into Matewan, and the engineer and passengers looked out, wide eyed, at the bodies lying in a row on the street before them. Sid, his guns back in his holsters, walked among them, searching the bodies. As he stood over the remains of Al Felts, he brandished the warrant for the detective's arrest and said, "Now, you son of a bitch, I'll serve it on you."

Thus ended the battle of Matewan as told by Lon Savage. The miners and their supporters had won the first battle – showing they were not afraid of standing up to the mine owners and their hired detectives-thugs. There would be more skirmishes, not the least of which would be in the courtroom, but they would come later.

Contemporary Media Coverage

Compared to the massive casualties in the recently concluded World War, the killings at Matewan were minuscule. But they were Americans killing Americans and that made the incident front-page news. Even the New York *Times*, the paper of record for most of the country, ran a seventeen-paragraph account, along with two sidebars, starting on page one.

Under its traditional stacked headlines, the highlights of the story were:

TWELVE MEN KILLED IN
PISTOL BATTLE IN WEST VIRGINIA

Fight Follows Ousting of Discharged Miners
from Coal Camp at Matewan

MAYOR IS AMONG THE SLAIN

Seven Detectives, Two Miners
and Two Citizens Are Others Killed

TROOPS RUSHED TO SCENE

Miners Are Said to Have Had Trouble
When They Joined the Union

Under the dateline of Charleston, the state capital, the gist of the story read:

Twelve men were shot to death in a pitched battle on the streets of Matewan, Mingo County, tonight between members of a private detective agency and members of a newly-organized coal miners union...of the dead, seven were members of the Baldwin-Felts Detective Agency of Bluefield, W. Va...the fighting took place near the Norfolk and Western station at Matewan just before the arrival of the 5:15 train for Kenova, on which the members of the detective agency intended to depart, according to information received at the office of Governor John J. Cornwall here.

Former employees of the Stone Mountain Coal Company, who were reported to have been evicted from company houses because they had joined a newly formed miners' union, are said to have opened fire on the detectives from buildings nearby. The detectives started to flee, firing as they ran, and the attackers followed. All of the detectives had been shot down before the firing ceased...Colonel Jackson Arnold, Superintendent of the Department of Public Safety of West Virginia, is tonight gathering his entire force, scattered over the State, to be rushed to the scene of the shooting.

Matewan is located along the Norfolk & Western Railroad, between Kenova and Bluefield and is on the Kentucky border line. The Nitro detachment of State police will be the first to arrive on the scene and will get there about 4 o'clock tomorrow morning.

With an assist from the Associated Press, details of the Massacre at Matewan were in newsrooms across the country. Nowhere was it a bigger story that in Bluefield, West Virginia, one of the headquarters of the Baldwin-Felts Detective Agency.

The Bluefield *Daily Telegraph* of May 20 devoted more than three-quarters of its front page to events in Matewan. A double-deck, all cap headline, screamed:

AT LEAST NINE PERSONS ARE KNOWN TO BE DEAD AS RESULT OF A PITCHED BATTLE IN STREETS OF MATEWAN

A six-line subhead gave the details of the shootings:

Six of Those Killed Were Special Agents of Baldwin-Felts Detective Agency, Including Albert and Lee Felts – Mayor of Mining Town Probably Fatally Wounded, Four Others Seriously and One Slightly Hurt, While Two Detectives Were Still Unaccounted for After Midnight.

Just who fired the first shot as evening was enclosing the train station at Matewan on May 19, 1920 will probably never be determined. The *Daily Telegraph* gives two versions on its front page.

In two of its Associated Press stories, one datelined Charleston and the other Matewan, Sheriff G. T. Blankenship, of Mingo County, was quoted as saying detective Albert Felts shot

Mayor Testerman with a gun hidden in Felts' coat pocket. Sid Hatfield then shot Albert Felts and the shootout followed, with up to 500 shots being fired.

In another story, not carrying a byline but probably also written by the staff of the *Daily Telegraph*, Albert Felts was reported to have been shot without warning by a man on whom Felts was going to serve a warrant. The story could not give an exact identification of the man said to have killed Albert Felts, but indicated that man also may have been killed in the fighting.

The story continued:

Passengers arriving here last night from Williamson, (County Seat of Mingo) and points in the Thacker district spoke of the tragedy as being a 'cold blooded' affair, and said an unfair advantage had been taken of the detectives who were brutally slain. A great number of shots had been fired from ambush, according to reports of the train passengers, and from the position of the bodies of the slain men they had evidently been picked.

The *Daily Mail*, published in the capital of Charleston, ran a more analytic story with its banner headline sharing space with two other items:

**PLOT IS BLAMED FOR MATEWAN SHOOTING;
BANKERS MAKE DRASTIC HALT IN CREDIT;
PENNSYLVANIA LEADERS TO RELIEVE TIE UP**

Down the right-hand column of the paper, the stacked head continued:

**LITTLE TOWN IS QUIET
TODAY AFTER KILLINGS**

**Charged That Effort Was Made to
Wipe Out Baldwin-Felts
Detective Agency**

**DETECTIVES ON WAY TO
STATION WHEN AMBUSHED**

**Said That Mayor Testerman and
Two Others Were Killed
By Stray Bullets**

EVICTIONS START TROUBLE

Real Beginning, However, Is Said
to Have Been in Attempted
Organization of Field

The *Daily Mail* story differed from the Bluefield *Daily Telegraph* account in saying that Mayor Testerman had been hit by a stray bullet and that the miners were planning to wipe out the entire Baldwin-Felts agency, though only a tiny fraction of the work force would be in Matewan that fatal day.

This paper supported the detective agency. Not until the 18th, and last paragraph, did it mention Mingo County Sheriff Blankenship's version that Albert Felts fired the first shot.

By the next day, the massacre had begun to fade from memory with the *Daily Mail* running only a small piece under the head:

SITUATION IN MATEWAN
REPORTED QUIET TODAY

Forty Members of State Police
Under Command of Colonel
Arnold Are In Charge

The four-paragraph story ended with "it was said no further trouble was anticipated in the county."

When Sid Hatfield married the widow Testerman, less than two weeks after the gun battle, a third theory of the incident emerged: That Hatfield started the shooting by killing Mayor Testerman so he could wed his widow Jessie.

With Matewan quiet and under control of the constabulary, the situation would be put on hold until the trial in Williamson.

The ironic part of the Massacre at Matewan is that had it not been for unintended consequences, the battle may never have taken place.

Logan County, directly to the north of Mingo County, was a stronghold of the mine owners. Don Chafin was the sheriff of Logan County and with his small army of deputies, most of them financed by the coal company owners, kept a tight lid on union and miner activities.

Mingo County's sheriff, George T. Blankenship, along with Mayor Testerman and Chief of Police Hatfield, sided with the miners.

Twenty-five years earlier Mingo County have been carved out of the larger Logan County and established its own government, setting up the eventual showdown between the miners of Mingo and the owners of Logan.

According to the 1920 census, Logan County had a population of some 41,000 while Mingo could count less than 27,000. Simple mathematics, together with the power of Sheriff Chafin, would tend to indicate that the sheriff's job, and power, of the greater Logan County would have stayed with Chafin and the coal mine owners. C. C. Testerman probably would not have been mayor of Matewan and Sid Hatfield would not have been chief of police. With Sheriff Chafin controlling a greater Logan County, the miners would have had no champions.

But one simple act of the government of West Virginia in 1895 did make the Massacre of Matewan, and the resulting battles between the miners and the owners, a bloody part of Appalachia history.

The Baldwin-Felts Detective Agency

Though called a detective agency, Baldwin-Felts was more involved in acting as a private police force for the railroads, providing security for the mine owners, and vigilantism.

The firm took the name Baldwin-Felts Detectives, Inc. in 1910 with founder William Baldwin running the railway portion of the business from Roanoke, Virginia. Partner Thomas L. Felts moved to Bluefield, West Virginia to handle mine security.

The first incursion between the men of B-F and miners took place in 1911-12 along Paint and Cabin Creeks when the miners tried to form a union (see above).

Baldwin-Felts did not limit its activities to West Virginia.

In the fall of 1913, the talents of B-F were called upon to break a strike called by coal miners in Ludlow, Colorado and to protect "scab" workers. They relished the job.

The men of B-F even fabricated an armored car known as the "Death Special" to roam the perimeter of miner's camps. Shots were often fired and miners were maimed with no legal retribution.

As the strike became more violent, Colorado Governor Elias Ammons called out the Colorado National Guard to support the detectives.

The Ludlow Massacre took place on April 20, 1914. Shooting and scuffling took place all day. Three miners were found shot to death.

Also among the dead were four women and ten children who had been hiding in a pit beneath a tent. They died of suffocation when the tent caught fire.

The death toll climbed as fighting in and around Ludlow continued until President Woodrow Wilson sent federal troops into the area to replace the National Guard and disarm the strikers.

In his book *Blood Passion*, Scott Martelle estimates that at least 75 people, miners and their families, guardsmen, and bystanders were killed. Included was Baldwin-Felts detective George Belcher.

Belcher had fashioned an early version of an improvised flak jacket girdling his body with metal bars. Thus protected, he felt invulnerable as he patrolled in and around Ludlow. He was wrong. The jacket did its job, but Belcher was killed by a single shot to the back of the head.

Altogether, more than 400 miners were arrested. More than 300 were indicted for murder while 22 National Guardsmen were tried by court-martial. One striker was found guilty but his conviction was overturned by the Colorado Supreme Court.

None of the detectives were charged with crimes. The strike was eventually broken and numerous strikers were replaced by non-union workers. The men of B-F were free to return to West Virginia where their next major confrontation was the Massacre to Matewan.

Don Chafin

With the possible exception of the Baldwin-Felts toughs, Don Chafin was, to the striking miners, the most despised man in West Virginia.

Don Chafin was one of eleven children born to Francis and Esther Chafin. Francis Chafin served as an officer with the Confederates in the American Civil War and was sheriff of Logan County from 1894 to 1898.

The younger Chafin was elected sheriff of Logan County in 1912 at the age of 25. As state law prohibited back-to-back elections to that office, he took the job of county clerk in 1916 but was also sworn in as a deputy sheriff.

Chafin recaptured the top job in 1920 by a huge majority. He could do no wrong in the eyes of the mine owners and the "better people" of Logan County.

Writing in a small booklet entitled *The Incomparable Don Chafin*, life-long friend George T. Swain commented that though the sheriff was not highly educated, he did take some courses at what is now Marshall University in Huntington and what is now Mountain State College in Parkersburg. The job of sheriff of Logan County paid $3,500 per year. But by the age of 30, Chafin had a net worth of a quarter-million dollars, or more. How could that have happened?

The coal mine owners had a system by which they paid into a central fund a set amount for each ton of coal brought to the surface. As the county governments in West Virginia at the time operated on a shoestring, this money was used by local sheriffs to hire additional deputies beholding to the mine owners. Each deputy was paid a salary. Anything extra ended up in the accounts of the sheriff. Chafin's "army" at times grew to more than 300.

In his book *Life, Work and Rebellion in the Coal Fields*, author David Corbin wrote that while sheriff, Chafin was also paid almost $3000 per *month* by the Logan County Coal Operators' Association to keep a lid on the county, i.e., keep the United Mine Workers of America out.

Though the coal mine wars sputtered out in the mid-1920s, Chafin remained active in politics and was a delegate to the 1924 and 1928 Democratic National Conventions. Fearless and pugnacious, he also found time to be a sometime bodyguard for heavyweight boxing champion Jack Dempsey. Sheriff Chafin would be a key player in the Battle of Blair Mountain.

The Death of "Smilin' Sid"

Sid Hatfield and 22 others were scheduled to go on trial during the dreary winter months of 1921 in Williamson, county seat of Mingo County. The sole charge was the murder of detective Albert Felts. The defendants had little to worry about in this case.

Sid Hatfield could have been tried later for the deaths of the other detectives and the murder of Anse Hatfield, a friend of the Baldwin-Felts men, who was killed in August of 1920. Sid had been charged with that murder as well. But those cases would be in the future.

As was shown in the case of the nineteenth-century filibuster William Walker (see chapter three), appearing before a sympathetic jury is vital. Walker was repeatedly found not guilty of violating neutrality acts when the evidence strongly indicated otherwise because the public felt his cause was just.

The same could be expected in Mingo County where sentiment was strongly against the Baldwin-Felts detectives.

The trial was a sensation in southwestern West Virginia. People chugged in by car, rode horses and mules, or walked through the snowy and muddy countryside to the courthouse.

In a move which, though not unprecedented, was certainly unusual, the coal operators added "muscle" to the country prosecutor's office by hiring four "special" prosecutors – a former judge, a former justice of the state supreme court, a counselor working for the Williamson Coal Operators Association, and a veteran criminal lawyer.

The United Mine Workers of America, collecting money from its membership, provided two veteran attorneys, John J. Conniff and Harold W. Houston, to represent Sid Hatfield and the other defendants. R.D. Bailey was on the bench for the trial with Colonel Herman Hall, commander of the federal soldiers enforcing martial law in Mingo County at the time, at his side.

Picking a jury was the next hurdle. More than 400 possible jurors were examined, including one who said he was certainly impartial, favoring neither the hard-working miners nor the Baldwin-Felts "thugs".

The jury, 12 white men, had to be satisfactory to Sid Hatfield and his fellow defendants – nine farmers and laborers, one illiterate backwoods man and two teachers.

The trial dragged on through March. Each witness seemed to have seen something different.

The most disturbing witnesses had to be Charles E. Lively.

Lively had carried a union card for almost 20 years and was a constant agitator, trying to get miners to join the movement. He even opened a restaurant in Matewan that served as an informal meeting hall for the miners, an excellent place to pick up bits of gossip and intrigue.

But Lively was playing a double game – working as well for the mine owners as a spy, and being paid $225 per month, plus expenses, about three times what a miner could scratch out using a pick and shovel in the pits.

He testified that several of the defendants had told him of their roles in the killing of the detectives. The problem with his testimony was that he was in Charleston trying to worm even deeper into the union movement when the shootout took place. At best, his words were hearsay.

His testimony did present a problem for Sid Hatfield, partly of Sid's own making.

Twelve days after Mayor Testerman was killed, Hatfield and the widow Testerman traveled to Huntington and were married.

The prosecution, using Lively as their witness, painted a picture in which Sid Hatfield had actually killed the mayor so that Jessie would be free to marry him. Lively testified that Sid Hatfield had said previously that he would like to marry but someone was standing in his way. Was that someone the dead mayor?

As spring was breaking along the Tug River, the verdict came in. The defendants were found not guilty on all charges. Each defendant had to post bond pending possible prosecution for the killings of the other detectives.

Sid Hatfield and the others returned to Matewan as heroes. They had stood up against the might of the coal operators and had won. Hatfield was mobbed by supporters as he got off the train from Williamson. It took him an hour to get to his home.

Sid Hatfield, not yet 30, was enjoying his notoriety as a local Robin Hood. The mayor who succeeded C. C. Testerman had named a new chief of police for Matewan but Sid kept wearing a badge as he was the new constable of Magnolia District.

"Smilin' Sid" entertained the visiting paparazzi by being photographed with a gun in each hand, or one on each hip. He even traveled to Washington to testify about conditions in the coalfields.

But the young constable was not in the clear.

Doubtless at the urging of business interests in the state, a law was passed allowing for local juries to be impaneled including members from adjacent counties. This simply meant that if Sid Hatfield were to be tried again in *friendly* Mingo County, some the jurors could be from *unfriendly* Logan and McDowell Counties. Pro-mine owner jurors, and "special prosecutors" financed by business interests, spelled *potential* trouble. But first Hatfield would have to contend with *real* troubles.

While in Washington testifying before the Senate, word came of a criminal conspiracy indictment, in hostile McDowell Country, southeast of Mingo County.

The case was almost a year old. The charge was blowing up a coal tipple in the mining camp of Mohawk. Hatfield was among the 30 suspects.

Hatfield made the trip to McDowell's county seat Welch for the trial. Against his better judgment, he had agreed to go to the courthouse unarmed. He feared for his safety but another Hatfield, a distant relative named Sheriff William Hatfield of McDowell Country, had guaranteed his safety. By some strange quirk, the sheriff was not in Welch when Sid Hatfield and his party arrived, but was out of town "taking the waters."

The date was August 1, 1921. In addition to Sid and Jessie Hatfield, Ed Chambers, Sid's best friend, and his wife made the trip.

Unnoticed by the Hatfield party as they walked through town, a group of Baldwin-Felts detectives lounged around the courthouse. As the Hatfields and Chambers headed up the courthouse steps, shots rang out. The number of detectives firing is in dispute but there was no question that four bullets tore into Sid Hatfield.

In his book *The Battle of Blair Mountain*, author Robert Shogan credits Charles Lively, Bill Salter, and George Pence, all B-F detectives, with the murders of Sid Hatfield and Ed Chambers.

Thus ended the short, but adventuresome life of Sid Hatfield. Thousands of mourners paid their respects to Sid and Ed Chambers. Authorities were prepared to deal with a backlash but there was none, at the time. But the memory of "Smilin' Sid" would cause an even greater outrage among the miners culminating at the Battle of Blair Mountain.

Freedom Fighter or Terrorist?

Sid Hatfield was back in the headlines again on August 2, 1921. As Welch is only some 25 miles from Bluefield, the *Daily Telegraph*, rushed a front-page, staff-written story, into print under banner headlines:

SID HATFIELD AND ED CHAMBERS SHOT TO DEATH IN WELCH

Two of Alleged Principals in Matewan Tragedy Accompanied by Wives Were Mounting Steps Leading to McDowell County Court House When Pistol Battle That Cost Two Lives Broke Out

FIVE MEN ARRESTED IMMEDIATLEY BUT ONLY C.E. LIVELY AND GEORGE PENCE ARE HELD AFTER PROBE

The main story covered three full columns, counting the jump to page nine. Three additional items also appeared on page one.

The primary story read in part:

Sid Hatfield and Ed Chambers were shot to death in a pistol fight on the steps of the McDowell County court house in Welch yesterday morning at 10:35 o'clock. Five persons were arrested immediately after the shooting and were held pending an investigation. These were C.E. Lively, George Pence, H.H. Lucas, Robert Day and Wm. Salter. Late last night following an investigation by Prosecuting Attorney G.L. Counts, Lucas, Day and Salter were released.

Hatfield, accompanied by his wife, and Ed Chambers, and his wife, arrived in Welch yesterday morning on train No. 4 from Matewan. Leaving the station they went immediately to Ellwood Hotel and remained there until about 10:30 o'clock when they started for the court house...upon reaching the steps leading up to the court house Chambers and his wife stepped in front and immediately behind them walked Hatfield and his wife. They had just reached the first landing when the shooting started. At the head of the steps were Lively, Pence, Lucas, Day, L.H. Ellis, a state policeman, C.M. Samson and B.C. Gallamore.

Chambers and Hatfield were well on the landing when the shooting occurred. Chambers was several feet to the left of Hatfield and when he fell his body remained on the landing. Hatfield tumbled backward and his body rolled down the steps almost to the bottom of the recess in the street well...Chief of Police Walter Mitchell who was just across the street from the court house said he was unable to say who fired the first shot. It sounded like a volley, he said, and in turning towards the scene, he said he saw Chambers and Hatfield and their wives standing on the landing of the steps. The shooting was still in progress. He said he saw both Hatfield and Chambers fall and the firing ceased.

"I then rushed to the steps,"' Chief Mitchell said, "'and reached Hatfield first. I removed his body from the steps to the recess in the street well." Chief Mitchell said he found a .38-caliber, two-inch barrel revolver, in the right front pocket of Hatfield's trousers and also picked up another .38-caliber revolver by his side. The one in his trousers had not but fired but there were four empty chambers in the other revolver, the chief said. He also said he found another .38-caliber revolver lying beside Chambers' body and it was said to have been fired all the way around.

At the general offices of T.L. Felts here (Bluefield) yesterday, it was stated that numerous alleged threats had been made by Sid Hatfield against the life of Lively since his identity was revealed during the trial of Hatfield and others for the murder of Albert and Lee Felts in a street battle at Matewan, Mingo County,

May 19, 1920 during which seven Felts men were slain and three other persons killed, including Mayor Testerman.

A companion story read:

SHOOTING CAUSED
LITTLE MORE THAN
FLURRY AT WELCH

Some Excitement Resulted
Large Crowd Was Quickly
Dispersed

CORONER'S JURY TO DECIDE
WHO TO HOLD FOR TRIAL

Story of Tragedy on Steps of
McDowell County Court
House as Furnished to
Associated Press by Its
Correspondent at Welch.

(By the Associated Press)

Welch, W. Va., Aug 1. – Sid Hatfield's career in West Virginia ended today on the courthouse steps of this village. It remains for a corner's jury who shall be held for trial on a charge of having fired the shot that ended the life of the picturesque figure in the industrial strife in Mingo County. C.E. Lively, a private detective, is being held pending an investigation...the shooting, though creating some excitement, did not cause more than a flurry, and the large crowd in Welch for the trail was dispersed quickly by local authorities. The charge on which Hatfield was to have been tried was in connection with the shooting up of Mohawk, W. Va., about a year ago.

Those who saw the bodies of Hatfield and Chambers after the two men had been shot at the court house entrance positively asserted that the smile of the Matewan ex-chief of police remained even in death. That smile has been the subject dwelt upon by all who came in contact with Hatfield and earned for his the sobriquet of "Smiling Sid."

A three-paragraph story from Matewan reported that all was quiet in the hometown of Hatfield and Chambers. A two-inch story from Huntington, West Virginia, indicated that Mrs. Hatfield had no comment on the shooting of the day before.

The killings of Sid Hatfield and Ed Chambers were featured in the New York *Times* of August 2 but from a different perspective.

SAYS SID HATFIELD
WAS VICTIM OF PLOT

Prosecuting Attorney Accuses Two
Men of Killing West Virginia
Gunman in Cold Blood.

Special to the New York Times

CHARLESTON, W. Va. Aug. 2 –A carefully arranged plot apparently was revealed today by the authorities investigating the shooting at Welch yesterday of Sid Hatfield and Ed Chambers of Mingo County, according to counsel for the United Mine Workers.

Evidence uncovered by Prosecuting Attorney G.L. Counts indicated that the victims were shot without warning and at a time when Hatfield was unarmed, according to an unofficial statement.

The Coroner's Jury rendered a verdict which said the men were killed by persons unknown.

Prosecuting Attorney Counts said he had established the following facts in connection with the shooting: Sid Hatfield and Ed Chambers were shot to death on the steps leading to the court yard at Welch. Hatfield and Chambers, with their wives on their arms, were ascending the steps slowly on their way to the Court House, Hatfield to answer an indictment, Chambers as a witness when, without warning, they were shot by C.C. Lively, 'Buster' Pence, and probably others assembled at the top of the steps. These men were deputy sheriffs.

Chambers, while sinking from several shots, tried to draw a gun from his inside coat pocket, but got it only partly out when he rolled lifeless down the steps. At that point Mrs. Chambers pleaded with Lively not to shoot her husband any more, but Lively plunged down the steps and, placing his gun close to Chambers' head, just back of the ear, fired two more shots into the prostrate man.

Then it was that Mrs. Chambers struck Lively with her umbrella, and not before.

Hatfield was lower down on the steps and attempted to retreat, but the first shot fired at him struck him in the arm, the second across the lower part of the breast, and then, as he turned, three more shots were fired into his back, the latter proving instantly fatal. He made no attempt to draw a gun.

"There was no altercation whatever," said counsel for miners. "Neither man nor woman had made any demonstration. They were ambushed while peacefully on their way to a court of justice, and were murdered in cold blood by Baldwin-Felts thugs."

The *United Mine Workers Journal* agreed with this assessment writing, "Hatfield was a member of the United Mine Workers of America. He was a quiet, unassuming man of 26 years, good-natured and always wearing a smile. He never hunted trouble but never backed away from any danger. His fearlessness and indomitable courage was a thorn in the side of the gunmen system of Mingo and McDowell Counties." It went on to say that he was the subject of frame-up as a way to get him out of the way.

Resolutions of support for Sid Hatfield and letters of outrage and sympathy poured into the *Journal* that was able to publish only a small portion of the correspondence.

Lively and Pence were released under $10,000 bail to answer to the October Circuit Court Jury.

How can the statements of witnesses saying both Hatfield and Chambers were armed and fired several shots be reconciled with the findings of the prosecuting attorney?

McDowell County was "coal company" territory. Perhaps the witnesses were confused. But the situation could also have been that the citizens in and around Welch were tired of the "Terror of the Tug," as Sid Hatfield was often called, and were not unhappy to see him dead, and they did not want blame placed on the Baldwin-Felts men of nearby Bluefield.

In life Sid Hatfield had been the miner's matador, dueling with the twin bullies who had made their lives miserable – the mine owners and the Baldwin-Felts detectives.

In death Sid Hatfield became the miner's martyr, dead before he had reached the age of 30.

Word spread from hollow to hollow that Sid and his best friend, Ed Chambers, had been killed in Welsh – murdered as far as the miners were concerned. It was time to act.

The battle lines were being drawn.

The coal owners had on their side the sheriffs they had put into office around the state and the bands of "deputies" paid by the mine owners. For backup they had the resources of the Baldwin-Felts. When all else failed, they hoped they could count on the United States Army.

They also got help from an unexpected source – the "better people" of West Virginia – shop owners, businessmen, farmers and even students and scores of women and girls.

Why would this segment of society have sided with the mine owners, often unfeeling, rich men from out of state, against working persons like themselves? More than once a mine owner was heard to ask, following a mine accident, "did we lose any mules?"

Two reasons help explain why so many citizens of West Virginia sided with the operators – fear and a poor choice of neck wear.

The miners were armed with high-powered rifles, pistols, and even squirrel guns. Some wore the GI issue they brought home from World War I. But the most common "uniform" was a pair of blue bib overalls and a red bandanna – earning them the nickname "rednecks".

That was enough for the "better people". The miners were not just rednecks, they were *reds!* – Socialists, revolutionaries, Communists. They had to be stopped. Fear, manipulated well, is a most powerful emotion.

The Red Scares

Fear is the incubator of hysteria as witnessed during the two "red scares" of the twentieth-century.

The best known took place during the decade after the victory in World War II. By mid-century Americans had ample reasons to be edgy.

In 1949 the Soviet Union had entered the atom club with the help of spies in both Great Britain and United States. The United States was "fighting" a cold war with the Soviet Bloc that had rattled an "Iron Curtain" down on Eastern Europe, walling parts or all of eight countries off from the West.

The red tide was lapping at the shores of France, Italy, Greece and Turkey.

China was "lost" in 1949 with the Communists forcing the Kuomintang government of Chiang Kai-shek into exile on Taiwan. An increasingly unpopular stalemated war was being fought in Korea.

Fear, like parched leaves in the forest in the middle of a severe drought, was all around. All that be needed to set it off was a spark.

That spark's name was Senator Joseph McCarthy.

McCarthy, who lied on his application to Marquette University Law School, also fudged his World War II record claiming to have been a combat gunner – he actually spent most of the war behind a desk.

Nevertheless, "Tail Gunner Joe" was elected in 1946 as the Republican junior senator from Wisconsin. His first four years in the Senate were lackluster. He needed a gimmick to be reelected in 1952 – and the fear of Communism was it.

He began his "crusade" in Wheeling, West Virginia, February 9, 1950, holding up some sheets of paper that he claimed contained the names of Communists working for the U. S. State Department. He hammered on this theme across the country, though he never made a list public and the allegations shifted from "Communist" to "subversive" to "security risk." Numbers fluctuated.

The scare tactic worked: Professors lost their chairs, politicians accused of being soft on Communism were defeated. Actors, writers and producers were blacklisted. Reputations were savaged. The country lived in fear for five years.

McCarthy finally overreached by challenging the Army over the promotion of an alleged "pink" dentist and the Army's refusal to give preferential treatment to a draftee, G. David Schine, who had worked for the senator.

After a 36-day televised hearing which drew an audience of some 20 million, the drama ended, McCarthy had been made to look ridiculous, and the red scare had about run its course.

The low point of the hysteria was when a baseball team grew two appendages.

For as far back as the 1920s, the National League team in Cincinnati, a city with a long and proud baseball heritage, had been known as the Reds. The Queen City was the first community to have an entirely professional baseball team, the 1869 Red Stockings. That summer the team, nine players and a substitute, was paid $9,200. During the year in which San Francisco Giants slugger Barry Bond broke Hank Aaron's home run record, his salary could be calculated at more than $10,000 per *inning*.

In the best traditions of professional sports, the Red Stockings bolted their home city and were reconstituted two years later as the Boston Red Caps. And after playing under names like the Bees, Beaneaters, and Robins, the team has now morphed into the Atlanta Braves.

In 1953, ownership in Cincinnati buckled and changed the nickname of the team to the *Redlegs!*

Destructive as the red scare of the 1950s was to reputations and livelihoods, the earlier iteration following World War I was even worse.

There were two primary factors governing the post World War I red scare – the success of the Soviet revolution in Russia and the mistrust of aliens living and working in the United States.

Americas, and particularly President Wilson, were not comfortable siding with imperialist Russia in World War I, anymore than was the case of joining with the Soviet Union in World War II

The western nations were pleased when the liberal government of Prince Georgi Lvov and Alexander Kerensky took power in Russia in February 1917; not so when that shaky government was toppled by the Soviets in October of that year. The Soviets' separate peace with Germany was a further outrage to the Western Allies.

The war lurched to a conclusion with the signing of the Armistice on November 11, 1918. America wanted to "bring the boys home" and demobilize as quickly as possible – except for those the few thousand Americans stuck in northern and eastern Russia (see chapter two).

Something wasn't quite right. The Soviet menace had seeped out of Russia and was taking root in Europe. Hungary had a short-lived Soviet government. The red scourge was threatening Bavaria, France, Italy, and the rest of Germany. Would the United States be next?

The dual answer was to establish super-patriotic societies and to scapegoat foreigners and radicals.

Groups that fit the "radical" franchise were members of the Communist and Communist Labor parties, anarchists, bomb throwers, labor leaders, non-conformists and though its presidential candidate Eugene V. Debs has received almost a million votes in 1912 – the Socialists.

Many solutions were offered – deportation of troublemakers, revolutionaries and non-conformists – imprisonment, vigilante justice and gulag-like exile. Senator Kenneth McKellan of Tennessee suggested that radicals be held without trial at the mid-Pacific island of Guam! The island had been used to hold Philippine resistance leaders during the Insurrection of 1899-1902.

To give these various actions the sanction of legality, a bundle of laws including the Espionage Act and the resurrection of the Alien and Sedition Acts were implemented at the start of America's entry into World War I. These gave the government some tools with which to prosecute those felt to be hampering the war effort.

Attorney General A. Mitchell Palmer was changed with identifying and capturing subversives.

The dragnets brought in thousands of suspects, from perennial Socialist Presidential candidate Debs to the janitors who swept up the halls where suspect groups met. To Palmer, this hard-line crackdown was seen as a path to the 1920 Democratic nomination for President. Though he was one of the favorites for the nod, he failed to gain the two-thirds majority needed to win.

Most of the thousands of suspects were subsequently released. Some 850 were eventually deported – but none to Guam!

Even legitimately elected officials were not spared.

Victor Berger had been elected in 1910 as a member of the House of Representatives from the 5th District of Wisconsin (Milwaukee) – the first Socialist to serve in that body.

Berger was an outspoken vocal critic of World War I and voiced his opinion in his newspaper the Milwaukee *Leader*. He ran afoul of the law and lost his second class mailing privileges in 1917, effectively silencing his publication.

In the spring of 1918 he entered a three-cornered contest to fill a vacant senatorial seat in Wisconsin. Though he was indicted just ten days prior to the election of conspiracy to violate the Espionage Act, he won more than 26 percent of the vote.

On November 6, 1918, Berger was again elected as representative from the 5th District in Wisconsin but before he could travel to Washington, he was found guilty of violating the Espionage Act.

He was sentenced to 20 years at hard labor at Fort Leavenworth, Kansas by Federal Judge Kenesaw Mountain Landis, who would later become commissioner of baseball.

Berger was freed on bail and served no prison time. He moved on to the Nation's capital to resume serving in the House of Representatives.

In May 1919, the 66th Congress refused to seat Berger. A special election was called in Milwaukee to fill the seat and Berger won with more than 60 percent of the vote. Again Congress failed to allow him to take his seat, leaving the citizens of a large portion of Milwaukee without representation.

Eugene Debs, also convicted of violations of the Espionage Act, was not as fortunate as Berger and served 32 months of his 20-year sentence in prison. He ran for president for the fifth time in 1920, campaigning from his cell in the federal prison in Atlanta, Georgia, and got almost a million votes.

209

While all of this was taking place, the state legislature of New York refused to seat five Socialist politicians from greater New York City though the Socialist Party was recognized as a legitimate entity in that state.

These elections were reminiscent of what took place in the Cabin Creek area of West Virginia in 1912 when Socialist candidates swept all local contests, gathering more votes than the Democrats and Republicans combined. The winners were denied the opportunity to serve.

The only real differences were that the disenfranchisements in Congress and New York State were done in legislative chambers – in West Virginia it was done at the point of a bayonet.

The super patriot right needed a hero and got one in Ole Hanson.

Hanson was mayor of Seattle, Washington when an International Workers of the World-inspired general strike shut down the city. Hanson brought in extra police and soldiers from what is now Fort Lewis, to break the strike. His actions led to a short-lived boomlet for president in 1920.

With all of the violence and as the "red" hysteria about to hit its peak in 1920 as a backdrop, the West Virginia miners made a very poor choice in choosing to wear bandanas of that emotionally-charged color RED!

Revolt of the "Rednecks"

Officials in Welch assured the miners that the men who killed Sid Hatfield and Ed Chambers would get a "full dose" of McDowell Country justice. This raised a "red" flag for the miners as they could be quite certain that McDowell County justice would mean acquittal for the Baldwin-Felts men. They would be proven correct when Charles Lively and the other Baldwin-Felts detectives pleaded self-defense and were found not guilty at the same McDowell County Court House where Sid Hatfield and Ed Chambers had been shot and killed.

If the deaths of Hatfield and Chambers were to avenged, the miners would have to do it themselves.

For once in their lives the miners felt they had power. No longer could they be intimidated by the thugs of Baldwin-Felts, the corrupt sheriffs and the mine owners.

After a couple of false starts in which the miners were talked into putting down their guns and going home, the forces of the owners overplayed their hand at a place called Sharples resulting in the death of an undetermined number of miners. This time there would be no turning back.

From Cabin Creek and Paint Creek, from Lens Creek and along the Kanawha River they came in knots of 20, 30, 50. Some walked, others carjacked "tin lizzies" and rode to the front.

Others commandeered trains, loaded them with the miners and supplies and joined the march. At times the miners would fashion their own trains, hooking various cars together as needed. The most graphic scene was a train of lumber cars filled with miners and their weapons.

Actual numbers are impossible to prove. The miner "army" was estimated at being some 10,000 or more, most the men wearing blue bib overalls and the trademark red bandanna. They were armed with shotguns, rifles and revolvers. They even brought a machine gun out of hiding from the days of the strike at Paint and Cabin Creeks and stole a Gatling gun.

Much time and research has gone into determining who was the "generalissimo" of the marchers. Again, no determination has been accepted.

The miner army was made up of many small bands of marchers. They knew what the wanted – to swoop down on Logan County and hang Don Chafin from a sour apple tree, free their friends in the Mingo County Jail, overturn martial law in Mingo County and maybe burn the court house in Logan County for good measure.

But they did not have a strong military-like organization. They were loosely organized along union local lines.

They felt they had the initiative and had Sheriff Chafin and his band of defenders outnumbered, if not outgunned. The state government, though solidly behind the mine owners, was weak and had not even reconstituted the state's National Guard, as it should have following the end of World War I.

Sheriff Chafin had three small aircraft that flew reconnaissance missions and even dropped some crude pipe bombs that, though echoing through the hills, did no damage. The miners had no air wing.

The showdown was going to be at Blair Mountain, on the border of Boone and Logan Counties, which blocked the way to the city of Logan and Mingo County. Chafin had vowed that no army was going to march through his county!

Chafin and his defenders had the advantage of the high ground where they dug trenches, threw up barricades, and placed machine gun nests. Volunteers joined the defenders, including some Junior ROTC cadets from Charleston. Help from out of state swelled the ranks of the miners. Prospects of an all-out battled loomed.

To differentiate themselves from the miners, the defenders wore white armbands. Another red-white split like the monarchists and Bolsheviks in Russia (see chapter two) and the forces of General Walker and the reactionaries in Nicaragua (see chapter three).

Considering the number of rounds fired by both sides, casualties were fairly light. Again, no definite totals could be established. At times the miners felt they had lost hundreds of their numbers, probably greatly overestimated. The defenders also suffered deaths with the exact total impossible to determine.

Local doctors climbed among the hollows and ridges to treat the wounded. The defenders stationed women and girls, wearing caps with red crosses on them, at improvised hospitals and feeding stations. The wives and daughters of the miners were at their own locations, wearing caps bearing logos of the union.

To some of the "better people," the battle was a bit of a lark. They munched on chunks of baloney wrapped in slabs of home-baked bread, all washed down with grape soda pop or sarsaparilla.

The defenders were panicky. Fearing that the town of Logan would be sacked, the mine owners begged West Virginia politicians to again call on the federal government to send in the Regular Army.

The fighting raged along a 20-mile front for some two weeks. Some 500 square miles of southern West Virginia were in play. Estimates of shots fired range up to a million!

To the miners it was a struggle for their union and a better life. For the owners, it was an attempt to break the union and remain in control. The tipping point came when Regular Army troops were alerted from as far away as Ohio, Kentucky, and New Jersey to pack up and be ready to move into southwestern West Virginia.

Johnnie Comes Marchin' In

The state militia and Regular Army had yo-yoed into and out of the coalfields from 1912 to 1921 almost as often as the Navy and Marines had dropped anchor in Haiti and Nicaragua.

Periods of Military Intervention in West Virginia

Time Period	Component
September-October 1912	West Virginia Militia
November 1912-January 1913	West Virginia Militia
February-June 1913	West Virginia Militia
October-November 1919	U. S. Army
August-November 1920	U. S. Army
November 1920-February 1921	U. S. Army
August-November 1921	U. S. Army

Republican Governor William Glasscock had put the coal-fields under state-administered martial law three times before leaving office in 1913. His decrees made it possible for Mother Jones to have been tried by court-martial and not in a civil court.

Henry Drury Hatfield took office as governor in March 1913. He was a medical doctor who had been born in Mingo County and had worked as a physician in the coal pits among the poor miners. The governor had settled the differences between the factions and worked hard to keep the peace between the miners and the coal mine owners.

The coalfields were generally quiet during and right after World War I. Coal was needed to fuel the American industrial machine as 70 percent of the nation's energy came from that source, with West Virginia contributing 25 percent.

The mine owners profited from the increased demand for their product with the price increasing by some 400 percent. The miners were lucky if they could count an extra 30 percent in their pay envelopes.

At the end of the war, the mine owners wanted to cut wages and eliminate unions; the workers wanted to hold on to their gains and wanted more. Scattered fighting, strikes, and Matewan brought military law back to West Virginia.

Federal troops dropped into Mingo County for the first time in late August 1920, complete with machine guns, a cannon, mules, and campaign hats. One of the largest detachments was stationed at Matewan where the massacre had taken place three months earlier. The soldiers were a curiosity to the miners and their families but didn't seem like a threat.

They did keep a lid on passions and in early November the troops were withdrawn with the job of policing Mingo County returning to the state police.

Another pull of the yo-yo string and the federals were back.

Governor John Cornwell declared Mingo County in a "state of rebellion" and put it under the control of the commanding general of the Fifth Corps Area.

Colonel Herman Hall, commander of the 19th Infantry Regiment, who had been selected by the commander of Fifth Corps Area to administer Mingo County, set up his headquarters in the county courthouse. It was in capacity that Colonel Hall would sit on the bench at the trial of Sid Hatfield and friends.

The soldiers were popular with the residents of Mingo. Officers' wives helped distribute toys, candy and nuts to the children of the miners at Christmas time. For the time being, things would be relatively quiet in southwestern West Virginia.

That quiet was to be shattered in August of 1921 when the miners, enraged that state-imposed martial law would not be lifted, rallied at Mermet, just south of the capital of Charleston, and prepared to march to Logan to avenge the death of Sid Hatfield.

West Virginia again asked for federal troops. Secretary of War John Weeks, feeling the state was not doing enough to cope with its own problems, hesitated. He did order the 19th Infantry to be ready to march but first sent World War I hero Brigadier General Henry Bandholtz to investigate and make a recommendation.

The situation moved quickly in the summer of 1921 with federal troopers following this sequence:

August 26, 1921: As West Virginia Governor Ephraim Morgan and Army Deputy Chief of Staff Major General James G. Harbord were discussing the need for troops, orders went out to prepare for infantry action and air support.

August 27, 1921: Two miners are killed by a posse of 70 to 100 deputies and state police near the village of Sharples. Miners who had planned to return to their homes resumed plans to march to Logan.

August 29, 1921: Governor Morgan repeats his request for federal help, saying "outside" forces from Indiana, Ohio and Illinois were fanning the flames of insurrection

September 1, 1921: President Warren Harding's proclamation demanding the miners put down their weapons and return home was dropped in leaflet form along the lines of the strikers.

September 1, 1921: Troops of the 19th and 10th Infantry Regiments from Ohio, the 40th Infantry of Kentucky and the 26th Infantry of New Jersey are readied to move to the coal fields.

U. S. Army Units Deployed to Blair Mountain

Unit	Home Base
10th Infantry	Columbus Barracks, Ohio
19th Infantry	Camp Sherman, Ohio
26th Infantry	Camp Dix, New Jersey
40th Infantry	Camp Knox, Kentucky
Chemical Warfare Unit	Edgewood Arsenal, Maryland
88th Aero Squadron	Langley Field, Virginia

September 1, 1921: Brigadier General Billy Mitchell was ordered to send 21 aircraft of the 88th Aero Squadron to Kanawha Field near Charleston, to stand by for orders. General Mitchell advocated the use of poison gas and artillery to root out the miners. Considered to be a "loose cannon", parading around with a chest full of ribbons, and wearing spurs, he was pointedly directed NOT to make the trip. Most of the planes either got lost or crashed and airpower played almost no role in suppressing the rebellion.

September 1, 1921: Four DeHavilland DH-4B bombers, outfitted with nose and tail machines guns, and carrying tear gas and fragmentation bombs, fly from Washington, DC, to Charleston.

September 3, 1921: Federal troops spread out in West Virginia. A detachment of chemical warfare soldiers from Edgewood Arsenal, armed with tear gas, moves into the state.

The miners were more than willing to fight Don Chafin and his deputies, the Baldwin-Felts detectives, the state police, and the "better people" of West Virginia, but they were not going to fire upon the United States Army. The rebellion was against the mine owners and the corrupt sheriffs, not the United States.

Mountaineers have always been patriotic. They broke away from Virginia and set up a separate state rather than fight against the Union in the Civil War.

During the World War I era, citizens of West Virginia made up about 1.3 percent of the American population; during the "Great War" 2.6 percent of the soldiers listed as killed in action or missing (and presumed dead) were from the Mountaineer state, notwithstanding that miners could have avoided the war as "critical workers."

Many of the miners had fought in World War I. They swapped stories with the Doughboys and treated them like long-lost friends.

With the U.S. Army in the state, the rebellion sputtered out in September. The end came in this sequence:

215

September 4-8, 1921: The miners willingly surrendered to the U.S. Army. They either turned in their weapons or hid them in the hills and returned to their homes.

November 3, 1921: The State of West Virginia and the U.S. Army met to plan for the withdrawal of federal forces from the state.

December, 1921: The last federal soldiers, members of the 10th Infantry, packed up and returned to their home base in Ohio.

Winners and Losers

The only victories the miners could claim were their pride in standing up for their rights and the publicity that had been gained for their struggle to unionize and have a better life.

In the short run, the union in West Virginia was broken. Membership dropped sharply. The mine owners, with their private armies of deputy sheriffs and detectives, were once again *the* law in the coalfields. Not until the New Deal of President Franklin Roosevelt did the miners obtain unlimited rights of unionization for which many fought and some died.

The exact death toll in the years of off and on fighting will never be known. Some researchers estimate that hundreds were killed, on all sides, with many being buried in secret to prevent the "enemy" learning of the casualties they had caused. Men were killed in knots of two or three and maybe a dozen at a time. Few of the killers, on either side, were convicted.

The U.S. Army suffered no ground deaths though five aviators were killed when their plane crashed.

U.S. Army Fatalities in the Great Coal Mine Wars

First Lieutenant Harry Speck	Medford, Oregon
Second Lieutenant William Fitzpatrick	Medford, Oregon
Sergeant Arthur Brown	Rural Kentucky
Corporal Alexander Hazelton	Wilmington, Delaware
Private Walter Howard	San Francisco, California

The men were killed on September 3, 1921 while flying near Drennan, West Virginia in a Martin MB-2 bomber in support of the U. S. Army's efforts to disarm the dissident miners.

Hazelton survived the crash and died later; the others perished on the spot. The plane was returning to its home station near Washington, DC when it encounter rough weather, nose-dived into the ground and burst into flame.

Loose Ends

Both Merle Travis and Tennessee Ernie Ford have been elected to the Country Music Hall of Fame. Travis, who was tarred as a subversive during the Senator McCarthy red scare, was inducted in 1977, seven years after becoming a member of the Nashville Songwriters Hall of Fame. Travis even lent his musical talents to the 1953 movie *From Here to Eternity* playing *Reenlistment Blues.*

Tennessee Ernie Ford was inducted into the Country Music Hall of Fame in 1990. He was awarded the Presidential Medal of Freedom in 1984 and has three stars on the Hollywood Walk of Fame – for his work in radio, records, and television.

Mother Jones gave her last speech, a "fiery one", at the age of 100 in Silver Spring, Maryland. She died seven months later and is buried in the Union Miners Cemetery at Mount Olive, Illinois, a city in the southern Illinois coalfields. She spoke at the dedication of the cemetery and requested six years before her death that she be buried among "her boys." Her grave, in the only cemetery in the country owned by a union, is among those of the victims of the Virden, Illinois, mine riot of 1898 and is adorned by a $16,000 marker purchased by the Progressive Mine Workers of America, a group which had splintered off from the United Mine Workers.

Her gravesite is marked with a bronze tablet that reads:

Mary "Mother" Jones
Born May 1, 1830
Died November 30, 1930

She Gave Her Life To The World Of Labor, Her Blessed Soul Is In Heaven. God's Finger Touched Her – And Now She Sleeps

She is featured on the six by 12 foot bronze bas-relief dedicated in Virden in October 2006 as the "Battle of Virden Monument."

Her funeral in 1930 in Mt. Olive drew thousands of mourners who overflowed the mass at the Ascension Church for, as she was known by the miners and their families – the "Eastern Irish woman". The crowd was sometimes compared to that which welcomed home the body of President Abraham Lincoln in nearby Springfield some 65 years earlier.

Mother Jones' name also lives on in the form of a progressive magazine by that name published in San Francisco. The magazine in pro-environment, sides with the working man, and is against war and imperialism, the type of causes Mother Jones would no doubt support.

Police Chief Hatfield and Mayor Testerman fought side by side in the battle against the Baldwin-Felts detectives at the shootout at Matewan. They are still side by side, being buried in adjoining plots in the Buskirk, Kentucky cemetery. Also interred in the cemetery in Buskirk is Ed Chambers who was murdered along with Sid Hatfield on the steps of the courthouse in Welch.

Hatfield's gravesite is adorned with a three tiered black granite stone with the wording:

TO THE MEMORY OF
SID HATFIELD
MAY 15, 1893
AUG 1, 1921

Under a head and shoulders etching of the "Terror of the Tug" is this epitaph:

DEFENDER OF THE RIGHTS
OF WORKING PEOPLE
GUNNED DOWN BY FELTS
DETECTIVES ON THE STEPS
OF THE McDOWELL COUNTY COURTHOUSE IN
WELCH, W. VA. DURING
THE GREAT MINE WAR

Chiseled into the pedestals are the words:

WE WILL NEVER FORGET

HIS MURDER TRIGGERED
THE MINERS' REBELLION AT THE
BATTLE OF BLAIR MOUNTAIN

Sheriff Don Chafin, who was "the law" for years in Logan Country, ran afoul of authorities during prohibition for turning a blind eye to the operation of a tavern in Barnabus known as the Blue Goose. If or not he was a silent partner is still up for discussion. Federal Judge George McClintie sentenced Chafin to two years in jail and fined him $10,000. He was released from the federal prison in Atlanta after just ten months. The incident did little to damage his image as being "Mr. Law and Order" and he continued to accumulate wealth as a businessman. He lived until 1954 and had amassed a fortune said to have been more than a million dollars.

Charles Lively, credited with being one of the shooters who killed Sid Hatfield and Ed Chambers in Welch, pleaded self-defense and was found not guilty. In later life he worked around the mines as a railroad detective and a hotel manager.

The twice-widowed Jessie Testerman married two more times and lived to a ripe old age in Kentucky and is buried in the same cemetery as Sid Hatfield and Mayor Testerman.

William Baldwin died in March 1936; Thomas Felts passed on a year later. With the deaths of the founders of the Baldwin-Felts Detective Agency, operation of the firm went to Estil Meadows. Rather than have the agency investigated by the National Labor Relations Board, Meadows dissolved the organization and destroyed the files.

In his book *The True Story of the Baldwin-Felts Detective Agency*, author John A. Velke III wrote that through the life of the company, 234 men and two bloodhounds were on the roles as employees. Of 43 clients, 21 were coal operators and six were government agencies.

Senator Joseph McCarthy died in disgrace after having been censured by the Senate in December of 1954 by a vote of 67 to 22. On May 2, 1957 he passed away in Bethesda Naval Hospital of what was described as "acute hepatitis." Pulitzer Prize winning journalist Haynes Johnson, in his work *The Age of Anxiety,* disputes this, writing that the senator died of cirrhosis of the liver, a victim of acute alcoholism.

G. David Schine, the most famous Army private until the drafting of Elvis Presley, finished his military career, serving part of it as a military policeman, and was honorably discharged. He worked in the movie and music industries and was Executive Producer of the Academy Award-winning film *The French Connection.*

Socialism in Milwaukee survived both the World War I red scare and McCarthyism.

Victor Berger's conviction for violating the federal Espio-nage Act in 1917 was overturned on appeal in 1921 and he was again elected to the House of Representatives in 1922. He was reelected in 1924 and 1926. He was seated for the three terms without incident.

Frank P. Zeidler, also a Socialist, served as Milwaukee's mayor as recently as 1960 and was his party's candidate for president in 1976.

Ole Hanson resigned after serving as mayor of Seattle for less than 18 months citing health reasons and the need to rebuild his finances. He became a hit on the lecture circuit. In his book *Red Scare, A Study in National Hysteria 1910-1920,* Robert Murray writes than Hanson earned almost $40,000 during seven months criss-crossing the nation explaining the dangers of bolshevism; the office of mayor of Seattle paid $7,500 per year.

The yellow dog contract, first used by the Hitchman Coal Company in Wheeling in 1907, and upheld as constitutional by the U.S. Supreme Court in 1917, also has passed from the scene, being outlawed by the Morris-LaGuardia Act of 1932. The National Labor Relations (Wagner) Act of 1935 gave added safeguards to workers wanting to join unions.

The Red Men, now known as the Improved Order of Red Men and the Degree of Pocahontas, have some 25,000 members scatted in 18 states, mainly in the South and Southwest. Its library and museum are at its headquarters in Waco, Texas.

The organization, which once had a membership of a half-million, including Sid Hatfield, still has a number of secret rituals and ceremonies. The membership rules have been changed with the minimum age now being 16 and the word "white" has been dropped from requirements to join, though current or past members of the Communist Party are still barred.

Baseball players had to wait another 40 years before being freed from the reserve clause but for modern athletes, it was worth the wait.

A ruling was made by a labor arbitrator in 1975 saying players would be free to sell their services to the highest bidder after an initial number of years with the team which first signed the player, usually four. The better players are now free to look for the best financial deal.

For the players it has been a bonanza. In 1970 the baseball minimum wage was $12,000 and the average salary was slightly less than $30,000. By 2000, the minimum was $200,000 and the average was more than $1,199,000!

The warehouse in which the St. Valentine's Day Massacre took place in Chicago has been torn down. The land is now used as a park.

The company store has gone the way of windup Victrola and the kerosene lamp. Some still be can found, but as tourist attractions only.

Matewan today, while still lacking a stoplight, does have three restaurants, two banks, a bed and breakfast and a clinic. Highlights of the year in the town are the May and October reenactments of the May 19th massacre; a replica of the scene is located in a local museum. A Wal-Mart is just 15 miles away, in South Williamson, Kentucky.

And finally, Cincinnati had a double amputation in 1960 – the "legs" were severed from the National League baseball team that is once again the "**Reds**."

PRIMARY SOURCES

Linda Akinson, *Mother Jones*, Random House, 1978

David Alan Corbin, *Life, Work and Rebellion in the Coal Fields*, University of Illinois Press, 1981

David Alan Corbin, editor, *The West Virginia Mine Wars, an Anthology*, Appalachian Editions, 1990

Richard B. Drake, *A History of Appalachia*, University of Kentucky Press, 2001

Ray Ginger, *The Bending Cross: A Biography of Eugene V. Debs*, Russell and Russell, 1949

Elliott J. Gorn, *Mother Jones: the Most Dangerous Woman in America*, Hill and Wang, 2001

Theodore Graebner, *The Secret Empire; A Handbook of Lodges*, Concordia Publishing House, 1927

Seymour Hersh, *The Dark Side of Camelot*, Little Brown & Company, 1992

Hayes Johnson, *The Age of Anxiety – McCarthyism to Terrorism*, Harcourt, 2005

Howard B. Lee, *Blood Letting in Appalachia*, West Virginia University Press, 1969

Dr. Allen H. Loughry II, *Don't Buy Another Vote, I Won't Pay for a Landslide*, McClain Printing Company, 2006

Richard D. Lunt, *Law and Order versus the Miners, West Virginia 1907-1933*, Anchor Books, 1979

Scott Martelle, *Blood Passion, the Ludlow Massacre and Class Warfare in the American West*, Rutgers University Press, 2007

John McCain with Mark Salter, *Hard Call, Great Decisions and the Extraordinary People Who Made Them*, Twelve, 2007

Charles H. McCormick, *Seeing Reds*, University of Pittsburgh Press, 1997

Sally Miller, *Victor Berger and the Promise of Constructive Socialism 1910-1920*, Greenwood Press, 1973

Howard W. Moore, *Plowing My Own Furrow*, W.W. Norton, 1985

Robert K. Murray, *Red Scare: A Study of National Hysteria*, University of Minnesota Press, 1955

Heather Cox Richardson, *West from Appomattox, the Reconstruction of America after the Civil War*, Yale University Press, 2007

Thomas C. Reeves, *A Question of character, A Life of John F. Kennedy*, Free Press, 1991

Lon Savage, *Thunder in the Mountains*, University of Pittsburgh Press, 1990

Robert Shogan, *The Battle of Blair Mountain*, Westview Press, 2004

Edward M. Steel, Jr., editor, *The Court Martial of Mother Jones*, University of Kentucky Press, 1955

Edward M. Steel, Jr., editor, *The Speeches and Writings of Mother Jones*, University of Pittsburgh Press, 1988

Ken Sullivan, editor, *The Goldseal Book of the West Virginia Mine Wars*, Pictorial Histories Publishing Company, 1991

George Swain, *The Incomparable Don Chafin*, Ace Enterprises, 1962

John A. Velke III, *The True Story of the Baldwin-Felts Detective Agency*, self-published, 2004

William Joseph Whalen, *Handbook of Secret Organizations*, Bruce Publishing Company, 1966

Theodore White, *The Making of the President 1960*, Atheneum, 1961

MEDIA SOURCES

Bluefield (WV) *Daily Telegraph*
Charleston (WV) *Daily Mail*
Charleston (WV) *Labor Argus*
Chicago *Tribune*
New York *Times*
United Mine Workers Journal
Welch (WV) *News*
Williamson (WV) *Daily News*

INTERNET SOURCES

As.wvu.edu
Civilwarliterature.com
Eh.net
Geocities.com
Globalsecurity.org
Historicalbaseball.com
Home.inn.ne
Matewan,WV, homepage
Newyouth.com
Ourdocuments.gov
Phrases.org.uk

Prairieghosts.com
Reference.com
Rootsweb.com
WVminesafety.org
Usinfo.state.gov
UTress.org